THE ROOTS OF RHETORIC

THE ROOTS OF RHETORIC

Politics of Nuclear Weapons in India and Pakistan

Haider K. Nizamani

India Research Press
New Delhi

Published by

India Research Press
B-4/22, Safdarjung Enclave, New Delhi – 110 029.
Ph.: 6196234; Fax : 4618637
e-mail : bahrisons@vsnl.com

2001

South Asia Edition © India Research Press
2001 © India Research Press, New Delhi.
ISBN : 81-87943-21-1

Cataloging in Publication Data
Nizamani, Haider. K.
The Roots of Rhetoric : Politics of Nuclear Weapons in India and Pakistan /
by Haider K. Nizamani.

Includes bibliographical references and index.
ISBN : 81-87943-21-1
1. Politics. 2. Nuclear Weapons – India / Pakistan.
3. South Asia Security. 4. India / Pakistan - Politics and government.
5. India / Pakistan Military Relations. 6 Title.

Printed in India by Focus Impressions, New Delhi – 110 003.

The Roots of Rhetoric : Politics of Nuclear Weapons in India and Pakistan
by Haider K. Nizamani.

This edition by arrangement with Greenwood Publishing Group Inc., Westport, CT, USA.
Reprinted from the Praeger Publishers edition, published in the USA.

India Research Press
B-4/22, Safdarjung Enclave, New Delhi – 110 029
Ph.: 6196234 Fax : 4618637
e-mail : bahrisons@vsnl.com

About the Author

HAIDER K. NIZAMANI is Postdoctoral Fellow at the Center for Nonproliferation Studies, Monterey Institute of International Studies.

About India Research Press

- ....AND THE ANSWER IS A PINEAPPLE Rs. 595
  Claudia Hyles
- THE SUSTAINABLE LIVELIHOOD SERIES :
  - 1-a SUSTAINABLE LIVELIHOODS AND PROJECT DESIGN IN INDIA *by Cathryn Turton*
  - 1-b THE REALITY OF TRYING TO TRANSFORM STRUCTURES AND PROCESSES : FORESTRY IN RURAL LIVELIHOODS *by Mary Hobley, Dermot Shields*
    Combined Edition Rs. 295
  - 2 DO THE POOR MATTER? A COMPARATIVE STUDY OF EUROPEAN AID FOR POVERTY REDUCTION IN INDIA
    Aidan Cox, Steen Folke, Lau Schulpen, Neil Webster, Rs. 295
  - 3-a ENHANCING LIVELIHOODS THROUGH PARTICIPATORY WATERSHED DEVELOPMENT IN INDIA *by Cathryn Turton*
  - 3-b PANCHAYATI RAJ AND WATERSHED MANAGEMENT IN INDIA : CONSTRAINTS AND OPPORTUNITIES *by Pari Baumann*
    Combined Edition Rs. 295
- LAHORE - 1947 *by Ahmed Salim and others* Rs. 250
- DEMOCRACY- a failure, SHEFOCRACY- the solution, for human welfare Rs. 495
  by Rabin Mukherjee
- SECURITY IN THE NEW MILLENNIUM : Views from South Asia Rs. 495
  by Rajesh M. Basrur
- INDIA-SRILANKA RELATIONS and SRI LANKA'S ETHNIC CONFLICT DOCUMENTS - 1947-2000 (set of 5 Vols.) Rs. 5,500
  Avtar Singh Bhasin

Volume - 1
- Section - I : Political Relations
- Section - II : Maritime Boundary and Fishing in the Palk Strait

Volume - 2
- Section - III : Economic Trade Relation
- Section - IV : Persons of Indian Origin

Volume - 3
- Section - V : Building up of the Ethnic Problem
- Section - VI : Indian Involvement in Ethnic Problem

Volume - 4
- Section - VII : India-Sri Lanka Peace Accord And Its After Month

Volume - 5
- Section - VIII : De-induction of the Indian Peace Keeping Force
- Section - IX : Nineties — The Decade of Hope and Despair

FORTHCOMING BOOKS :

- BATTLES THAT CHANGED HISTORY : A historical survey of wars in the sub-continent
- KATHA SAGAR : Collection of Stories *by* Prem Chand
- HANKLYN JANKLIN : A Mumble-Jumble of Indian words
- QUIZ MASTER (OMNIBUS) : Student's Guide to Success

Contents

Acknowledgments

I have accumulated many professional, personal, and monetary debts in the process of working on this project. The list of names is too long to be mentioned, but without the help from the following this book would never have seen the light of the day.

Brian Job has encouraged and advised me patiently over the last five years to grapple with security issues. Ayesha Haider, my friend and critic, chose to put up with me with all my faults during these years. Tahir Suheil read an earlier draft, offered valuable comments, and asked difficult questions. Peter Kracht and Lisa Webber, at Praeger, showed immense empathy for a debutante author like me and helped bring the project in the book form to the reader. Numerous family members and friends have always been there for mc whenever I needed their support.

I thank you all for your support, and am solely responsible for any faults in the book.

Chapter 1

Nuclear Weapons and Discourse Analysis

> For the six men who assembled in the sitting room of the prime minister's official residence . . . that hot Monday afternoon, it was a tense wait. Three simultaneous nuclear explosions rocked the scorching sands of the Pokhran test range in the Rajasthan desert at 3:45 P.M. Exactly ten minutes later, the phone rang in the adjoining room. The prime minister's Principal Secretary Brajesh Mishra lifted the receiver hesitantly to hear an excited voice cry "Done!" Putting the caller on the hold, Mishra reëntered the room. Picking up the receiver, Atal Bihari Vajpayee, in an emotion-choked voice, thanked the two scientists who made it happen. L. K. Advani was seen wiping away his tears.
>
> —*India Today*, May 25, 1998

India and Pakistan became de facto members of the international nuclear club by conducting ten nuclear explosions within a span of twenty days in May 1998. These explosions shattered more than just the grounds of the test sites. Precipitated by a fragile coalition government in New Delhi, led by Hindu nationalist Bharatiya Janata Party, the overt embracing of nuclear weapons by the two poverty-stricken, hostile neighbors is a result of the dynamics of internal politics. Analysts, experts, journalists, and policy-makers—both in the subcontinent as well as abroad—share the belief that nuclear programs of Islamabad and New Delhi enjoy a consensus in these societies as the guarantors of national security and symbols of national power. In spite of the professed significance of domestic factors as the determinant of nuclear postures of India and Pakistan, the existing literature does not tell us in systematic and comparative terms how an issue requiring considerable scientific know-how has become so popular in the subcontinent.

India and Pakistan have not used nuclear weapons in the literal sense of dropping atomic bombs on each other's population centers, but these bombs have been put to political use by both countries. Wrapped in the reverent cloak of patriotism, nuclear weapons have helped revive plummeting political fortunes of some political parties and relegated their opponents to potential foreign agents. It requires familiarity and conformation to rules of the game before one can safely participate in the nuclear debate in India and Pakistan. If the successful explosion of Indian nuclear devices can bring tears of joy to the eyes of L. K. Advani, home minister of India and a leading light of the Hindu nationalist movement, then there is little room in such a political milieu for those who would decry the act of overt nuclearization by India as a manifestation of military adventurism for political expediency. Similarly, the nuclear tests by Pakistan are celebrated by its leaders as a scientific feat. Yet a country where 70 percent of the people are still illiterate, voices challenging the validity of official claims can be silenced in the name of national pride.

These paradoxes call for a serious attempt to understand the dynamics of the nuclear politics in the subcontinent. By questioning what is taken for granted about the nuclear discourse in the subcontinent, I attempt to grapple with some crucial questions, which, hitherto, have not been adequately dealt with by security analysts concerned with politics of the nuclear issue in South Asia. How has the nuclear issue evolved over the years into the political giant it is today in India and Pakistan? How and in what forms has it assumed a life of its own? And finally, in what ways and to what extent does the politics of the issue serve the interests of defining the respective national identities of India and Pakistan as distinct from the Other/Enemy; namely, its close relationship with the politics of identity and security? In the end I may not be able to come up with satisfactory answers, but the salience of these questions warrants an exploration for answers by going beyond the disciplinary confines of strategic studies.

Existing literature on the nuclear issue lacks a comparative account that explains its rise as a symbol of sovereignty and security in the subcontinent. There are either accounts of developments of nuclear policies and installations in the two countries, or a barrage of accusations against each other or by Western analysts in the name of history.[1] Explanations offered by available scholarly writings are unable to account for the salience of the domestic factors because an overwhelming number of analysts stick to the conceptual outlook of the mainstream deterrence theory. Limits of the deterrence model, as we shall see below, cannot in any meaningful way explain the domestic dynamics of the nuclear issue. On the other hand, scholarship most notably associated with the works of Barry Buzan has tried to go beyond the traditional deterrence theory by looking inside the workings of the Third World state to understand the dynamics of security in the non-Western world. Although not extensively used by experts dealing with the South Asian security issues, my argument is that there are inherent limitations that make Barry Buzan's "weak state" framework insufficient to understand the nuclear discourse in India and Pakistan.

It is hardly surprising that given the power-centric and policy-oriented nature of modern security studies, debates have been dominated by American scholars and largely exist within the scope of temporal interests defined by the American state.[2] In such an intellectual environment, a critical analysis of issues affecting the Third World has always been a problematic enterprise. One is always confronted with questions such as: Are the theoretical bases meant to explain the trends in the Western world fit for analyzing the issues facing the non-Western world? Is the Third World a unique category, which merits a separate analytical framework? Can the West-centered tools of analysis be modified and used to answer security questions specific to the Third World? The theoretical ground-clearing work starts with locating the position of the Third World in traditional security studies. This is followed by a brief critical look at the conceptual models of "weak states," which claim to rectify the theoretical shortcoming of traditional strategic studies. Finally, I spell out the key features of the discourse analysis methodology that I have employed to study the dynamics of nuclear politics in the subcontinent.

THE THIRD WORLD AND TRADITIONAL SECURITY STUDIES

The neorealist view of the workings of the international system and validity of the concept of deterrence holds sway over most scholars addressing the issue of nuclear weapons in the subcontinent. In this scheme, the focus of security studies is the study of the threat, use, and control of military force, and any effort to broaden the notion of security by studying "non-military" sources of threats is equated with the act of destroying intellectual coherence of the discipline.[3] This section briefly outlines the key features of this theory as expounded by Kenneth N. Waltz, indisputably the most influential and an eloquent contemporary proponent of this theoretical perspective.[4]

Neorealism emphasizes the systemic forces that states are subject to in the international system.[5] A system refers to a group of parts or units whose interactions are significant enough to justify seeing them in some sense as a coherent set. A group of states form an international system when "the behavior of each is a necessary factor in the calculations of the other."[6] A system comprises a structure and interacting units. Leaving aside characteristics of units (states) for the sake of elegance and parsimony, states are assumed as basic units of the international system.[7] Structure in the Waltzian sense refers to two things. One, it is a compensating device that works to produce a uniformity of actions despite a variety of inputs; two, it is a set of constraining conditions.[8] Therefore, a structure is defined by the arrangement of its parts.

Three criteria are used by Waltz to differentiate the international system from the domestic system, namely, an ordering principle, functional differentiation, and the distribution of capabilities. Hierarchy is the ordering principle in a domestic system. Constituting units in such a system tend to specialize in their respective functions. The international system differs fundamentally in its ordering principle because it is an anarchical system. Given the anarchical nature of the system, states must rely on the dictum of self-help to ensure their survival. By virtue of this, all states are functionally alike in the international system, and are "distinguished primarily by their greater or lesser capabilities."[9]

Due to the anarchical nature of the system and because units are functionally alike, the international system is defined by the arrangement of its parts, and only the changes of arrangement are structural changes.[10] Existence in such a system of self-help requires constant balancing on the part of the units. The result is the balance-of-power principle as the pillar of neorealism. In such a system, cooperation is hampered by the dictum of "relative gains," which guides states in coping with other units in the system.[11] By his own account, Waltz's theory is not aimed at explaining every outcome in international politics, but only a few important parts of that reality. Concerned with capabilities defined in terms of power, neorealism is meant to be a great power politics theory. In spite of being a theorist of great power politics, Waltz's ideas on the role of nuclear weapons as war preventers on the global scale have profoundly influenced the writings on the nuclear issue in the subcontinent.

NUCLEAR WEAPONS: WHO SHOULD OR SHOULD NOT HAVE THEM?

The neorealist argues that peace—understood in terms of the absence of a major war among great powers—in the post–World War II era has prevailed because of the bipolar international system and the advent of nuclear weapons as a means to deter the enemy.[12] The effectiveness of nuclear weapons in ensuring peace between two superpowers during the Cold War was taken as almost an article of faith among realists.[13] What made nuclear weapons qualitatively different from other weapons systems? If these weapons could lead to peace between the enemies in the Western world, could they have a similar effect in the non-Western world?

According to neorealist theory, territorial security becomes the key objective of national states in an international system based on the dictum of self-help and every state pursues deterrence policies best suited to its circumstances. Realists minimally define security as "the protection of the homeland from military attack," and deterrence as a means to stop others from doing something by frightening them.[14] The stabilizing role of nuclear weapons is due to the political effects their introduction has produced on statecraft.[15] Given their immense destructive capacity, which can be inflicted in a very short span of time, the use of force between two nuclear powers lies in preventing the outbreak of war rather than the traditional preoccupation with winning the war.[16] This makes nuclear weapons effective deterrents. Since the costs of risking a nuclear retaliation are very high, "states are not likely to run major risks for minor gains."[17] In a world of conventional weapons, according to Waltz, adversaries usually resort to war through miscalculations. Nuclear weapons make deterrence transparent because one "is uncertain about surviving or being annihilated."[18] In the certainty that the losses will invariably outweigh the gains of fighting, nuclear powers desist from waging war with each other.

These statements appear rational as a result of the universal nature of the assumptions of neorealism. Taken to the logical conclusion, it is not difficult to see that the thermonuclear weapon system, which made miscalculation next to impossible in the East-West context, will also serve the same purpose if applied in the context of the non-Western world. At this point fundamental differences emerge between a vast majority of strategic analysts of the West, especially the United States, and most of their counterparts in South Asia.

Waltz becomes almost a solitary voice in the United States when he suggests that the spread of nuclear weapons in the Third World would lead to the same results as it did in the Western world. The majority of realists find faults with this position and consider the acquisition of nuclear weapons by the Third World countries as an ominous prospect.[19] The West, especially the United States, fears that unstable regimes in the Third World sometimes led by "rogue" and "authoritarian" leaders may resort to the nuclear option to settle unresolved questions. Reflection of this is evident from outright sensational accounts based on historical inaccuracies to instituting measures to prevent Third World countries from acquiring nuclear weapons.

William Burrows and Robert Windrem epitomize sensationalism in their declaration that "the Indian subcontinent is the most dangerous place on Earth."[20] They discount the plausibility of deterrence as the main objective behind Pakistan and India's nuclear programs and suggest that the sole purpose of nuclear weapons in the subcontinent is genocide.[21]

Even a scholar like George Perkovich, who does not yield to sensationalism, argues that in the aftermath of the Cold War, "the chance of local nuclear conflict among undeclared nuclear weapon powers has grown." Considering the relationship between India and Pakistan as "fraught with uncertainty," he thinks that "the danger is especially acute in South Asia."[22] Similarly, a study group of leading U.S. South Asianists noticed "the dangers of continued nuclear developments in the subcontinent" and called for American "efforts to discourage and deter the Indian program to *produce* and *deploy* nuclear weapons."[23] An overwhelming majority of studies on the nuclear issue in South Asia conducted by American scholars are more concerned with what is described as serving the U.S. policy goals in the region rather than undertaking disinterested analyses. Stephen P. Cohen, renowned South Asian security analyst, best sums up this point by maintaining that "one would be foolish to advocate a policy which did *not* serve one's country's interests."[24] However, there have been exceptions to this rule and recently Devin Hagerty, critically examining the dynamics of nuclear deterrence in South Asia, went beyond the dictates of policy goals. Analyzing the strategic relations between Pakistan and India in light of the various perspectives for and against the value of nuclear weapons as stabilizers, Hagerty concluded that the presence of the nuclear factor has prevented interstate war between the two countries.[25]

Kenneth Waltz finds the most vocal adherents in the subcontinent, and a few like Hagerty in the West. Waltz favors the spread of nuclear weapons to other countries, including Third World states, on grounds that the historical evidence only documents states with specific security needs to have kept the nuclear option open. As long as the nuclear option remains an effective deterrent, they are unlikely to abandon it. Advocates of nuclear deterrence in principle accept this but they argue that due to the unstable nature of regimes and leaders in the Third World, the probability of the use of nuclear weapons increases manifold in such regions. Waltz discounts this argument by maintaining that as far as the rationality of leadership is concerned, doubts about the sanity of Third World leaders are indicative of "the old imperial manner" rather than a statement of truth.[26] This view, as I show in the relevant chapters, has become a standard argument for proponents of the nuclear option in South Asia.

In spite of claiming to be an all-encompassing framework to explain deterrence policies, this perspective is obviously not meant to address the domestic sources of the nuclear discourse in the subcontinent. Given the importance of the domestic realm for understanding the nuclear discourse of India and Pakistan, we have to see if theorists who look inside the state to explain security policies can be of some help.

THIRD WORLD SECURITY

Analysts concerned with the causes of war and conditions of peace in the postcolonial world argue that assuming states as unitary actors hampers our understanding of the security dynamics of a vast majority of Third World countries where war is mostly intrastate rather than interstate and security policies are aimed at safeguarding the existing regime rather than the nation. Problematizing the nature of the Third World state, Barry Buzan and Kal Holsti, two leading exponents of the new wave of Third World security, conceptualize the international system in terms of "strong" and "weak" states where peace prevails in the former and the latter are the venue of societal disintegration and warfare. They raise important conceptual questions by offering a provocative reading of the security dilemmas of the postcolonial world. I argue that this perspective has a limited explanatory value due to its orientalist tendencies, circular logic, symptomatic approach, and latent ahistoricism.[27]

A state is denominated "weak" by juxtaposing it to the "strong state" of the West. A weak state is perceived as an entity containing "various combinations of the following characteristics."[28] First, "the ends or purposes of governance are contested . . . (and) the lines separating the state from civil society are blurred." This exacerbates regime legitimacy. Second, "there are two or more nations within the state." Of these, "one or more are commonly constructed as minorities not equals." Third, "the government apparatus is 'captured' or held by one group, which systematically excludes others." Fourth, "the government is 'captured' by a family or clan for the primary purpose of personal enrichment." Fifth, "major communal groups or ideological groups or nations identify with, or are loyal to, external states and/or societies; or significant segments of the population owe primary or exclusive loyalty to primordial groups." Sixth, "the state is incapable of delivering basic services or providing security and order for the population." Seventh, "the government relies primarily on violence, coercion, and intimidation to maintain itself in power." Eighth, which Holsti considers a fundamental distinction, "the state lacks legitimacy" and the authority of the ruler is always in question. Holsti argues that the postcolonial nationalist leaders' right to rule "was seldom validated by elections or plebiscites." As a result, "many of the new states are 'weak'—not militarily, but in the sense that significant sectors of the population do not identify strongly with the post-colonial state."[29] This situation leads to isolation, disenfranchisement, and often brutal persecution of large sections of the population in these societies. Consequently, what a "weak state" regime portrays as "national security" priorities may not be shared by large segments of the population. Buzan also considers the distinction between "weak" and "strong" states as a vital factor to any analysis of national security.[30] His list of characteristics of a weak state includes "a high degree of state control over the media" and "a conspicuous role for political police in the everyday lives of citizens" as hallmarks of a "weak" state.[31]

Imagine something exactly opposite to the above narrative and what we have is a "strong" (read Western) state. Therefore, "strong states contain characteristics opposite of those found in weak states, as well as others."[32] Hence, "in most modern industrial societies . . . there is a consensus that the purpose of governance is to help provide 'the good' life for the individual," where power rotates among different social groups, "and no group faces systematic persecution or denial of civil liberties and political office."[33] Even if the existing practices of the Western societies were taken as fixed givens, the discriminatory exclusion of lesbian and gay communities—the group that comes immediately to mind—in the United States through systematic laws against same-sex marriages provides a marked contradiction to the above claim. The point is not to find faults with what are ideally described as the characteristics of "strong states." It suffices to say that the yardstick of measuring is firmly fixed with reference to the assumed practices of the contemporary Western states.[34]

For the purposes of this study, I will concentrate on the reasons given by these authors to explain the relative "weakness" of the postcolonial states and their consequent security dilemmas. Buzan is of little help in this regard, because assuming the unproblematic nature of these characteristics, he concludes rather desperately that "whatever the reasons for the existence of weak states, their principal distinguishing feature is their high level of concern with domestically generated threats to the security of the government."[35] Such a conception is a result of "dehistoricizing the state" in which Buzan "renders them [states] permanent, tying his analysis to the structural presumptions of an unchanging anarchy and the permanence of state security problems."[36]

Holsti goes beyond just observing that regions of "weak and failed states" are a prime location of war, and offers a tentative explanation of the "weakness" of the postcolonial world. According to him, the modern Western states are based on two different "foundations of legitimacy: "historic-civic" (examples, France, Spain, Sweden) and "natural" (Finland, Hungary, and the Baltic states). In the former the state molded the modern territorial nation, and in the latter the nation (as defined and even created by ruling elite) helped create the state.[37] States based on the "natural" foundations refer to "nations based on consanguinity and/or language and religion," as against those that are based on the principle of history and territory (contiguity).[38] In Europe two "hybrid" states (i.e., Yugoslavia and Czechoslovakia) were creations of diplomats and "not the results of some 'natural' community to sovereign statehood." These "fictions" could not be turned into civic or "natural" communities by seventy years of iron control and "we are now seeing the results."[39]

The above model does not consider the varied forms of state formation processes in the postcolonial world, and Holsti concludes, "this is exactly the problem faced by many contemporary post-socialist and Third World states." They did not meet the "civic" or "natural" criteria of state legitimacy at the time of independence.[40] Such a situation arose because the ex-colonies' claims for statehood were based primarily upon negative grounds, namely, anticolonialism or anti-Sovietism, rather than on the positive achievements of a historical community and its citizenship or on the "natural" bonds formed through history, consanguinity, language, and/or religion. Bureaucrats or diplomats in London or Paris drawing straight lines on maps carved these states out.[41] Therefore, at the time of independence, these states lacked statehood, which is defined in terms of a defined territory, skills and organizations to administer a permanent population, and the capacity to enter into treaty relations.[42] One important reason for this was the colonial regimes' failure to build the foundations of statehood.

When the leaders of national liberation movements spoke of "self-determination," they hardly did so in the name of a "people" because no such "people"—meaning a "natural" community—existed. There were, rather, congeries of communal-religious groups, ethnicities, tribes, clans, lineages, and pastorals that wandered freely. Lacking "natural' communities or a national history of uniqueness that might legitimate their claims to statehood, they had to rely on the territorial creations and concoctions of the colonialists to define their hoped-for communities.[43] Therefore, postcolonial states "owe their creation more to the international community than to their own artificial communities."[44] As a result, the security policy of these states is not a response to external threats, but a weapon to quell threats that are rooted within the spatial boundaries of the respective state.[45]

The above formulation is an example of security orientalism, and its grand generalizations do not necessarily accurately depict either the history or the present status of all postcolonial societies. With these fundamental conceptual problems, it is unlikely to shed light on the nuclear discourse in India and Pakistan. In what follows, I rely on the subcontinent's encounter with colonialism and its postcolonial dilemmas to ascertain the relevance of the "weak state" model.

DISTINCT PROBLEMATIC OR SECURITY ORIENTALISM?

For Buzan and Holsti the "weak states" are perceived as fixed entities in the global system. What is defined as a "weak" state turns out to be more of a symptomatic mixing of causes with effects rather than an analytical tool.[46] Ironically, the analyses of Third World security since Buzan's pioneering work have assumed this dichotomy without critically examining it, thus reifying a questionable assertion.

In defining a "weak" state causes are mixed with effects without clearly defining the relationship. For example, a weak state is one where the question of legitimate use of force is unresolved (an effect), and the colonial demarcation of boundaries is to be blamed for a number of problems faced by these states (a cause). Others echo this concern by arguing that "legitimacy—that authority which rests on the shared cultural identity of ruler and the ruled—is the most precious resource of any regime" and states are "weak" in the Third World because regimes are constantly faced with legitimacy crises.[47]

Dichotomizing states into binary opposites on the basis of such characteristics is indicative of "logocentrism," which in this specific context becomes security orientalism.[48] Logocentricism views the world in practical oppositions such as domestic/international, core/periphery. Encountering such oppositions, "the logocentric disposition inclines a participant in the regime of modernity to impose hierarchy, . . . (in) which one side can be conceived as a higher reality."

A model based on logocentric procedure divides countries on the basis of their characteristics and establishes dichotomies of Us and Them, good and bad, and so forth. The Other is judged and classified to be "weak" in the context of how much different it is from Us (i.e., the "strong" West). The more striking the differences are, the weaker that state is. Hence, the difference itself becomes an explanation. This, in short, is security orientalism, which juxtaposes the mature West with the infantile non-West and subordinates the latter into perpetual contrast with the former. The Pakistani state acts the way it does because it is "weak," and its weakness is based upon its differences from the "strong" West. The weak states model's view of the non-Western world is a result of what T. N. Madan has aptly termed as three deceptions. First, they have had their traditions tampered with, eroded, and invented, often with the help of anthropologists and historians. Second, they are deceived societies as they have their present transformed into a permanent transition: the developing societies will forever remain developing societies if they are to catch up with the so-called developed but, in fact, runaway societies. The seven industrialized countries (G-7) are like the constellation of seven stars that point to the fixed pole star, but the goals of development do not remain fixed, they recede further away. Finally, these societies are deceived for the third time because their future has been preempted.[49]

Given epistemological privileging of the West over the rest, the "weak states" model can hardly help us understand the nuances of nuclear discourse in the subcontinent except by blaming the outcomes on the weakness of the Indian and Pakistani states. Rather than indulging in such circular logic, we have to locate the rise of the nuclear weapons politics by situating it in the context of attempts by the postcolonial dominant episteme to create newer versions of national selves. It is here that I go beyond the disciplinary confines of security studies and delve into relevance of discourse analysis to shed new light on the nuclear issue. The focus is on the processes that constitute the political world of an issue.

DISCOURSE ANALYSIS AND NUCLEAR POLITICS

The appendix in George Orwell's novel *Nineteen Eighty-Four* is a good place to find some clues to understanding and deciphering the nuances of nuclear politics in Pakistan and India. For traditional security analysts Orwell may appear an unlikely help because he was no expert on nuclear weapons or security studies. But he understood the value of symbols and language to sustain certain types of thinking and suppress others. One form of it he ingeniously described as *Newspeak* has a striking resemblance to the nuclear discourse in Pakistan and India.

Newspeak was the official language of Oceania and had been devised to meet the ideological needs of Ingsoc, or English Socialism. In the year 1984 there was still no one who used Newspeak as his sole means of communication, either in speech or in writing. The leading articles in the *Times* were written in it, but this was a *tour de force* that could only be carried out by a specialist.[50] Newspeak was meant to serve two purposes: first, "to provide a medium of expression for the world-view and mental habits proper to the devotees of Ingsoc," and second, "to make all other modes of thought impossible." The words were assigned special meanings to meet these ends. When the language is considered a social reality rather than mere words, it is studied as a discourse. In a political world discourses are "sets of statements which give expression to the meanings and values of an institution. Beyond that, they define, describe and delimit what it is possible to say and not possible to say (by extension possible to do and not to do) with respect to the area of concern to that institution."[51]

I conceptualize security discourses as a framework through which the constant articulation of external dangers is used to carve out and maintain a particular version of national identity for a state. Neither the sources of the danger nor the identity it supposedly threatens is static. The goal of negotiating and striking a delicate balance between the imagined community and the reality of existing heterogeneity often propels security discourses in such a manner that externalizing the danger to the imagined community becomes one common feature of security policies. Analyzing the discourse of security policies one would ask, "How, from the welter of information and interaction among states and their representatives, are threats constructed, and mobilised against?"[52] Once understood in terms of discourse, the language employed by security analysts and policy-makers becomes more than an objective analysis or representation of a state's national interest. Discourse analysts see such statements by decision-makers and analyses by experts as expressions of particular interests and justifiers of a distinct regime of practices or truth. As this discourse is conducted within the context of the respective societies, we have to keep in mind Foucault's following observation:

> Each society has its regime of truth, its "general politics" of truth: that is, the types of discourse which it accepts and makes function as true; the mechanisms and instances which enable one to distinguish true and false statements, the means by which each is sanctioned; the techniques and procedures accorded value in the acquisition of truth; the status of those who are charged with saying what counts as true.[53]

The nuclear discourse in the subcontinent also has its "general politics of truth" in which certain types of statements are made to function as true and thus serve as informal rules by which some statements are designated as accurate reflections of national interests and others as antinational viewpoints. This general politics of truth sanctifies certain means of inquiry and dismisses others. This in turn creates the Pundits and *Dalits* (Untouchables) in the nukespeak hierarchy of the subcontinent.

The question of truth is not isolated from issues of power and right. In the triangle of truth, power, and right Foucault observed a close relationship where "there can be no possible exercise of power without a certain economy of discourses of truth which operates through and on the basis of association."[54] To put it simply, "we are subjected to the production of truth through power and we cannot exercise power except through the production of truth."[55] The discourse of truth is not a mere linguistic construction but an engine of power whose effects can be felt at different levels. As such it is through discourses of truth that we are judged, condemned, classified, determined in our undertakings, and destined to a certain mode of living or dying.[56]

An analysis of a regime of discourse, in this case the nuclear discourse in Pakistan and India, questions the objectivity of so-called self-evident truths regarding a subject matter by viewing them as products of specific historical circumstances and statements that are subject to manipulation. However, these discourses once in place have the capacity to manipulate participants in that area, as well as influence the shape of things to come there. Hence, it is a mutually constitutive process where both the agency and the structure shape and reshape each other. This mode of inquiry is suited to undertake projects aimed at writing histories of the present. It is the topical nature of nukespeak in the subcontinent that warrants accounting for its underlying rules, both formal and informal, that enable nukespeakers to prescribe the forms of thinking, writing, and policy-making possible on the issue. Such an effort is a history of the present because it tackles an issue that preoccupies the political agendas of contemporary Pakistan and India. Viewed as a discourse, politics of nuclear weapons in Pakistan and India can meaningfully be considered as political practices central to the constitution, production, and maintenance of their national identities by invoking the themes of threats and dangers.

Read in conjunction with Foucault's notion of discourse, Tzvetan Todorov's case study of the encounter between Europeans and native Americans helps significantly to contextualize the nukespeak in Pakistan and India.[57] According to Todorov, the Other can be conceived as an abstraction—other in relation to myself, or else as a specific group to which I do not belong. This group can be interior to society—blacks during the apartheid regime in South Africa or women in modern societies—or it can be near or far away from the territorial limits of a country. Danger emanated for the United States during the Cold War from the geographically distant Soviet Union, which was considered to be an "evil empire." Similarly, for Pakistan it is India that becomes the main danger to its independent identity.

Todorov's study of two forms of relationship between the colonizer and the colonized as a model to understand the dynamics of one's relationship with the Other can further help us in contextualizing nukespeak in the subcontinent. On the one hand, the colonizer saw the colonized as a human being, having the same rights as himself. The colonized was not seen as an equal but rather identical, which led to assimilation. For example, native Americans were seen as an equal by the European missionaries provided they embraced Christianity and became the same as enlightened Europeans. Or else the colonizer started from difference, which was immediately translated into terms of superiority and inferiority.[58] In both forms, what is denied is the existence of a human substance truly other, something capable of an independent being, not merely an imperfect state of oneself. When the Europeans started from difference, the Other was perceived and portrayed as an inferior. Once the difference was cast in terms of inferiority and superiority, the feeling of superiority engendered a paternalistic behavior.[59] The dominant security discourse in postcolonial India and Pakistan exhibits this trend whereby the Other is portrayed as an inferior. An expression of this in the case of Pakistan's dominant discourse is equating all Indians with Hinduism, a religion that they consider inferior to Islam. On the other hand, for the state-managers of India, in contrast to their democracy, Pakistan is seen as the outcome of a parochial idea based on religion, which serves as a fertile ground for dictatorships. In Pakistan and India these two forms become two edges of the same sword. These contrived monoliths suppress difference within their territorial limits in the name of Islam and secularism, respectively, and deny any similarity with what is considered as external/dangerous/inferior.

Nuclear discourse is an integral part of this gamut of the dominant discourse in Pakistan and India. As the following chapters illustrate, nuclear politics cannot be divorced from the issue of identity in both countries, but the task of turning the dominant episteme into a normal and unquestioned world-view of the constituent populations is far from being over. For proponents of the dominant discourse in Pakistan, the self implies an identity based upon Islam as a unifying religion and Urdu as the national language of the country. Heterogeneous societal reality asserts itself to defy such a national identity. Dynamics of these contradictions enmesh internal and external in two ways. By portraying India as a danger to the Pakistani identity—read Urdu and Islam—India is projected as a monolithic Hindu entity primarily interested in destroying Pakistan. Any internal resistance to the national identity based upon Urdu or Islam as the sole defining factor is interpreted as the doing of India. This scheme denies the fact that where there is a use of power (which is often coercive) to forge an identity, resistance to it is immanent in the process. This denial results in marginalizing, isolating, and in some cases violently suppressing movements or voices that do not fall within the orbit of the dominant lore about national identity. In this triad, internal dissent is invariably tied to the external enemy. A Pathan secessionist becomes an Afghan agent and a Sindhi separatist an Indian agent. The same can be said of India in its relations with Pakistan. The latter is equated with difference. Difference is equated with "theocracy" as compared to the pluralist and secular basis of India. These Pakistani characteristics become a danger to the secular Indian identity. Kashmiri militancy is attributed to the malicious designs of Pakistan rather than resistance to the failure of Indian identity to correspond with the Kashmiri reality.

The nuclear discourse in the subcontinent, especially that of Pakistan, is closely tied to this process in which the nuclear option is portrayed as a guarantor of the independent identity of an Islamic Pakistan against the evil designs of heathen India. The dominant Indian nuclear discourse strives to use the official policy on the issue as a sign of India's assertion as a regional power capable of resisting the global power structure. Those sections of the intelligentsia who do not subscribe to the dominant discourse within both countries are portrayed as either actual or potential agents of external powers or as novices who do not comprehend what is in the national interest.

The methodology of discourse analysis will help in answering the following important questions regarding the politics of nuclear issue in Pakistan and India: Who decides what is in the national security interest of Pakistan and India? How are external threats used to define the Self? How is the liaison established between internal dissent and external dangers? How has the nuclear option emerged as a means to cope with threats to national security? In attempting to answer these questions I have tried to be empirical but not empiricist. At best, an attempt has been made to cast a detached look at the interplay of forces that have played a constitutive role in the present shape of the nuclear discourse in the subcontinent. This, then, is the study of the creation and use of threats to consolidate particular "national" identities in the subcontinent. The salience of the nuclear issue is explored in the matrix of creating national identities by invoking the theme of internal and external enemies.

Before embarking on our encounter with nukespeakers, we should have an idea which sections of the Indian and Pakistan societies constitute the core custodians of the dominant security discourse.

WELCOME TO THE WORLD OF NUKESPEAKERS

The notion of "epistemic communities" is a useful starting point to identify segments of the societies in Pakistan and India that constitute the core of the nukespeakers.[60] The basic argument here suggests that "control over knowledge and information is an important dimension of power" and that "networks of knowledge-based experts—epistemic communities" play an important role in defining the rules of the game in a given issue area. Peter M. Haas describes an epistemic community as "a network of professionals with recognized expertise and competence in a particular domain or issue area." Such a community may consist of "professionals from a variety of disciplines and backgrounds," who share a set of common characteristics. They include:

> (1) a shared set of normative and principled beliefs, which provide a value-based rationale for the social action of community members; (2) shared causal beliefs, which are derived from their analysis of practices leading or contributing to a central set of problems in their domain and which then serve as the basis for elucidating the multiple linkages between possible policy actions and desired outcomes; (3) shared notions of validity—that is, intersubjective, internally defined criteria for weighing and validating knowledge in the domain of their expertise; and (4) a common policy enterprise—that is, a set of common practices associated with a set of problems to which their professional competence is directed.[61]

Other likely characteristics of an epistemic community can be shared "patterns of reasoning" and "a policy project drawing on shared values." Usually the number of members in epistemic communities is relatively small by virtue of the same world-view (or *episteme*).[62] Inclusion in an epistemic community goes hand in hand with the exclusionary criteria inherent in such a notion. Terms of inclusion are set through subjective understandings rather than referring to any "objective" or "scientifically proven" tests. This becomes abundantly clear in the following chapters when we discuss the nuclear discourse in the subcontinent.

Two surveys of the Indian elite's opinion on the nuclear issue conducted in 1969–1970 and 1994 identify groups who constitute the core of dominant discourse.[63] Ashis Nandy in 1969–1970 termed such groups "the strategic elite" of India. It comprised "political ultra-elites, counter elites, interest group elites, opinion leaders, scientists in power and specialists in international relations, strategic studies and military affairs."[64] David Cortright and Amitabh Mattoo, while soliciting the views of the Indian elite on the nuclear issue almost a quarter century later, divided the elite into eight categories (i.e., arts and sports, academic and science, bureaucrats and diplomats, businesspersons, journalists, lawyers, medical doctors, and armed forces and police personnel).[65] Mattoo's apt observation that the nuclear "discourse is controlled by a handful of scholars and former military and government officials, who, until recently did no more than justify official policy" is crucially important for the purpose of this study.[66]

I focus primarily on the words and works of a handful of individuals constituting the respective epistemic communities that have appropriated the nuclear discourse in Pakistan and India. A clarification of the multiple roles assumed by the same individual in the dominant discourse is called for. Unlike in North America, where a division of intellectual labor is the norm, the intellectual scene in the subcontinent is markedly different. Individuals assume multiple roles that blur the lines between various groups specified as the dominant elite in Pakistan or India. For example, the undisputed champion of contemporary Indian nukespeak, Krishnaswami Subrahmanyam, has served as an official in the ministry of defense (a bureaucratic post), was the director of a leading think tank (the Institute for Defense Studies and Analyses) from where he contributed regularly to the Indian newspapers (a media position), and contributed as a defense expert to academic journals.

If a few individuals in each country have appropriated the nuclear discourse by assuming multiple roles, then other groups mentioned by Cortright and Mattoo have played little public role in shaping the contours of the nuclear discourse. Foremost among them are sports figures, medical doctors, and businesspersons, who have largely been silent on the issue. People from these backgrounds are conspicuous by their absence in this study.

This study is divided into seven chapters. After this theoretical ground clearing, the following four chapters rewrite the history of the evolution of nuclear discourse in India and Pakistan with two chapters on each country. Chapter Six is about the dissenting narratives in the nuclear discourse, and in the final chapter I summarize and assess the key themes that emerge during the study.

A ROAD MAP

Chapter One offers a critique of commonly used theoretical criteria for the study of the nuclear and Third World security. The general assumptions of neorealism inform not only the nuclear deterrence literature in general, but also enjoy a near intellectual monopoly over the discussion of the nuclear issue in South Asia. Then I discuss the works of scholars like Barry

Buzan and Kal Holsti who have emphasized that neorealist framework lacks adequate theoretical tools to help us analyze the "distinct Third World security problematic." Finally, I outline the feature of the methodology of discourse analysis employed in this book to study the politics of the nuclear issue in the subcontinent.

The second chapter tells the story of Indian nuclear discourse from its inception in the late 1940s to the nuclear explosion in 1974. By focusing mainly on Jawaharlal Nehru's views on independent India's status in the world and the importance, or lack of it, attached to the nuclear option in determining India's position in the world community, I set the stage for analyzing later developments in Indian nukespeak. Nehru did not see any role for nuclear weapons in India and during his rule (1947–1964), New Delhi practiced "nuclear celibacy." We continue the story of Indian nukespeak when the celibacy slowly gave way to ambiguity in the late 1960s. The chapter ends with a discussion of the nuclear discourse that followed in the wake of the Indian nuclear explosion in 1974. Chapter Three focuses on the present stage of the Indian nuclear discourse. We will see how the nuclear option became an integral part of the discourse that identifies India as a major power. In today's India, the nuclear option has become a credible means to ward off immediate geostrategic threats and a symbol of India's independence and autonomy in international affairs. This is a complete U-turn from the policies pursued during the Nehru years. The discussion will also show how Pakistan has become a more credible source of threat for the Indian "strategic elite" as compared with the Chinese threat.

Chapter Four discusses the dynamics of nukespeak in Pakistan from the 1960s to 1977. It traces the emergence of the nuclear issue from its absence in the strategic discourse to the new vigor it achieved during late Zulfikar Ali Bhutto's regime (1971–1977). The discussion starts with the centrality of the Indian threat invoked by General Ayub Khan (Pakistani head of the state during 1958–1969), and the absence of the nuclear option as a means to deter this threat. This brings us to the 1971 Bangladesh civil war and the war with India as decisive events in terms of both the unresolved identity issue of Pakistan and Islamabad's inability to deter India. We will see how the issues of identity, security, and threat were fused in this period. This is followed by an examination of Z. A. Bhutto's thinking on the nuclear issue, and the way the nuclear factor entered into the dominant political discourse of Pakistan. I conclude the story of the first phase of nukespeak in Pakistan with the analysis of Pakistani reaction to the 1974 Indian nuclear explosion, and the transformation of the nuclear issue by the military regime after 1977 into a litmus test of patriotism. In Chapter Five, I analyze how the nuclear issue was utilized by Zia-ul-Haq's military regime to boost its legitimacy by portraying it as a means to consolidate Islamic identity for Pakistan against Hindu India. The chapter ends with a survey of the nuclear discourse in contemporary Pakistan.

Chapter Six discusses the dissenting narratives in the nuclear discourses of India and Pakistan. In spite of the dominant discourses' claims about the unanimity of views on nuclear programs within India and Pakistan, a closer look suggests that there is a section of intelligentsia in both countries that dares to oppose the so-called consensus. These voices range from Pulitzer Prize winner novelist Arundhati Roy in India to Pervez Hoodbhoy, a leading physicist, in Pakistan. In this chapter I contexualize the limits of the dissenting voices in influencing the nature and direction of the nuclear discourse in the subcontinent.

The final chapter consists of the summary and assessment of the themes discussed in the preceding pages. This is done by comparatively highlighting the similarities and differences between the nuclear discourse in Pakistan and India. Keeping in mind the exploratory objective of the study, I attempt to show how the reading offered in this book contributes to a better understanding of the dynamics of the nuclear issue in the subcontinent.

A NOTE ON SOURCES

Availability and importance of the material in each case determine selection of the sources. Literature covered in the theoretical chapters relies heavily on the writings of a select group of individuals whose works are widely used in theoretical treatment of Third World security issues.

In the case of Indian nukespeak, the words and works of Nehru and Homi Bhabha are extensively used in discussing the nuclear discourse up until 1965. In the absence of an identifiable community of security issues experts, these two individuals held sway over the nature and direction of the early nuclear discourse. From the late 1960s onward, an embryonic community of security experts started to take shape in India. Over these years K. Subrahmanyam has consistently and prolifically written about the nuclear issue, and is rightly considered by friends and foes alike as the leader of the nuclear hawks in India. His works, therefore, are cited extensively, along with those of other leading nukespeakers, in the chapter on the modern Indian nukespeak. Most material in the Indian case cited in the study, barring the 1990s, relies on books published in India. Most of the relevant sources are compilations of newspaper and research journal articles written by leading members of India's strategic community.

The source material to study the Pakistani nukespeak is, much to the dismay of students and analysts, scattered because little effort has been made to compile it into book-length studies. Therefore, I had to scan through academic journals and archives of the leading English daily of Pakistan, *Dawn*, to narrate the story of the Pakistan nukespeak. Unlike Subrahmanyam of India, Pakistan's epistemic community of nukespeakers has no one dominant figure that can claim or be credited with the status of the flag-bearer. These differences in the sources give the two case studies a distinct character.

However, in both case studies I have tried to limit the discussion of the works of nonresident Pakistani or Indian authors writing on the nuclear issue to a minimum for the simple reason that such writers do not operate within confines of the power relations that drive the nukespeak in the subcontinent. Their influence in terms of shaping the contours of nukespeak in Pakistan or India is also nonexistent. This, however, does not imply that such works should not be taken seriously.

NOTES

1. For a history of India's nuclear program see Ashok Kapur, *India's Nuclear Option: Atomic Diplomacy and Decision Making* (New York: Praeger, 1976), and George Perkovich, *India's Nuclear Bomb: The Impact on Global Proliferation* (Berkeley: University of California Press, 1999). For a history of Pakistan's program see Akhtar Ali, *Pakistan's Nuclear Dilemma: Energy and Security Concerns* (Karachi: Economic Research Unit, 1984); for a sensational analysis of the nuclear issue in the Third World see Steve Weismann and Herbert Krosney, *The Islamic Bomb* (New York: Times Books, 1981); and for a recent work on the dynamics of nuclear strategy in the subcontinent see Devin Hagerty, *The Consequences of Nuclear Proliferation: Lessons from South Asia* (Cambridge: MIT Press, 1998).

2. For a brief overview of the American influence on the theoretical activity in International Relations (IR) see Steve Smith, "Paradigm Dominance in International Relations: The Development of International Relations as a Social Science," in Hugh C. Dyer and Leon Mangasarian, eds., *The Study of International Relations: The State of the Art* (Basingstoke, UK: Macmillan; in association with *Millennium: Journal of International Studies*, 1989), pp. 3–27; Ekkehart Krippendorff, "The Dominance of American Approaches in International Relations," in Ibid., pp. 28–39.

3. Stephan Walt, "The Renaissance of Security Studies," *International Studies Quarterly* 35:2(1991), pp. 212–213.

4. Kenneth N. Waltz, *Theory of International Politics* (Reading: Addison-Wesley, 1979). Since its publication this volume has become a common referent for both adherents and opponents of modern Realism. However, Waltz calls his theory "structural" and other variants of Realism as "reductionist" theories. But the Waltzian theory is better known as "neorealism," a term coined by Richard Ashley. See Richard K. Ashley, "The Poverty of Neorealism," in Robert O. Keohane, ed., *Neorealism and Its Critics* (New York: Columbia University Press, 1986), pp. 255–300. Citations of Waltz's works are reproduced from the above volume.

5. Kenneth N. Waltz in Robert O. Keohane, ed., *Neorealism and Its Critics*, (New York: Columbia University Press, 1986), pp. 34–47.

6. Barry Buzan, Charles Jones, and Richard Little, *The Logic of Anarchy: Neorealism to Structural Realism* (New York: Columbia University Press, 1993), p. 29.

7. Ibid., p. 71.

8. Waltz, in Keohane, *Neorealism and Its Critics*, p. 62.

9. Waltz, "Political Structures," in Keohane, *Neorealism and Its Critics* pp. 81–92.

10. Ibid., p. 72.

11. Relative gains can be defined as a situation in which "a state worries about a division of possible gains that may favor others more than itself." Waltz, Ibid., pp. 102–103. For more on this see, Joseph M. Grieco, "Anarchy and the Limits of Cooperation: A Realist Critique of the Newest Liberal Institutionalism," *International Organization* 42:3 (summer 1988), pp. 485–507.

12. Kenneth N. Waltz, "The Emerging Structure of International Politics," *International Security* 18:2 (fall 1993), pp. 44–47.

13. It will be nearly impossible to list all the major names and their works in the present context. Along with Waltz, Robert Jervis' works neatly summarize this argument. See Robert Jervis, *The Meaning of Nuclear Revolution: Statecraft and the Armageddon* (Ithaca, NY: Cornell University Press, 1989).

14. Robert J. Art and Kenneth N. Waltz, "Technology, Strategy, and the Uses of Force," in Robert J. Art, and Kenneth N. Waltz, eds., *The Use of Force: International Politics and Foreign Policy*, 2d Ed. (Lanham: University Press of America, 1983), pp. 4 and 10. However, these definitions are functional at best and vary from author to author even among those adhering to the same theoretical perspectives. For a recent attempt to clarify and adequately explicate the concept of security, see David A. Baldwin, "The Concept of Security," *Review of International Studies* 23 (1997), pp. 5–26.

15. Robert Jervis, "The Political Effects of Nuclear Weapons," *International Security* 13:2 (fall 1988), pp. 80–90.

16. Ibid.

17. Scott Sagan and Kenneth N. Waltz, *The Spread of Nuclear Weapons: A Debate* (New York: W. W. Norton, 1995), p. 5.

18. Ibid., p. 7.

19. For a representative sample see Robert Jervis, "The Future of World Politics: Will It Resemble the Past?," *International Security* 16:3 (winter 1991–1992), p. 26. Jervis sees the prospect of the spread of nuclear weapons as a major threat to U.S. security in the post–Cold War period.

20. William E. Burrows and Robert Windrem, *Critical Mass: The Dangerous Race for Superweapons in a Fragmenting World* (New York: Simon & Schuster, 1994), p. 351.

21. Ibid.

22. George Perkovich, "A Nuclear Third Way in South Asia," *Foreign Policy* 91 (summer 1993), p. 85. For a more recent view of Perkovich on the subcontinent and the likely role of the United States see George Perkovich, "India, Pakistan, and the United State: The Zero-Sum Game," *World Policy Journal* 13:2 (summer 1996), pp. 49–56.

23. See Selig Harrison, and Geoffrey Kemp, *India and America after the Cold War* (Washington, DC: Carnegie Endowment for International Peace, 1993), p. 36. For a complete list of members of the study group, which comprised academics and practitioners, see, Ibid., pp. 57–62.

24. Stephen P. Cohen, "Preface," in Stephen P. Cohen, ed., *Nuclear Proliferation in South Asia: The Prospects for Arms Control* (Boulder, CO: Westview, 1991), p.

xiv; see also Stephen P. Cohen, ed., *The Security of South Asia: American and Asian Perspective* (Urbana and Chicago: University of Illinois Press, 1987).

25. Devin T. Hagerty, *The Consequences of Nuclear Proliferation: Lessons from South Asia* (Cambridge, MA: MIT Press, 1998).

26. Sagan and Waltz, *The Spread of Nuclear Weapons*, p. 13.

27. My use of the term orientalist is based upon Edward W. Said's thoughts. See Edward W. Said, *Orientalism* (London: Penguin, 1978). "*Orientalism* is the generic term . . . to describe the Western approach to the Orient. It is the discipline by which the Orient was (and is) approached systematically, as a topic of learning, discovery, and practice" (p. 73). The project is based upon creating binary opposites where "the Orient is irrational, depraved (fallen), childlike, 'different'; thus the European (in our case the Western) is rational, virtuous, mature, 'normal' " (p. 40).

28. K. J. Holsti, "War, Peace, and the State of the State," *International Political Science Review* 16:4 (1995), pp. 331–332.

29. K. J. Holsti, *International Politics: A Framework for Analysis* (New Jersey: Prentice-Hall, 1995), p. 55.

30. Barry Buzan, *People, States, and Fear: An Agenda for International Security in the Post-Cold War Era* (New York: Harvester Wheatsheaf, 1991), p. 97.

31. Ibid., p. 100.

32. Holsti, "War, Peace, and the State of the State," p. 332.

33. Ibid., p. 333.

34. The term "Western" is quite problematic as well. Here, it refers to the countries of Western Europe, the United States, Japan, and white settler colonies (i.e., Canada, Australia, and New Zealand).

35. Buzan, *People, States, and Fear*, p. 90.

36. Simon Dalby, "Security, Modernity, Ecology: The Dilemmas of Post–Cold War Security Discourse," *Alternatives* 17 (1992), p. 106.

37. Holsti, "War, Peace, and the State of the State," p. 327.

38. Ibid., pp. 325–326.

39. Ibid., p. 327.

40. Ibid.

41. Ibid., p. 327.

42. Ibid., p. 329.

43. Ibid., p. 328.

44. Ibid., p. 329. Robert H. Jackson argues that most states of Africa, especially sub-Saharan Africa, not only owe their creation to the international community but survive mainly due to the "sovereignty" norm propounded by the international community. See Robert H. Jackson, "Quasi States, Dual Regimes, and Neoclassical Theory: International Jurisprudence and the Third World," *International Organization* 41:2 (autumn 1987).

45. Steven R. David, "Explaining Third World Alignment," *World Politics* 43 (January 1991), pp. 233–242.

46. The point of mixing causes with effects is made in another context by Yael Tamir, "The Enigma of Nationalism: Review Article," *World Politics* 47:3 (April 1995), pp. 418–440. But such confusion is common in the perspective of the "weak states" model.

47. Thomas G. Weiss and Meryl A. Kessler, eds., *Third World Security in the Post–Cold War Era* (Boulder, CO: Lynne Rienner, 1991), pp. 23–24.

48. On "logocentrism" see Richard K. Ashley, "Living on Borderlines: Man, Poststructuralism, and War," in James Der Derian and Michael Shapiro, eds., *International/Intertextual Relations: Postmodern Readings of World Politics* (Lexington: Lexington Books, 1989). pp. 261–262.

49. T. N. Madan, "Anthropology as Critical Self-Awareness," in D. L. Sheth and Ashis Nandy, eds., *The Multiverse of Democracy: Essays in Honour of Rajni Kothari* (New Delhi, Thousand Oaks, London: Sage, 1996), p. 263.

50. There is no substitute for reading the appendix and the novel itself to appreciate Orwell's critique of the totalizing effects of the language forms that rely on dualism to condone certain types of views as true and çondemn the other forms as false and dangerous. George Orwell, *Nineteen Eighty-Four* (First published by Martin Secker & Warbrug in 1949). I have used the Penguin Books 1984 edition (p. 257).

51. Gunther Kress, "Discourses, Texts, Readers and the Pro-nuclear Arguments," in Paul Chilton, ed., *Language and the Nuclear Arms Debate: Nukespeak Today* (London, Dover: Fraces Press, 1985), p. 68.

52. Keith Krause, "Critical Theory and Security Studies," YCISS Occasional Paper 33, 1996, p. 16.

53. Ibid., p. 73.

54. Michel Foucault, "Two Lectures," in Michael Kelly, ed., *Critique and Power: Recasting the Foucault/Habermas Debate* (Cambridge, MA: MIT Press, 1994), p. 31. Foucault delivered "Two Lectures" in 1976 and they offer a very good overall view of his research strategies.

55. Ibid.

56. Ibid., p. 32.

57. Tzvetan Todorov, *The Conquest of America: The Question of the Other*, Richard Howard, trans. (New York: Harper–Perennial, 1992 edition).

58. Ibid., pp. 3–42.

59. Ibid., p. 38.

60. The term "epistemic communities" is, like all other social constructs, a contested concept. I have relied on the definitional aspects discussed in Peter M. Haas, "Introduction: Epistemic Communities and International Cooperation," *International Organization* 46:1 (winter 1992), pp. 1–36; and Emanuel Adler and Peter M. Haas, "Conclusion: Epistemic Communities, World Order, and the Creation of a Reflective Research Program," Ibid., pp. 367–390.

61. Haas, "Introduction: Epistemic Communities," p. 3.

62. Ibid., p. 27.

63. The survey in 1969–1970 was conducted by the eminent Indian scholar Ashis Nandy and the findings were published in Ashis Nandy, "The Bomb, NPT and Indian Elite," *Economic and Political Weekly*, Special Issue, 7:31–33 (August 1972), pp. 1533–1540; and Ashis Nandy, "Between Two Gandhis: Psychological Aspects of the Nuclearization of India," *Asian Survey* 14:11 (November 1974), pp. 966–970. The Fourth Freedom Forum and Joan B. Kroc Institute commissioned the 1994 survey for International Peace Studies. Results and analyses of the survey are published in David Cortright and Amitabh Mattoo, eds., *India and the Bomb: Public Opinion and Nuclear Options* (Notre Dame, IN: University of Notre Dame Press, 1996). A similar survey of the Pakistani elite was commissioned by the above institution in 1996. Samina Ahmed and David Cortright, eds., *Pakistan and the*

Bomb: Public Opinion and Nuclear Options (Notre Dame, IN: University of Notre Dame Press, 1998).

64. Nandy, "Between Two Gandhis," p. 966.

65. Cortright and Mattoo, *India and the Bomb*, p. 117.

66. Amitabh Mattoo, "India's Nuclear Status Quo," *Survival* 38:3 (autumn 1996), p. 46.

Chapter 2

From Celibacy to Explosion: Nuclear Discourse in India, 1947–1974

Indian identity is a work in progress. "Midnight's children" started their "tryst with destiny" in the name of democracy, secularism, and nonalignment.[1] Although officially still wedded to those ideas, India today is armed with nuclear weapons, distrusted by neighbors as a regional hegemon, plagued by the rise of Hindu fundamentalism, and feared by various identity-based movements as an oppressive federation. Nuclear weapons once dubbed as "evil" by Jawaharlal Nehru, independent India's first prime minister, are now a symbol of national sovereignty and strength in Atal Bihari Vajpayee's India. This chapter documents the post-1947 Indian leadership's opposition to nuclear weapons and ends with a shift in that policy that culminated in the so-called peaceful nuclear explosion in Pokhran in 1974. It shows how the nuclear weapons option was gradually converted from a national anathema into a strategic alternative by investing new political meanings to it.

The nuclear issue is situated within the framework of the dominant security discourse in India. The potency of the nuclear discourse lies in its close relationship with the notion of national interests, which, in turn, rely on constant reference to enemies. Neither these interests nor threats to them are objective, or hanging out there, only to be recognized by patriots. In the real world both the interest and enemies are created and recreated through conscious efforts. The nuclear weapons option is one of the modern innovations used in security discourses to ward off threats. Political dynamics determine the value assigned to nuclear weapons or to the option of having them. This chapter shows how the nuclear weapons option gradually entered the dominant security discourse in India. This background sets the stage for the next chapter in which the present-day facets of the dominant narratives regarding the nuclear weapons option are explored.

The Indian nukespeak privileges the dominant discourse of security in the name of national interests. The historical roots of these arbitrary assertions made in the name of India's national interests are analyzed with the help of the methodology of discourse analysis. The dominant security discourse in India, of which nuclear weapons have become an integral part, is guided by a variety of factors ranging from an aspiration to great power status to allocating blame to the adversaries (Pakistan being the major one) for the nuclear imbroglio in South Asia. Chapters Two and Three look critically at the regime of truth regarding India's security with special reference to the nuclear issue. The following questions serve as the framework to explore the manner in which the nuclear issue has entered the security discourse. What is India's status in the comity of nations? What dangers does India face and why? How should it ward off these dangers? Where does the nuclear factor fit into this matrix? Answers to these questions will help in understanding the changing nature and political value of the nuclear factor in the context of Indian identity as envisaged in the country's dominant security discourse. This identity is defined in negative terms, that is, what it is not, by referring to the Others (both internal and external) of India. These Others by implication become threats to the Indian identity. The dominant security discourse maintains that external enemies threaten India. These enemies foment troubles within India to achieve their objectives. Therefore, internal dissent is no more than an extension of some foreign hand. The methodology of discourse analysis enables us to situate the value of the discussion of threats in the dominant discourse as an integral aspect of identity formation on a particular line in postcolonial India. Here, Pakistan emerges as the most dangerous of all threats because it strives to Balkanize India. The Chinese threat would be invoked from time to time but could never achieve the political value that the Pakistan factor has acquired. The West also emerges as a force that tries to undermine India through coercive diplomacy and other means.

The thoughts of Jawaharlal Nehru, independent India's first prime minister, regarding India's international status with special reference to his views on India's two important neighbors, namely, Pakistan and China, are an appropriate starting point to tell the story of the Indian nuclear discourse. Following this is the background of Indian nukespeak starting with a brief account of the period marked by what G. G. Mirchandani aptly terms "nuclear celibacy," that is, from independence in 1947 until Nehru's death in 1964.[2] Coincidentally, the Chinese joined the nuclear club later in the same year. Nehru's death and the Chinese explosion resulted in a shift in the official policy with the introduction of an element of nuclear ambiguity and emergence of some, hitherto peripheral, voices in favor of exercising a nuclear option in the wake of the Chinese threat. The third part of the chapter discusses marginal voices in the Indian security discourse in support of the nuclear option especially in the wake of defeat at the hand of China in a brief border war in 1962. By the late 1960s an imperceptible shift had occurred in the official Indian stand on the nuclear issue: from unequivocal nuclear abstinence to guarded ambiguity. This is followed by an account of nukespeak leading to the so-called peaceful nuclear explosion by India in May 1974. It was during this period that the nuclear program increasingly became enmeshed in the jargon of national security against enemies. This ultimately led to the Pokhran nuclear explosion in May 1974. This chapter ends with a discussion of the explosion and its immediate effects on the nuclear discourse in India.

INDIA'S INTERNATIONAL STATUS

Nehru can be credited with personifying the dominant discourse that shaped the post-1947 Indian identity, in terms of its internal as well as external parameters. Two aspects of his thoughts merit a close look. First, how did he define the international status of independent India and what practical means did he utilize to ensure that status? Where did nuclear weapons fit into this equation? Second, how did he portray Pakistan and China? Nehru's characterization of India's role in the international system serves as the bedrock that is widely used to induct nuclear weapons into modern India's panoply.

In Nehru's episteme India's position in the world hierarchy was that of a great power. Such a status was portrayed as a manifest destiny that the country could not escape even if it wanted to. However, nuclear weapons were not a pressing need of this great power, whereas Nehru's portrayal of Pakistan as an intimate yet puzzling Other on the one hand and his depiction of China as a friendly country up until the 1950s have had a lasting impact on India's strategic discourse where Pakistan continues to be the ideal candidate to identify as an enemy in the Indian nukespeak. These two interrelated themes of the dominant security discourse of India as expounded by Nehru merit detailed discussion.

In January 1947, prior to India's formal independence in August 1947, Nehru declared it a "great country, great in her resources, great in manpower, great in her potential, in every way."[3] Considering the key conflict in the world to be between the atomic bomb and the spirit of humanity, he foresaw an independent India representing the spiritual rather than the atomic side of humanity. Two years later, India's emergence in world affairs was construed to be of "major consequence in world history."[4] Nehru is almost apologetic for being at the helm of affairs of the country when it was "growing into a great giant." Considering himself and his team as men of small stature, he pledged that "in spite of our own smallness, we have to work for great causes and perhaps elevate ourselves in the process."[5]

The international role of India was perceived in no other terms but as an influential global actor. Nehru gingerly avoided calling India the leader of Asia, but at the same time acknowledged that "a certain special responsibility is cast on India. India realizes it, and other countries realize it also. The responsibility is not necessarily for leadership, but for taking initiative sometimes and helping others to co-operate."[6] Below the surface of Nehru's modesty was the message to others that justified India's external policy as a moral mission on the one hand, and on the other infused the sense of special responsibility among Indians. The Indian policy of special global responsibility became popularly known as nonalignment in the polarized world of the early Cold War years.

Assuming the major power role without resorting to a traditional military buildup was more a result of India's military weakness than guided by a belief in the cherished ideal of nonviolence.[7] India's global role was based upon the twin strategies of becoming a mediator between the two hostile superpowers and a leader of the postcolonial world. Cultural diversity of the country was seen as an advantage that could enable her "to be a bridge to join warring factions and to help in maintaining the most urgent thing of today and the future—the peace of the world."[8] Gradually the hope for a mediator's role would fade in the background with more emphasis on being a Third World leader. Indian foreign policy during the Nehru period is described as a "search for [an] equitable global system, populated by non-aligned states and genuine disarmament."[9] The internal and external realms were intertwined in this explanation and India's defense policy was "geared to the threat from Pakistan and the danger of communist subversion within India."[10] The language of dangers and threats came as a convenient link to tie the external with the internal affairs.

Sometimes even Nehru castigated internal opponents of his foreign policy as lesser Indians. He had a definite criterion by which to judge a person's patriotism in India. A true Indian must believe in "India's progress, economically and otherwise, and India playing a part in the freedom of the world and the preservation of peace in the world."[11] Keeping these objectives in mind, whose parameters were certainly going to be defined by Nehru, he saw no scope of difference on foreign policy issues, and those who differed with these ideas were "individuals or groups who think in terms of other countries and not primarily of India at all."[12] Since such people did not qualify as Indian patriots, any possibility of interaction with them was deemed very difficult.

Although popularly regarded as a leader who went beyond traditional means of conducting foreign policy, Nehru also used the theme of internal and external dangers to define India's position in the world. While internal detractors on foreign policy issues were portrayed as the custodians of foreign interests (alluding to the communists in India as followers of the Soviet and Chinese instructions); external adversaries, especially Pakistan, were depicted as the unpredictable Other. Echoing the dominant views in India on the formation of Pakistan as an historical aberration, Nehru in June 1948 depicted Pakistan as a "breakaway part of India."[13] This background put Pakistan in a special category because "all the people of India" were completely shocked and emotionally upset over "the way Pakistan was formed and India was divided."[14] Such characterizations suggest at least two things. First, claiming that *all* people of India were upset over the creation of Pakistan effectively marginalizes the huge number of Indian Muslims who wanted an independent country. Second, the creation of Pakistan is always projected as the division of an Indian whole. This binary opposition between the whole and the part always sees Pakistan as a part of what ideally should have been *Akhand Bharat* (whole India).

Since Pakistan's existence boiled down to that of a wayward child in the greater Indian family, it was only natural for New Delhi to be keenly interested in the affairs of Pakistan despite a proclamation that "it is not our policy to criticize the internal affairs of Pakistan."[15] Referring to the political difficulties faced in the newly formed state by the Pashtun nationalist leader Khan Abdul Ghaffar Khan, who was a Congress ally in prepartition days, Nehru saw it fit to express an interest in the Khan's cause because he was one of India's "colleagues and friends" and it would be "inhuman of us to forget these friends."[16] Such statements laid the foundations of a persistent use of the Pakistan factor in India's dominant security discourse. Nehru's characterization of Pakistan hence contradicted the Indian claims that New Delhi did not believe in interfering in other countries' internal affairs.

As compared with Pakistan, Nehru viewed the People's Republic of China in markedly different terms. It was considered a friendly country with a different political system but with problems similar to India's. In Nehru's notion China was a great power and preceded India in international hierarchy. "Leaving these three big countries, the United States of America, the Soviet Union and China, aside for the moment, look at the world. There are many advanced, highly cultured countries. But if you peep into the future and if nothing goes wrong—wars and the like—the obvious fourth country in the world is India."[17]

Nehru suggested that India could learn a great deal from the Chinese revolution because both faced similar problems such as huge peasant populations, technological backwardness, and an urge to attain higher standards of living.[18] These views were best echoed in the slogan of *Hindi Chini Bhai Bhai* (Indian and Chinese are Brothers) coined during Chou En-Lai's trip to New Delhi in 1954. Nehru claimed that during 2,000 years of mutual relations between China and India "there is no record of war between us."[19] This assertion would be contradicted in 1962.

The zeal of Sino-Indian brotherhood was dampened in the late 1950s by a growing divergence of views on the issue of international boundaries.[20] Occasional skirmishes in the mountains between the Chinese and Indian forces became routine from 1959 onward. In spite of these tensions, Nehru trod on a delicate diplomatic path when commenting on the issue. Rather than criticizing China he told his countrymen in 1959 that "I do not think war will come." He used nationalist rhetoric in somewhat abstract terms, but emphasized that "if war is thrust upon us, we shall fight, and fight with all our strength. But I shall avoid war, try to prevent it with every means in my power. There are, however, some things which no nation can tolerate. Any attack on its honor or the integrity of its territory, no nation tolerates, and it takes risks, even grave risks, to protect them."[21] Yet China was not rapped in the manner used to condemn Pakistan. Even when the war broke out in 1962, Nehru's words were more those of an individual in a pensive rather than a combative mood. Expressing shock over what he called the Chinese invasion of India, he said:

> Nothing in my long political career has hurt and grieved me more than the fact that the hopes and aspirations for peaceful and friendly neighborly relations which we entertained and to promote which my colleagues in the Government of India and myself worked so hard ever since the establishment of the People's Republic of China, should have been shattered by the hostile and unfriendly twist given in India-China relations during the past few years.[22]

Comparison of Nehru's thoughts on Pakistan and China makes it clear that the former has always been easier to identify as an enemy. China appears more like a distant giant, disagreements with whom are mainly due to misunderstanding. Even the brief border war with China came as a departure from the norm of peaceful relations that lasted over 2,000 years. The same, however, cannot be said in Pakistan's case. This brief account of the international status of India as envisaged by Nehru will serve as background to understand the dynamics of present-day nukespeak in India.

"NUCLEAR CELIBACY": 1947–1964

Nehru viewed atomic energy as a harbinger of progress for India while expressing contempt for its military uses on moral grounds. That remained the extent of nuclear weapons in Indian politics, both at home and abroad.[23] With no identifiable group of strategic experts at that time, this section discusses the role assigned to the nuclear factor by newly independent India's two key personalities, namely, Nehru and Homi Bhabha, a leading scientist.[24]

Development and industrialization were synonyms for Nehru. A developed India meant a heavily industrialized country in the Nehruvian model. He considered nuclear energy as a panacea to meet India's power requirements to embark on the path of industrialization. Vijay Laxmi Pandit, an exponent of Nehru's views, aired these aspirations in the UN General Assembly as early as 1948, suggesting that India was an "under-developed and under-powered country in whose economy, it is our belief, atomic energy will play an important role."[25] India's ruling elite eschewed the military use of atomic energy and considered it an evil that the country would not harbor. However, an immense potential was seen in its peaceful uses, especially to meet energy needs of countries like India. The choice was between developing India (read industrialization) and using atomic energy as a means to achieve that or remain "under-developed and under-powered." Nehru saw more use of this energy for a "power-starved and power-hungry country like India" than industrially advanced countries like France or the United States.[26]

The mantle of making scientific sense of Nehru's political case for India's atomic needs fell on the shoulders of Homi Bhabha, India's foremost atomic scientist and Nehru's close associate. Bhabha expressed concern over the disproportionately higher amounts of energy used by the West to sustain its existing living standards. He argued that to make such living standards possible for the rest of humanity, countries like India should "turn to atomic energy for a solution." Convinced that atomic energy would be a cheaper and more efficient means with which to meet power needs, Bhabha saw immense potential for India in the atomic field especially because of its well-developed pool of scientists and large deposits of atomic raw materials, especially thorium.[27]

Having no doubts about the peaceful nature of the Indian program, Bhabha claimed that India "unhesitantly" accepted the Canadian condition of peaceful uses while accepting the latter's help in the atomic field.[28] The Nehru-Bhabha belief in the potential uses of atomic energy for India's economic development was evident when by 1959 the Atomic Energy Establishment in Trombay staffed over 1,000 scientists. Bhabha was sure that given India's huge population nuclear power was the only viable energy option. He suggested that "by the end of the century atomic energy will be supplying a major part of the total power production, and practically all the increase from this period will be covered by nuclear power."[29] Ironically, India entered the new millennium as a power-starved but nuclear-armed country. The energy efficiency of atomic power became an article of faith for early Indian policy-makers. Nehru viewed military uses of such a technology with contempt. The dominant security discourse in India during the Nehru years primarily echoed what he postulated as the country's national interests.

India's answer to end the arms race during the 1950s was advocacy of suspension and eventually banning of nuclear tests, followed by a dismantling of weapons systems, and finally a declaration by the nuclear powers not to manufacture atomic weapons in the future. However, Nehru was not sure what role India could play in this regard except putting forward such proposals.[30] During the 1950s the nuclear issue was primarily the concern of a few diplomats assigned duties to represent India in the Conference on Disarmament or a very select group of scientists at India's Atomic Energy Commission headed by Dr. Homi Bhabha. Voices in favor of India making nuclear weapons were conspicuous by their absence.

The Indian dream for Third World leadership came to a violent end when the People's Republic of China and India fought a brief but decisive war in 1962 over disputed borders. China scored a decisive victory and forced hitherto anti-Western India to seek military assistance from the West and embark upon the road of beefing up its defense expenditures. Nehru's deteriorating health after the defeat symbolized a nation in pain. Two years after defeating India in the war, China acquired nuclear weapons in October 1964. Nehru died in May 1964 after leading India for seventeen years. Under the changed circumstances "nuclear celibacy" gave way to "nuclear ambiguity" at the government level, whereas more radical voices arguing in favor of nuclear weapons started to appear on India's political horizon. The following section discusses early nukespeak in India. The taboo surrounding the military aspects of nuclear technology in India's political discourse slowly gave way to discussions about the potential deterrence value of nuclear weapons.

NUKESPEAK ON POLITICAL MARGINS

Defeat at the hands of the Chinese was a severe blow to the dominant security discourse of India in which New Delhi was viewed as a self-proclaimed leader of the Third World. Two years after the Sino-India war, China joined the nuclear club in October 1964. The public reaction to the Chinese detonation in India was "surprisingly inchoate and scattered."[31] The reason why this reaction was inchoate and scattered has to do with the lack of political importance hitherto attached to the nuclear issue in the Indian security discourse. The mainstream political leadership at that time had not used the nuclear issue as an instrument of domestic politics for consolidating their patriotic credentials or condemning their opponents. Moreover, there was no epistemic community that made its living by writing as experts and true patriots on the importance of the nuclear option as a means to enhance India's image and decry nuclear threats posed by China or Pakistan. There were, though, some voices arguing for India to go overtly nuclear for strategic reasons. This section briefly situates those voices in the framework of the Indian security discourse.

The official Indian position on the Chinese detonation of the atomic device reflected the lack of political value of the nuclear issue in the dominant security discourse of India. Less than a month before the Chinese explosion, a debate on external affairs in the Indian parliament had no reference to any aspect of nuclear politics. Swaran Singh, then External Affairs minister, spoke 15,000 words on foreign policy but did not comment on news reports of a possible Chinese explosion and its repercussions for India.[32] When the Chinese detonated their atomic device in October 1964, defense minister Y. B. Chavan maintained that the Chinese threat to India emanated from conventional weapons; the introduction of the nuclear factor would not make a big difference.[33] Mirchandani, documenting the reaction in the leading Indian dailies, did not find the situation much different from what Chavan had described. Prime Minister Lal Bahadur Shastri condemned the Chinese test as a disservice to the cause of international peace, but vowed that India would not emulate China.[34]

Although India's political leadership ruled out any immediate strategic use of the nuclear option in the country's defense planning, Bhabha, shortly before Nehru's death, had started to speak publicly about the value of nuclear weapons as a possible effective deterrent. In a paper presented at the Pugwash Conference on Science and World Affairs in February 1964, Bhabha argued that nuclear weapons with an adequate delivery system would enable a state to acquire "absolute deterrence even against another having a many times greater destructive power under its control."[35] Acknowledging nuclear weapons as great equalizers, he viewed the conventional superiority of a big country like China as "a danger to its smaller neighbors." He said such a danger could be averted either by establishing an effective collective security arrangement or by resorting to nuclear deterrence. Bhabha hinted at the possible value of such weapons for India by noticing the failure of collective security arrangements to prevent wars. He also maintained that dual uses were inherent in atomic knowledge. It appears that the deteriorating health of Nehru had resulted in the loosening of his grip over India's atomic establishment. After Nehru's death in May 1964, the theme of dual uses of atomic knowledge and the possible deterrence value of nuclear weapons became quite recurrent in Bhabha's writings until his tragic death in an air crash in January 1966.[36] Although he did not advocate a fundamental shift in the existing policy of nuclear celibacy, Bhabha's later views did pave the way for India's dominant security discourse to adopt official ambiguity on nuclear matters.

Amid the morally high-sounding policy of abstinence there were some voices on the Indian political scene proposing the nuclear course for India. One leading exponent of the nuclear option was the Jana Sangh, the Hindu fundamentalist political party and precursor of the present-day Bharatiya Janata Party (BJP). The party demanded an indigenous nuclear weapons program in the wake of the Indian defeat in 1962. The Jana Sangh's ideas revealed ingredients of nukespeak based upon a Hindu ideal of the Indian identity. Ramachandra Bade, one of the fourteen Jana Sangh MPs in the

489 member Lok Sabha, proposed Indian development of nuclear weapons in 1963 saying that "only those who wish to see Russians or Chinese ruling India will oppose the development of nuclear weapons."[37] The external and internal realms were intimately linked in the Jan Sangh's view.

The suggestion that opposing the nuclear option amounted to inviting Russian or Chinese rule was targeted at two sections within India. First, various communist factions formed the second largest bloc of M.P.'s at that time in the Indian parliament and they all opposed the nuclear weapons option. The Jana Sangh portrayed them as no more than Indian stooges of the two major communist powers. Second, the party was also taking a shot at Nehru, who was firmly against nuclear weapons and was seen by many as a politician with socialist orientations. For the Jana Sangh the opponents of the nuclear weapons option could be either Russian or Chinese agents, leaving out any possibility that they were American spies or Western agents. Such a selective demonization was quite intentional because anti-American rhetoric was used by Nehru to enhance India's international stature as an independent center of decision-making.

The Jana Sangh had to offer some positive rationale for putting India on the nuclear course beyond dubbing opponents as external agents. The urgent reason cited was to equip the Indian army with nuclear weapons because they represented the most modern arms available to the state. Such weapons would, according to the Jana Sangh, enable India to conduct international affairs from a position of strength.[38] The theme of a strong Indian voice in global affairs was a common goal that the Jana Sangh shared with Nehru, the arch figure of India's dominant security discourse. However, the Jana Sangh's means to achieve that also included nuclearizing India.

In leading English-language dailies of India during that period there was little space allocated to the discussion of the Chinese test and its repercussions for India. Similarly, the so-called experts on security issues had not made the nuclear issue their main concern as yet. Shyam Bhatia attributes the absence of the Jana Sangh's concern among the scholarly community to "a lack of interest and inadequate discussion of the nuclear issue."[39] The situation was compounded by a lack of technical information on the matter. *International Studies*, the leading Indian journal of foreign affairs at that time, did not publish a single article on the nuclear issue between 1959 and 1964, and there were hardly any books published on the subject. This situation was indicative of the apolitical nature of the nuclear issue rather than a lack of technical information available to scholars. The select group of people who became experts on the nuclear issue did not attain that status by virtue of having access to the select circle of individuals who made technical and political decisions regarding the nature and direction of India's nuclear program or because they had any accurate technical knowledge of the matter. Their claim to expertise rested rather on the political use they made of the nuclear issue in India's political discourse. Ashok Kapur explains the general public's lack of interest as due to "the low level of literacy" where "one does not expect the lay public in India to take an interest in foreign defense issues."[40] This observation is more reflective of the author's own biases of trusting literate over illiterate in the matters of politics; but it is belied by the Indian, or for that matter Pakistani, illiterates' enthusiastic participation in the political process.

Officially, India still strove to obtain "positive security assurances" to meet possible nuclear threats. Positive security assurances mean formal "declarations that nuclear-weapon states will come to the assistance of any non-nuclear-weapon state threatened with nuclear weapons."[41] This policy of acquiring positive security guarantees would eventually amount to informal treason in the eyes of experts who would insist on having indigenous means to ensure national security. However, by the end of 1964, Lal Bahadur Shastri did slightly alter India's earlier position of absolute "nuclear abstinence" by suggesting that if the need arose, India might favor a peaceful nuclear explosion (PNE). This change was apparently in response to Dr. Homi Bhabha's claim that India could be ready for a PNE by 1967 and the demand of a number of M.P.'s within the Congress party to seriously consider the nuclear option.[42]

India entered 1965 with an embryonic nuclear debate and the legacy of defeat by China. The tension between India and Pakistan steeply rose in this year ultimately culminating in the second full-fledged, although indecisive, conventional war between the two in September 1965. The war came as a boost for the pronuclear voices in India because Pakistan was easier to identify as an enemy than China. Friendly relations between China and Pakistan were further seen as a grand conspiracy to harm India. International efforts to institute a nonproliferation regime intensified during the same period. The Indian opposition to this regime, based upon the supposedly moral high ground, crystallized in this era and remains at the heart of the contemporary Indian security discourse. Immediately after the war with Pakistan, nearly 86 M.P.'s urged Shastri to opt for nuclear weapons on grounds that "the security of this country [India] can no longer be left to the mercy or whims of so-called friendly countries. India's survival, both as a country and democracy, casts a duty on the Government to make an immediate decision to develop our own nuclear weapons."[43]

Ambiguity replaced celibacy as a policy in Indian diplomats' presentations on the international stage. Badr-ud-din Tayabji, Indian representative at the International Atomic Energy Agency (IAEA) General Conference, in September 1965 hinted at the policy shift in New Delhi. Tayabji argued that if "China proceeded to stockpile atomic weapons it might not be possible for a number of countries, including India, which were capable of producing such weapons but which so far had refrained from doing so, to continue their present policy."[44] Vishnu C. Tridevi, Indian representative at the First Committee of the UN General Assembly, expressed more or less similar views a month later when he said that technologically India was undoubtedly "a very advanced nuclear capable country."[45]

The discourse demanding India's acquisition of nuclear weapons was premised upon two interconnected themes. First, the argument was made that genuine Indian national security could only be achieved through indigenous nuclear weapons and anything less would be mortgaging that security to external powers. That was the crux of the Jana Sangh position discussed earlier. Second, this time India's national security was seen in wider terms that went beyond ensuring territorial integrity and also included safeguarding the Indian political system based on constitutional democracy. According to this logic, the acquisition of nuclear weapons was to serve multiple functions, of which the smooth functioning of the democratic system was one. The issue of nuclear weapons was gradually becoming infused with nationalist pride. However, the government of India officially did not subscribe to this point of view and opposed an overt nuclear weapons program.

India refused to become a party to the Nuclear Nonproliferation Treaty (NPT) in 1967 and demanded a time-bound program for global disarmament. Officially, India considered the NPT as a discriminatory treaty against the developing countries on two grounds. First, the NPT institutionalized nuclear apartheid by dividing the world into nuclear weapons states (NWS) and non–nuclear weapons states (NNWS). Second, the treaty did not spell out clear mechanisms for the transfer of nuclear technology for peaceful purposes. This line of argument has become the hallmark of Indian nukespeak. One invariably finds a substantial discussion in most books dealing with the nuclear issue written by Indian writers allocated to the analysis of the "discriminatory" nature of the NPT and India's "principled" opposition to it. The Indian experts' views on the NPT will be discussed in detail later. Suffice it to say that opposition to the NPT would constitute a patriotic duty and support of the treaty could be construed as an act of possible national betrayal. Such voices had found their way into India's emerging community of nuclear experts. Sampooran Singh's *India and the Nuclear Bomb* published in 1971 is a good example of incipient Indian nukespeak. In the following section I look closely at Singh's nukespeak to show how the nuclear issue is used to perpetuate a particular security discourse in India.

NUKESPEAK ENTERS ACADEMIA

Vilifying the "enemies" by creating binary oppositions is the most convenient tool utilized by nuclear hawks. Concern with the alleged Sino-Pakistan collusion against India becomes the launching point to build the case for a nuclear-capable India.

The Chinese government is considered "intensely ethnocentric and expansionist with a dogmatic ideology." It is a totalitarian and "hegemonic" power that launched "a massive attack in 1962 and occupied our territory."[46] The condemnation of China is not restricted to attacks on its regime. It is also accused of training "hostile Nagas and Naxalites."[47] Demonizing the adversary in the above fashion implies that the enemy is not only dangerous by virtue of its characteristics per se and harboring intentions to cause military damage through territorial aggression, but it is also intricately involved in fomenting internal divisions within India. Denying any role played by the Indian authorities in failing to address the sociopolitical demands of either the Naga tribals or Naxalite guerrillas, the onus of unrest is squarely placed on China. This not only absolves New Delhi of any wrongdoing but also endorses violent suppression of internal dissent (in this case the Naga and Naxalite insurgencies) in the name of rooting out external conspiracy. Nuclear weapons are seen as cards that China can use "to win the psycho-political game" and also "an option to precipitate a crisis in which India could be blackmailed into paralysis."[48]

While the Chinese threat is explained through the Communist regime's attributes, Pakistan becomes a threat by virtue of its very existence. Its creation in 1947 is seen as the emergence of a theocratic state pitted against secular India. Pakistan is held responsible for "invading the state of Jammu and Kashmir" in 1947 and launching "an offensive in April and September 1965."[49] Such accounts are guided by a logocentric logic where binary opposites operate in such a manner that the opponent is always the embodiment of lesser and evil forces. Pakistani leadership is considered "unscrupulous" because it might try to "pressurize India to part ways with Jammu and Kashmir" and "may pose a nuclear threat to India."[50] This historical representation of Pakistan as the guilty party in the nuclear stalemate in the subcontinent would become a staple theme of Indian nukespeak. Interestingly, this early nuclear discourse was allocating responsibility to Pakistan well before Islamabad had embarked on its controversial nuclear path. Given the friendship between "expansionist" China and "aggressive" Pakistan, Singh's suggestions for India are unequivocal.

The case for acquisition of nuclear weapons proceeds with an appeal to what are considered obvious "truths." Paramount among them is the fact that "nuclear weapons are the supreme symbol of national self-reliance" and "the states without them tend to be ignored by those who have them."[51] Since China has them, the small Asian states "have no alternative to accepting China's supremacy and domination." The Indian role is seen in terms of a country capable of breaking "the myth of China's supremacy and will act as a deterrent to its expansionist policy."[52] Opting for nuclear weapons would not only serve as an effective deterrent against China but also enhance India's credibility vis-à-vis small countries like Nepal and Bhutan who "have begun to doubt the ability of India to protect and defend them."[53] It is obvious that India's interest in countering China's position is guided by the equally expansionist desire to hold sway over smaller neighbors. Hence, while accusing China of expansionism and hegemonism, the course charted for India entails the same objectives. The byword for hegemony here is India's ability to "defend" its smaller neighbors.

The twin strategies of the dominant discourse, that is, holding external adversaries responsible for internal chaos and conducting an ideological witch-hunt against domestic opponents of nuclear discourse, could be seen, as evidenced in Singh's work, at play in India by 1971. Antinuclear elements were portrayed as a group lacking "strategic understanding." Any deviation from the dominant path of thinking is relegated to naïveté rather than an alternative mode of thinking. In summarizing the benefits of nuclear weapons, Singh argues that they would "help to foster national pride and help to further internal unity."[54] This logic assumes that opponents of the nuclear option wanted to undermine the unity of the country and lessen its international status. As far as the costs of not developing nuclear weapons go, they are outlined as universal truths that India simply cannot ignore or escape. "Any nation state that does not develop national power commensurate with its size and population is not likely to be permitted to continue that way for long. It will be reduced in size and population to commensurate with its power."[55]

The symbol of national power commensurate with India's position was nuclear weapons. However, much to the dismay of the doomsday predictions of Singh, India has not been reduced in size or population in spite of not being a formal member of the nuclear club. Yet the use of the scare tactic that India's integrity can only be guaranteed by acquiring nuclear weapons will intensify with the passage of time in the Indian nuclear discourse.

India entered the 1970s on an upbeat note. A decisive victory against Pakistan in 1971 compensated a great deal for the stigma of defeat in 1962 and the indecisive war of 1965. Explosion of what it termed as a peaceful nuclear device in 1974 made the politics of the nuclear issue a lasting feature of the dominant security discourse in India. Krishnaswami Subrahmanyam epitomizes this dominant discourse on the nuclear issue in India.[56] His writings have left an indelible mark on Indian nukespeak in the last two decades, and that is why Subrahmanyam's prominence in this study becomes all too understandable.

THE ROAD TO POKHRAN

> India's role is not that of a middle power. Her area and population rule that out. India will, in the next two or three decades, become a major power, and if she fails to do that, external pressures will break her up.
>
> —K. Subrahmanyam[57]

The manifest destiny of India as a major power and images of its demise in case it does not become one remain at the heart of the security discourse propounded by India's strategic epistemic community. Such a discourse of national security is invariably and typically tied to privileging the self, condemning the other, and a constant reminding of external and internal threats. Writing just before Pakistan's humiliating defeat by India in December 1971, Subrahmanyam was still unsure of India's military might against Pakistan. However, he had no doubts about Pakistan and China's assistance to "the Naga and Mizo hostiles (*sic*)."[58] The solution to warding off such threats was simple: "it [India] must have adequate military power." The champion of the nuclear option in present-day India was aware of the value of nuclear weapons as a source of national power but was less emphatic in his demand to acquire them to show Indian power to the world. Outlining the external enemies' collusion with internal "enemies" to harm India, Subrahmanyam in a somewhat philosophical manner describes what is being threatened.

> India as a national idea is thousands of years old. Indianness which distinguishes the people of the subcontinent from the rest of the world exists. The crisis of Pakistan has been its inability to free itself from the Indianness and establish for itself a separate identity. At the same time, the nation state idea is comparatively new to India. The binding force for a composite nation like this [India] will be common historical memories, commonly shared goals and values, and above all, a sense of pride in belonging to a community. The last one does call for a development of national power. A nation without an image of power is not likely to induce such a pride.[59]

The assertion that contemporary India may be a new entity as a national state but it is based upon a thousands-of-years-old idea of Indianness is axiomatic in this scheme rather than subject to scrutiny. It is conveniently forgotten that the very idea of nation in its modern sense is a recent invention. Stretching it over "thousands of years" sanctifies the present arrangement as the recent stage of an eternal situation and any deviation from it as a sign of momentary aberration.

This brings us to the overriding concern in India's security discourse in which Pakistan is portrayed as an aberration from the Indian norm. That deviation becomes a danger to the fragile Indian identity that continues to grapple with strains emanating from contending claims by various identities within the spatial boundaries of postcolonial India. Emergence of Pakistan as a separate state is viewed as a ploy to weaken India. Pakistan and India are usually cast in diametrically opposite terms in which the latter always represents the forces of good. The dark shadow of Pakistan always helps to illuminate the achievements of India. Even when the discussion is about democracy in India, Pakistan serves as an example that tried to do without it and "came to grief."[60] Similarly, India is portrayed as a resounding success as a federal polity by initiating the reorganization of states and Pakistan as a dismal failure. To assert such claims, the notion of instilling a sense of national pride through enhancing the image of national power comes in handy for strategic analysts. The nuclear program ultimately becomes a symbol of national power in the dominant security discourse.

Although India is juxtaposed as a secular and democratic unified whole pitted against an undemocratic and theocratic Pakistan, Subrahmanyam is aware of identity-based movements within India that assert contending identities. The case of the Indian Muslim community's reluctance to accept the secular claims of the Indian state is one of the constant reminders of New Delhi's failure to sell the secular dream to the Indian population. Subrahmanyam largely blamed Muslims for this situation. In 1973 he argued that "over the past 26 years of our secular life this largest minority has not moved closer to integration with the national polity, but has remained alienated."[61] Integration here implies assimilation and it is obvious that for Subrahmanyam secular is a synonym of Hindu. Alienation of Muslims is quickly dubbed as their emotional attachment to Pakistan, which makes them dubious Indians. It is claimed that the Indian army's triumph against Pakistan in 1971 "produced a traumatic effect on sections of the Muslim community in India."[62]

The insistence by Muslims on using Urdu language is considered a key evidence of this community's lack of allegiance to India and attachment to Pakistan. Contrary to claims of India being a composite multilingual and multiethnic state where various languages may flourish, the Indian Muslims' affiliation with Urdu is seen by Subrahmanyam as something that perpetuates communalism among them. As a result, they (Muslims) are held responsible for the rise of Hindu communalism in India.[63] His recipe to resolve the problem is as simplistic as his analysis. Muslims should "see how the Indian Christians have adjusted and integrated themselves with the mainstream of Indian life."[64] Once again, the term "Indian life" implies "Hindu life." Although it would be erroneous to assume that there is something undifferentiated called Hindu life, let alone Indian life, the talk of the new Indian identity at the expense of other contending identities in the mainstream discourse is a byword for upper-caste Hindu ethos.

The reason for outlining K. Subrahmanyam's views on issues like Indian Muslims and Pakistani and Indian nationalism is to inform the reader of the broader context in which Indian nukespeak operates. The talk of security is meaningless without threats, and the above-mentioned are some of the threats invoked by the Indian analysts.

Technological developments in the nuclear field and the emerging epistemic community of strategic analysts existed in somewhat mutually exclusive compartments in India. No event better illustrates that than India's first nuclear explosion in May 1974 in the desert of the state of Rajasthan. The Pokhran test, as it is popularly referred to due to the name of the village at the site, was euphemistically termed by the Indian government as a peaceful nuclear explosion (PNE). The test was a total surprise for the world as well as for the Indian security analysts. Retroactively, the Indian strategic community has regarded the explosion as a defining moment but at the time of its occurrence, none of the analysts had a clue to the impending development. Therefore, all accounts of the Pokhran explosion are *post facto*. This signifies that the politics of nuclear weapons is not dependent upon the actual technological developments or lack of them. Nuclear discourse operates in a broader context and the technological hallmarks are used as symbols and signs for political purposes. It is not imperative for strategic analysts to be aware of technological developments or be well versed in nuclear science in order to champion the nuclear cause. The technical information does come in handy but the stamp of expertise is bestowed or denied on the basis of which side is chosen in the regime of truth. That is solely a political issue and our concern here will be to analyze the political uses of the Pokhran test by the Indian security analysts.

Only a select group of people, who did not even include the minister of defense, knew in advance about the Pokhran test. According to Raja Ramanna,[65] then director of the Bhabha Atomic Research Center (BARC), only six people were present at the crucial meetings in which the decision about the explosion was made.[66] However, the international reaction to the test and the subsequent response of the Indian authors has become an integral part of the nuclear discourse. Our focus will be on the Indian security analysts' perception of the international reaction, especially that of Pakistan, and some important elements of their response.

REACTION TO POKHRAN

The standard Indian response to the West's condemnation of the Indian nuclear test was to castigate it as the advanced nations' determination to "crush India for its temerity."[67] The Western criticism is portrayed a hypocritical response of the developed world in the wake of a scientific stride by a Third World country. The Western suspicion regarding the military aspect of the Indian explosion is dismissed on the basis of the official Indian position that the Pokhran test was a peaceful nuclear explosion and nothing more than that. In spite of heavy security, reaching the level of paranoia, surrounding the test and the intricate link between the civilian and military uses of nuclear technology, Indian authors and decision-makers insist upon accepting the official stance of New Delhi at its face value. Anything else was either hypocrisy or an attempt to crush India.

International criticism of the Indian explosion was not confined to the West alone. Some developing countries expressed their concern over the Indian test in terms of it being a blow to international nonproliferation efforts and harmful for the South Asian security environment. Pakistan, understandably, reacted sharply to the Indian test and its reaction continues to evoke response from Indian analysts. Before discussing the Indo-Pakistan exchange on the issue in detail, I will document the Indian reaction to other critical voices on its test that emanated from other Third World countries.

When the Philippines questioned India's motives behind the test, Raja Ramanna was surprised by the reaction and saw it as a "part of the larger conspiracy to develop a rift in the cordial relations between India and the Philippines."[68] Ramanna blamed a senior Philippines diplomat for orchestrating the plot to sour good relations between the two countries. Disparaging another country's reaction is a hallmark of the Indian nuclear discourse. First, the very concern of a Third World country other than Pakistan about the Indian test becomes an anomaly in light of the Indian claim that its test symbolized the Third World's resolve against the nuclear odds. To resolve that anomaly without undermining the validity of the Indian claim, the next best option is to allege that the other Third World country was naive enough to become a tool in the West's conspiracy against India. The Philippines here is not the perpetrator of a plot against India but a mere passive actor deployed by the West. Furthermore, the country's position (in this case the Philippines') should not be taken seriously because the stance in question is that of a single official who was apparently working under the instructions of the West. In that whole scenario, the act, namely, the Indian nuclear explosion, that prompted the Philippines' reaction is eclipsed by the talk of international conspiracy and a critical assessment of the Indian step is deemed unnecessary. The awkward position of India in international atomic diplomacy is seen as the price for adhering to a principled nuclear stand based upon the equal right of all nations to exploit nuclear energy for peaceful purposes. The most common way to explain it is by creating a dichotomy of the West versus the non-West, where India symbolizes the true interests of the non-West.

The Indian strategic experts' response to the Pakistani reaction had a lasting impact on the nature and direction of the nuclear discourse in years to follow. Pakistan was portrayed as an unruly child whose objective in international forums dealing with atomic issues is to embarrass India. Such Pakistani tactics make things difficult for India, which has to cope with the West's "pressure to sign an unequal treaty (the NPT)."[69] In this process to "intimidate" India the West uses Pakistan. In Ramanna's opinion, Pakistan "was instigated by the others to make mischief."[70] Others relegated Pakistan's reaction as a "hue and cry" that was "part of the game her military allies may be playing."[71] Pakistan's concern over the Indian nuclear tests was reduced to a "ruse to follow her foreign policy goals."[72] This careful construction of the Other relegates it to an entity incapable of independent decision-making. Consequently, if Pakistan is assumed to be acting on the West's instructions then its protestations regarding India's actions become crocodile tears. In the end, the sum total of Pakistan's international diplomacy is negatively dubbed as "mischief" to convey that any criticism of India by its next-door neighbor merits no serious consideration. If Pakistan contended that the Indian test aggravated the regional security and posed a threat to its national security, Indians dismissed it as a figment of Islamabad's imagination. Some Indian authors eventually claimed that Pakistan's nuclear ambitions predated the Indian explosion; therefore, the responsibility for introducing the nuclear element into South Asian security rests with Pakistan and the Indian explosion had nothing to do with it. A detailed examination of these claims will shed light on the contents of present-day Indian nuclear discourse. The next chapter is devoted to this analysis, because such claims are at the heart of the latest phase of the Indian nukespeak that started in the late 1970s with a renewed interest in the so-called Islamic bomb of Pakistan.

NOTES

1. The phrase "a tryst with destiny" comes from Jawaharlal Nehru's speech delivered on the eve of India's independence on August 14, 1947. See Jawaharlal Nehru, *India's Foreign Policy: Selected Speeches, September 1946–April 1961* (Publication Division, Ministry of Information and Broadcasting, Government of India), n.dc p. 13. "Midnight's Children" comes from the title of Salman Rushdie's novel about the contemporary India. Midnight's Children has now become the byword for the generation of Indians born in the 1940s. See Salman Rushdie, *Midnight's Children* (London: J. Cape, 1981).

2. G. G. Mirchandani, *India's Nuclear Dilemma* (New Delhi: Popular Book Services, 1968), p. 49. This is one of the earlier and in-depth surveys of Indian opinion-makers on the nuclear issue. Mirchandani's book is an essential primer available to students of the nuclear debate in India.

3. Nehru, *India's Foreign Policy*, p. 13.

4. Ibid., p. 23.

5. Ibid.

6. Ibid., p. 44.

7. Shyam Bhatia, *India's Nuclear Bomb* (New Delhi: Vikas, 1979), p. 11.

8. Nehru, *India's Foreign Policy*, p. 134.

9. Ashok Kapur, *India's Nuclear Option: Atomic Diplomacy and Decision Making* (New York and London: Praeger, 1976), p. 6.

10. Ibid., p. 8.

11. Nehru, *India's Foreign Policy*, p. 152.

12. Ibid.
13. Ibid., p. 259.
14. Ibid., p. 42.
15. Ibid., p. 289.
16. Ibid.
17. Ibid.
18. Nehru at a press conference in November 1954, in A. Appadorai, ed., *Selected Documents on India's Foreign Policy and Relations: 1947–1972, Vol. I* (Delhi: Oxford University Press, 1982), p. 472.
19. Nehru's speech at a banquet held in honour of Chou en-Lai in New Delhi on June 26, 1954, Ibid., p. 468.
20. For various aspects of the Sindo-Indian dispute see Neville Maxwell, *India's China War* (London: Penguin, 1972); Alastair Lamb, *The China-India Border: The Origins of the Disputed Boundaries* (London: Oxford University Press, 1964); Ramakrishna Rao and R. C. Sharma, eds., *India's Borders: Ecology and Security Perspectives* (New Delhi: Scholars Publishing Forum, 1991).
21. Nehru, *India's Foreign Policy*, p. 363.
22. Nehru's letter to Chou En-Lai dated October 27, 1962, in A. Appadorai, *India's Foreign Policy*, p. 656.
23. Indian authors tend to offer an overestimated account of India's role in international atomic diplomacy to achieve genuine disarmament. J. P. Jain's *Nuclear India Vol. I and II* (New Delhi: Radiant, 1974) in two volumes is an excellent source about India's nuclear politics. Volume II is a collection of documents ranging from the details of discussions in Lok Sabha on the nuclear issue to submissions of Homi Bhabha at international forums. Ashok Kapur's *India's Nuclear Option* (1976) is a good overall history of India's nuclear diplomacy and the history of development of nuclear technology in India. For a highly one-sided account that portrays India as the undisputed leader of the Third World interests on the nuclear issue see K. K. Pathak, *Nuclear Policy of India: A Third World Perspective* (New Delhi: Gitanjali Prakashan, 1980).
24. (Dr.) Homi J. Bhabha (1909–1966) is rightly viewed as the architect of India's atomic energy program. The Cambridge-trained physicist as early as 1945 persuaded India's industrial giant, the House of Tatas, to establish the Tata Institute for Fundamental Research (TIFR), and in 1948 played a key role in setting up the Indian Atomic Energy Commission (AEC) in 1948. With his efforts the AEC decided to set up the Atomic Energy Establishment (AEE) at Trombay in 1954. The AEE was renamed Bhabha Atomic Research Centre (BARC) in 1972. Bhabha, a close confidant of Nehru, was at the helm of nuclear affairs of India until his death in an air crash in January 1966.
25. Vijay Laxmi Pandit, who was Nehru's sister, was India's leading diplomatic figure. She served as India's representative at the UN and ambassador to the United States. Because of her close ties with Nehru, who took a keen interest in India's external relations, she exercised considerable influence in India's early foreign policy making. Statement by Vijay Laxmi Pandit in the UN General Assembly, November 4, 1948, in J. P. Jain, *Nuclear India, Vol. II* (New Delhi: Radiant Publishers, 1974), p. 3.
26. While speaking in Lok Sabha in 1954. Nehru, *India's Foreign Policy*, pp. 191–192.

27. Homi Bhabha's presidential address at the First International Conference on the Peaceful Uses of Atomic Energy, August 1955. See Jain, *Nuclear India, Vol. II*, p. 14.

28. Bhabha speaking in 1957 at the IAEA conference. Ibid., p. 47.

29. Statement by Bhabha before the Atomic Industrial Forum Annual Conference, Washington, DC, November 1959. Ibid., p. 97.

30. Nehru, *India's Foreign Policy*, p. 200.

31. Bhatia, *India's Nuclear Bomb*, p. 109.

32. Mirchandani, *India's Nuclear Dilemma*, p. 24.

33. Ibid., p. 25.

34. Bhatia, *India's Nuclear Bomb*, p. 109.

35. See J. P. Jain, *Nuclear India, Vol. II*, p. 139.

36. Also see the draft of a talk by Homi Bhabha on All India Radio in August 1964 titled "Overview of Atomic Development in India," in Jain, *Nuclear India*, pp. 145–150.

37. Ibid., p. 109.

38. Ibid., p. 111.

39. Bhatia, *India's Nuclear Bomb*, p. 117.

40. Kapur, *India's Nuclear Option*, p. 178.

41. *The United Nations and Nuclear Non-Proliferation*, United Nations Blue Book Series, Vol. III (New York, 1995), pp. 18–19.

42. Bhatia, *India's Nuclear Bomb*, pp. 121–126.

43. Sampooran Singh, *India and the Nuclear Bomb* (New Delhi: C. Chand, 1971), p. iii.

44. See Jain, *Nuclear India, Vol. II*, p. 169.

45. Ibid., p. 173.

46. Sampooran Singh, *India and the Nuclear Bomb* (New Delhi: C. Chand, 1971), pp. 75–76.

47. Ibid., p. 77.

48. Ibid., p. 80.

49. Ibid., p. 80.

50. Ibid., p. 111.

51. Ibid., p. 97.

52. Ibid., p. 99.

53. Ibid., p. 102.

54. Ibid., p. 131.

55. Ibid., p. 132.

56. Krishnaswami Subrahmanyam is considered the flag-bearer of India's nuclear hawks. He has served as Secretary of Defense Production and Chairman of the Joint Intelligence Committee for the government of India. He was head of the Institute for Defense and Strategic Analyses, New Delhi. In the latter capacity this prolific writer became a key exponent of India retaining the nuclear option. At present he works with a Calcutta based NGO.

57. K. Subrahmanyam, *Our National Security* (New Delhi: Economic and Research Foundation, 1972), p. ix.

58. Ibid., p. 15.

59. Ibid., pp. 15–16.

60. K. Subrahmanyam, *Defence and Development* (Calcutta: Minerva Associates, 1973), p. 35.

61. Ibid., p. 77.

62. Ibid.

63. Ibid., p. 78.

64. Ibid.

65. (Dr.) Raja Ramanna (1925–) studied at King's college, London, for his doctorate. He became director of the BARC in 1972 and also served as Minister of State for Defense in 1990. He later became Director of the National Institute of Advanced Studies in Bangalore, India.

66. According to Ramanna, the following people participated in those meetings: Mrs. Indira Gandhi; P. N. Haskar, the former Principal Secretary to the Prime Minister; P. N. Dhar, the incumbent Principal secretary; Dr. Nag Chaudhary, Scientific Advisor to the Defence Minister; H. N. Sethna, then Chairman of the Atomic Energy Commission; and Ramanna himself. See Raja Ramanna, *Years of Pilgrimage: An Autobiography* (New Delhi: Viking, Penguin, 1991), p. 89.

67. Ibid., p. 92.

68. Ibid., p. 72.

69. Ibid., p. 83.

70. Ibid.

71. K. K. Pathak, *Nuclear Policy of India: A Third World Perspective* (New Delhi: Gitanjali Prakashan, 1980), p. 178.

72. Ibid., p. 180.

Chapter 3

Contemporary Indian Nuclear Discourse

The Atal Bihari Vajpayee government's induction of nuclear weapons in India's arsenal within two months of assuming power proved to be one of those rare exceptions when an Indian political party fulfilled one of its election promises. The nuclear explosions of May 1998 erased the thin line that divided the official Indian denial of possessing atomic bombs and the security discourse that considered retention of the nuclear option as an integral part of the Indian identity. The somber and reflective mood that characterized the fiftieth independence anniversary celebrations of India in August 1997 erupted into national outbursts of jubilation in May 1998 with nuclear fireworks. The atomic pill is now the medicine of choice for the dominant security discourse to revive the flagging national ego of the state. It has become a multipurpose drug to fight India's neighbors, internal dissent, and international inequities. This chapter is a discussion of trends that constitute the core of the contemporary nuclear discourse in India.

The kind of contempt that familiarity has bred between Pakistan and India is found in the latter's dominant security discourse. As demonstrated in the previous chapter, the discussion of the Chinese threat to India could never achieve the intensity that the Pakistan factor could bring to the strategic discourse in India. Pakistan permeates the security discourse of India as an all-encompassing "clear and present danger." Uma Bharti, a stalwart of Bharatiya Janata Party (BJP), captures that sentiment eloquently.

> Who is in occupation of our territory in Kashmir? Who is fuelling terrorism in the Valley? Who has forced lakhs of Kashmiris to flee

> their homes? Who engineered the Bombay blasts? Who is responsible for communal violence in different parts of India? Pakistan.[1]

How and why Pakistan assumes such characteristics in contemporary Indian nuclear discourse is the primary focus of this chapter. I will concentrate on the nuclear discourse since the 1980s when Pakistan's alleged Islamic nuclear bomb became a security concern of "secular and democratic" India. This is followed by a look at Indian nukespeak in the 1990s culminating in the May 1998 nuclear explosions.

The nuclear discourse "has been almost totally appropriated by a handful of scholars and former military officials and government officials who usually present no more than justification of official policy."[2] That is why in this chapter there is a conspicuous presence of the views of Krishnaswami Subrahmanyam, the undisputed nuclear ideologue of India's strategic epistemic community who chaired the National Security Advisory Board that presented the draft of India's nuclear doctrine in August 1999. It is an acknowledgment of the fact that he is a credible representative of the dominant discourse as well as a sign of how a select number of strategic luminaries almost single-handedly dominate the nuclear discourse in India.

Exploring possibilities of denuclearization in the region, Zafar Iqbal Cheema, a leading Pakistani defense expert, suggests that "the chances of denuclearization of South Asia are slim because of the level of nuclear weapons capabilities both countries have acquired."[3] This is so, but for fundamentally different reasons than those suggested by Cheema. The political investment of the voices of the dominant security discourses in India and Pakistan in the nuclear issue makes it immensely difficult for any government to abandon the nuclear option. This chapter expands this theme by highlighting factors that have turned nuclear weapons into a symbol of India's independent identity.

In the nukespeak of the 1990s, the China factor took the backseat mainly due to the improved relations between the two in the post–Cold War period. For most Indian nukespeakers the threat to national security now primarily emanated from Pakistan, whereby China's strategic collaboration with Islamabad made the situation even more difficult for New Delhi. This line of argument became the mainstay of Indian nukespeak when the NPT came up for indefinite renewal in 1995 and the CTBT was signed in 1996. India continued to decline to be a part of either agreement.

ISLAM, THE BOMB, AND PAKISTAN

The military coup in Pakistan in 1977 and the subsequent Islamization program put in place by General Zia-ul-Haq gave a new angle to the nuclear discourse in India. The Islamic bomb, a term coined by Z. A. Bhutto, became the new catchphrase of the Indian strategic community to highlight the dangerousness of Pakistan. Indian nuclear discourse since the 1980s has followed two textual strategies. It either started with a general negative characterization of political Islam and then viewed Pakistan as a part of that larger problem, or it focused on the dangerous aspects of Pakistan and then magnified them as an omen of a wider threat posed by resurgent Islam to India in particular and the world in general. In most Indian accounts, India would usually emerge as an innocent victim at the hands of global powers or Pakistani propaganda.

The other countries of the region generally see the Indian role in the South Asian security environment as an example of a regional hegemon. The strategic community in India is often puzzled by such concerns and quickly dubs them, as K. Subrahmanyam does, as ill-founded propaganda because "India does not have an imperial or expansionist history."[4] Such claims regarding Indian innocence are contradicted subsequently by him through assertions like these:

> The subcontinent is a strategic unity and India as the biggest nation has a special responsibility in ensuring the integrity of all states within the subcontinent especially against the inroads of extra-subcontinental powers.[5]

Pakistan is always seen as a power that inhibits India from exercising its rightful, read hegemonic, responsibility in the region. Subrahmanyam has no doubts that Pakistan's efforts are bound to fail because they contradict the laws of nature. India's dominance is "natural" because of its sheer size, which is ten times that of Pakistan.

Size is not the only factor invoked to justify what are considered by smaller neighbors as India's hegemonic aspirations. Issues of civilization and culture are brought in to demonstrate that South Asia is a single entity and the voices of separate national identities are a mere chimera. Since that singleness is seen as how India describes it, the others' efforts to evolve separate identities are characterized in the following way.

> Pakistani and Bangladeshis resent references to common cultural heritage, shared languages and ethnicity. Pakistan wants to identify itself with West Asia and Bangladeshis with Southeast Asia. The same is true of Sri Lanka. Nepalese want neutrality between India and China.[6]

Practically all South Asian neighbors of India barring Bhutan are condemned for harboring ill will against India because of their own complexes. New Delhi emerges as a victim of smaller neighbors' policies that are not even based on realities. If these neighbors think that India should not act like a big brother in South Asia then they are living in a utopia because "it does not occur to those who advocate that India should not behave as a great power that any other role for this country will not be credible."[7] Since those two factors are a given, R. R. Subramanian, another leading security analyst associated with Institute for Defense Studies and Analyses (IDSA), suggests that India "must project power equal to that of China."[8] Paradoxically no role except that of a regional hegemon is considered acceptable or credible by Indian analysts who assert that India is not vying for supremacy in South Asia. Such notions of great power identity are based upon the geographical size and mammoth population of India. Although India's huge population and vast geography are undeniable facts, it is quite difficult to be convinced by the Indian analysts' hegemonistic discourse that presents the vast pool of poverty-stricken Indian masses as a source of strength.

Nevertheless, India's neighbors are unlikely to comply with New Delhi's wishes and may try to look elsewhere for balancing against India. In order to deal with that situation, the only course suggested for India is to keep "defense equipment up-dated at the level of the rest of the world."[9] Even the remedy to counter smaller neighbors' concerns is militaristic. When Pakistan or any other neighboring country quotes instances like the Indian armed intervention in Sri Lanka or Maldives as examples of regional muscle-flexing, Indian authors argue that

> the Indian forces went to Sri Lanka and Maldives at the request of their respective governments, and also came back as and when the situation demanded. It spent huge resources in Sri Lanka, and faced heavy casualties too, in order to ensure the island nation's integrity, and still got the blame for hegemonistic designs.[10]

Rather than critically examining the historical context and New Delhi's pressures to get "invited" into tiny countries, D. D. Khanna and Kishore Kumar assume smaller neighbors' willingness to have Indian forces on their territory. Second, the Indian dominant discourse sees no hegemonic designs even when India took it upon itself to ensure other sovereign countries' integrity. We are all too familiar with the similar rationale given by the Soviets while intervening in Afghanistan and Hungary to legitimize their expansionist moves.

The doublespeak of portraying India as a genuine great power that has a "natural" right to correct wrongs in neighboring countries to ensure its legitimate interests is in marked contrast with claims that India does not harbor any expansionist or hegemonistic desires in the region. One way, although never fully successful, to resolve this contradiction has been through holding smaller countries responsible for leaving no room for India but to intervene in their internal affairs in a variety of ways. This unresolved contradiction is at the heart of the Indian nukespeak. The following section concentrates on the other side of the above coin, that is, what is it that makes Pakistan or others seem to be bad neighbors? The focus will be on Pakistan because it emerges as the main villain to Indian strategic community. Some aspects of this issue, like views on partition, have already been discussed in the previous chapter; here, the focus will be on the literature of the 1980s onward when the Indian strategic analysts' concern with the Pakistani nuclear bomb became central to their writings.

GRAND CONSPIRACY VERSUS NATIONAL AUTONOMY

Almost any discussion of Pakistan by the Indian strategic epistemic community addresses the issue of Islam and its role in shaping Pakistani domestic and foreign policies. In spite of the complexities and heterogeneous nature of Islam in India, let alone Islam in general, the Indian security analysts are usually content with stereotypes prevalent in the West about Islam. Foremost among them is the myth of the separation between the Church and state in Christianity and Hinduism, and the fusion of the two in Islam. This fusion allegedly exacerbates conflict between secularism and traditional values in Muslim countries. Because of a blurred line between the state and the mosque "in Islamic countries, the traditional opinion former in the society—namely the clergy—claim jurisdiction to determine the nature of the state and polity and not merely social and religious behavior."[11] The rise of Islamic fundamentalism is explained in terms of "the enormous wealth in the hands of the ruling elites of the Islamic countries as a result of oil price hike."[12] This explanation of a complex phenomenon like the rise of Islamist movements in different countries is a gross oversimplification. First, it wrongly correlates Muslim countries with oil. Countries where Islam is the dominant religion of a majority of the people are not necessarily oil rich. The three most populous Muslim countries, that is, Indonesia, Pakistan, and Bangladesh, cannot boast such a claim. Second, most populist Islamic movements are not found in the oil-rich Muslim countries. For example, the movements in Afghanistan, Algeria, or Lebanon have little or nothing to do with oil price hikes. As for the fusion between the mosque and the state argument, it is futile to make any sweeping generalizations because of the varied forms of governance throughout the so-called Islamic world.[13] Despite the glaring differences that divide the so-called Islamic world, some Indian authors promote the idea of a Muslim "sense of fellowship in the concept of *Millat*" (community), which is said to work against non-Muslims.[14]

The combination of the two factors—the uniqueness of Islam as a religion in which the temporal and spiritual realms are undifferentiated and the alleged sense of community among Muslims around the world—work as grounds to castigate contemporary Pakistan and the scope of its nuclear program. The event of partition still casts a long shadow on the Indian strategic community and the creation of Pakistan usually signifies a paradoxical situation for analysts. Seen as an "artificial" creation by a British-backed political party, that is, the All India Muslim League (AIML), and a theocratic state bent upon creating troubles for India, the accounts concerning Pakistan sometimes have a surreal air.

By the 1980s, Pakistan emerges in Indian security discourse as an unstable, unpredictable, and irrational country that intervenes in India's internal affairs with impunity and poses a nuclear challenge. Discussions about the two recent challenges to the dominant Indian identity by Sikhs in the Punjab and Muslims in Kashmir are seen as ploys of Pakistan to weaken India. General Krishnaswami Sundarji, former chief of staff of the Indian Army, has no doubt that the upheaval in Kashmir was created by the infiltration of regular Pakistani soldiers as volunteers in the valley. Not content with the performance of its soldiers, Pakistan also sends Afghan Mujahideen to Kashmir to fight a proxy war against India.[15] By establishing a link between the Pakistani army and the Afghan Mujahideen, the idea is to show that the domestic troubles of India are perpetrated by a grand coalition of different sources. In the post–Cold War period, the linking of the former Afghan Mujahideen and the Pakistani government in instigating troubles in Kashmir serves the purpose of portraying a grand alliance of Islamic fundamentalist forces. It is implied that such an alliance is certainly against the interests of a secular India in particular and the West in general.

Pakistan is portrayed as a danger with a long history of intervention in Indian internal affairs of which the current uprising in Kashmir is the most recent example. Some Indian experts argue that Pakistan has always "tried to capture Kashmir but the people of Kashmir and the Indian armed forces defeated such plans."[16] Any explanation of upheaval in Kashmir is reduced to the evil desires of Pakistan; and by doing that, an imaginary alliance is created between the Indian armed forces and the Kashmiri people. Those Kashmiris who resist the Indian armed forces, and this number is certainly quite high, by the above definition cease being Kashmiris.

Jasjit Singh, a retired Air Commodore who later became director of the IDSA, unequivocally holds Pakistan responsible for imposing three wars and two major skirmishes on India.[17] The reasons behind this situation include Pakistan's supposed efforts to Balkanize India and the vested interests in Pakistan that project India's military buildup as a threat without recognizing India's needs.[18] Subrahmanyam also echoes the same views and laments the fact that Pakistan has committed aggressions against India because it does not have "adequate respect for India's power."[19] This discourse on bilateral relations invests all responsibility for tension-ridden relations with Pakistan. Any movement within India to assert identities not endorsed by Delhi becomes the handiwork of Pakistan to Balkanize India. The military buildup of India is justified under all circumstances as a legitimate way to address its needs and no matter how genuine the Pakistani concerns, they are nothing but a lack of realization in Islamabad of India's needs.

Any discussion of the Pakistani nuclear program is preceded by such characterizations in the Indian strategic epistemic community where logocentric logic invokes the dangers of an artificial, theocratic, unstable Pakistan against a more natural, secular, and democratic India. The manner in which the nuclear issue is framed is an extension of the above parameters of security discourse where for some "the Pakistan bomb signifies many more things than the possession of a new weapon by a hostile nation, a nation which has not yet reconciled itself to its defeats and disintegration."[20] Indian alarmists have no doubt that the alleged Pakistani bomb "is meant for use against India in a not-so-distant future in a conventional war."[21]

These statements have the power to ring true if repeated endlessly in a regime of truth established in the name of national security. Indian strategic analysts sense a grand coalition between a theocratic Pakistan, communist China, and the capitalist United States to harm India; Pakistan "has been a partner in the neo-colonial design to keep the third world underdeveloped through her alliances with the West."[22] Pakistan's nuclear program becomes a vital component of a greater Western conspiracy to weaken the whole Third World in this scheme. No need is felt to back these assertions by unveiling the mechanisms of the conspiracy having such large-scale implications. K. Subrahmanyam did not credit the Pakistani nuclear program with the scale of undermining the whole Third World; however, the nuclear ambitions of the Zia regime were still seen in terms of Pakistan becoming "the defender of the Gulf area" assuming that "money will pour in from Muslim countries" to fund Pakistan's nuclear program.[23]

In sum, the Pakistani nuclear program is depicted as something more sinister than just a response to the Indian nuclear program. Whereas the Indian nuclear program is conceived in terms of a nationalist project representing the political will and scientific zeal of the Indian establishment, the Pakistani program has more to do with the conspiracy of India's adversaries, an undermining of the so-called Third World interests, and the ganging up of the Muslim world to acquire nuclear capability.

EVIL DESIGNS VERSUS NOBLE INTENTIONS

The Pakistani nuclear program is deemed a danger to India not only in terms of its wider scope but also because of Islamabad's malicious intentions. The intent of Pakistan is considered militaristic as against India's peaceful nuclear program. The broader scope and ill intentions coupled together, according to Indian nuclear discourse, make the Pakistani nuclear program a real danger for India.

A common method to ascribe ill intentions to the Pakistani nuclear establishment has been a spy-thriller mode of representing the career of Dr. Abdul Qadeer Khan, the controversial metallurgist who heads a nuclear research facility in Pakistan. One study argues that Dr. Khan acquired Dutch citizenship to gain access to secret information about nuclear installation designs while working as a researcher in the Netherlands, which was further made easier by "his command of German language."[24] What better proof can one look for of Dr. Khan's evil designs than his presence at the IAEA meeting in 1979 held in Salzburg as a member of the Pakistani delegation where he did not present any paper and asked just one question?[25] By this criterion, a good number of conference participants around the world would qualify as spies with ulterior motives. Reports about Dr. Khan's expeditions are splashed on front pages of the Indian print media. One headline in *Times of India* in 1996 read: "U.S. spies found bomb document in Pakistani scientist's luggage."[26] The story was not only an unconfirmed news item lifted from the *Washington Post*, but it also referred to an alleged incident that took place in the early 1980s. The report said that "during an overseas trip in the early 1980s, Pakistan's foremost scientist Abdul Qadeer Khan's luggage was secretly rifled by U.S. intelligence operatives who found a drawing of a Hiroshima-sized bomb that U.S. officials insist must have been supplied by Beijing." Others state with authority that Dr. Khan made secret notes of the complete design plans of the uranium enrichment process at the Almelo plant during his visit to the site.[27] Such thriller accounts report a wider network of Pakistani nuclear thieves across Europe. That network operated something like this:

> A secret buying network was established in 1975 in Europe to acquire nuclear technology, equipment, components of equipment and materials for reprocessing and for uranium enrichment. S. A. Butt was appointed In charge of Science and Technology at the Pakistani embassy in Brussels in July 1975. In February 1977, he was shifted to the Pakistani Embassy in Paris in the same position. He developed contacts with Belgo Nuclearie and SGN. Most of the purchases made by Butt in France related to reprocessing and only few were to the enrichment project. Ahmad Kamal, the Pakistani Charge Affaires in Paris, was involved in such deals. In January 1977 Ikram-ul-Haque of the Pakistani Ordinance Services was sent to Bonn, where he set up office at Watchberg Pech, 20 miles from the Pakistani Embassy. From there Ikram-ul-Haque placed orders for the enrichment project throughout Europe. The network was known as the Special Works Organization (SWO).[28]

Although some of the instances in the above account may have been just regular bureaucratic appointments or transfers, the author sees a grand scheme to acquire nuclear capability in every move. Any concrete or conclusive evidence, as usual, does not back these allegations. The ill intentions of Pakistan are not only manifest in the clandestine operations of its foreign missions and questionable ways of Pakistani scientists, but also in the greed-stricken mentality of its political leadership as against the moral superiority and far-sightedness of the Indian leadership. Prior to the May 1998 explosions, the Indian nuclear program was portrayed as patently civilian in nature guided by the vision of the Nehru-Bhabha team, whereas the Pakistani program was militaristic from day one.[29] This assumption is validated in two interestingly interrelated ways. First, the Indian strategic analysts discount the Pakistani claim that their program is a response to the security threats posed by Indian activities in the nuclear and conventional spheres and claim that the Pakistani nuclear program predates the Indian nuclear program. Second, the above point is stressed by the peculiar personality traits of the Pakistani leadership and their domestic needs.

The Indian nuclear explosion of 1974 is a watershed event in Pakistani dominant discourse that qualitatively changed the security environment of the subcontinent by introducing the nuclear factor, leaving no choice for the Pakistani decision-makers but to retain the nuclear option. This is not what prompted Pakistan to pursue nuclear ambiguity, according to the Indian authors. They argue that Pakistan introduced the nuclear factor in the region and Islamabad's nuclear ambitions predate the Pokhran 1974 test. K. Subrahmanyam uses deductive logic to argue that since Pakistan introduced F-104 aircraft, sophisticated tanks, and staged aggressions in 1947 and 1965, it would be perfectly reasonable to assume that Pakistan introduced the nuclear factor in the Indo-Pakistan relations.[30] This oft-repeated tactic of blaming Pakistan, not India, for introducing the nuclear factor usually makes a special reference to Z. A. Bhutto's role. Rikhi Jaipal, a leading strategic expert, argues that "it would be a mistake to imagine that Pakistan developed nuclear ambitions only after the Indian test explosion."[31] This assertion is made on the basis that since Z. A. Bhutto exercised considerable influence in foreign and defense policy-making in Pakistan during the 1960s, his penchant for nuclear means to meet the energy as well as security needs must have sown the seeds of Pakistan's nuclear program.

The Indian accounts conveniently forget that despite Bhutto's insistence on seriously exploring the costs and benefits of a nuclear program, General Ayub Khan, then president of Pakistan, never looked sympathetically into the matter and even naively maintained that Pakistan would buy nuclear weapons off the shelf if such a need arose.[32] For some Indian authors, Bhutto appears as a man obsessed with acquiring nuclear weapons well before India exploded its nuclear device.[33] For others, it was his personal greed that led to the nuclear stalemate in the subcontinent.[34] Those who are more generous say that Bhutto introduced the nuclear factor because of domestic compulsions.[35] In sum, it was one or the other aspect of Bhutto's personality or political expediency that introduced the nuclear factor into Indo-Pakistan interaction. India in these accounts emerges as a helpless bystander, which was dragged into the nuclear mire by Pakistan.

The Indian innocence is patent even in stories that hypothetically deal with situations of open nuclear confrontation with Pakistan. General K. Sundarji's fictional depiction of such a situation is pertinent in this connection.[36] He imagines two scenarios involving the use of nuclear weapons in an Indo-Pakistan conflict and its subsequent results. First, the Pakistani decision-makers, unsure about the Indian nuclear capabilities, launch a successful nuclear attack resulting in an unfair cease-fire imposed on India. The second scenario envisages India responding in kind and emerging victorious. In both situations, it is Pakistan who initiates the nuclear war. In both cases, the war is a result of Pakistan's unabated support for secessionists in Kashmir and its ignorance of the Indian ultimatums to desist from anti-India activities. So we need not be mistaken about the cause of the conflict in each case, that is, Pakistan's bid to Balkanize India.

In the first scenario of imaginary warfare where the Indian nuclear capability is not taken seriously, "Pakistan's consummate skills in propaganda" try to portray the insurgency in Kashmir as a popular uprising and it threatens to use all means to combat an Indian attack.[37] That is read as a threat of the use of nuclear weapons against India that creates panic in the Indian public, cities come to a grinding halt, economic activities are badly disrupted, and so forth. The conventional war starts in the plains and Pakistan immediately resorts to using nuclear weapons and targets defense establishments, initially killing 10,000 people. Pakistan claims that they had definite information about an impending Indian nuclear attack, which Sundarji considers "a masterpiece in disinformation."[38] Pakistan manages to win the international community's support and agrees to a cease-fire provided Indians surrender in Kashmir, withdraw from the plains, and agree to hold a plebiscite in Kashmir. Or else it (Pakistan) will continue nuking India. India is left with no option but to agree to the cease-fire offer. The Indian prime minister resigns after the disgrace. The whole situation turns out, after all, to be an imaginary Indian prime minister's nightmare. That calls for a fundamental reassessment of the Indian defense strategy against Pakistan. Before I move to the next scenario depicted by General Sundarji, it is worth pausing for a moment to highlight some elements of nukespeak in this portrayal.

It is Pakistan, that instigates violence and has the audacity to ignore the Indian ultimatum. Dismissing all the evidence available of nuclear-capable states' conduct during wars in contemporary history, it is presumed that the trigger-happy Pakistani decision-makers would use nuclear weapons at the first available opportunity. And not only will they be successful in crippling the Indian defense establishment, but they will be able to convince the world of the necessity of using their nuclear weapons through their "disinformation." Such accounts become possibilities only with the suspension of minimal logic while reading them. But we are told it was just an Indian prime minister's nightmare. A more realistic scenario, according to General Sundarji, proceeds on the following lines.

The Indian leadership is convinced of the minimum deterrence value of nuclear weapons and appropriate delivery systems. This is conveyed to Pakistan in clear terms along with a declared "no first use" policy, which puts Pakistan in a difficult strategic situation. Once again the starting point of the conflict is Pakistan's intervention in the Indian part of Kashmir; India issues an ultimatum to Pakistan to refrain from such activities or be ready for a full-scale war. Pakistan, as usual, does not heed the Indian voice and the war in the plains starts. Pakistani forces prove no match for the Indian army in the conventional realm. In desperation, Pakistan unleashes a nuclear attack hitting cities like Mumbai and Delhi. The Indian response is based upon the following dictum: "Our anger should be directed at those crazy decision-makers in Islamabad-Rawalpindi rather than at the people of Pakistan."[39] Instead of a massive response, India opts for a quid pro quo, and even there it decides to "spare Karachi because Indian Muslims' relatives live in the city."[40]

Here again India emerges as the considerate and saner country that keeps its cool even in the wake of a nuclear attack by the "crazy decision-makers" of Pakistan. Although Pakistan does not take into account the relatives of Pakistani Muslims who could have been killed in their nuclear attacks on Delhi and Mumbai, the Indians desist from attacking Karachi, the largest metropolis and business center of Pakistan, because it cares about Muslims. However, the care-for-Muslims factor hardly gets any attention by General Sundarji while discussing the uprising in Kashmir valley where Muslims are up against what they perceive to be Indian occupying forces. But we should not forget that partial historical amnesia is an essential condition of nukespeak.

Such an edifice of the Indian nukespeak based upon holding Pakistan responsible for the nuclear imbroglio in the subcontinent comes under stress when Pakistani officials unequivocally propose to sign the NPT if India does the same, or when they recommend declaring South Asia as a nuclear-weapons-free zone (NWFZ). Why would Pakistan, which is held responsible for aggravating the security scenario, come up with such drastic proposals? Do such proposals not belie the basis of the Indian allegations? Would acceding to these proposals not be a giant step toward significantly improving the security environment in the region? Or, at least, would that not expose Pakistani hypocrisy on the issue? It would be appropriate for students of India-Pakistan security relations to ask these questions when comparing the Pakistani proposals to the general trends of Indian nukespeak. For our purposes we will look into the works of the Indian "strategic fraternity" for answers to these questions.

All Pakistani proposals are considered nothing but a pack of unfeasible, impractical, anti-India, pro-West moves to undermine India's principled stand on the issue of proliferation. Therefore, when Pakistan advocates declaring South Asia a NWFZ and denuclearizing the Indian ocean, it is construed by Subrahmanyam as an indication of "the lack of contact with reality on the part of Pakistan's foreign policy establishment, its being conditioned by Western literature and its playing [the] role of surrogate of some great powers."[41] The cherished term among "realist" scholars of "national interests," which seems to be used to justify the Indian nuclear stance, does not find its way while describing Pakistani proposals to deal with the same issue. P. L. Bhola does not see these Pakistani proposals simply as a means of furthering the Western interests, but as a cloak to "conceal Pakistan's nuclear intentions."[42] He argues that when Pakistan made the NWFZ proposal in 1972, it "had already taken a secret decision to go nuclear."[43] Therefore, a proposal whose main purpose was to "mask the reality of Pakistan's nuclear program" rightly invoked a response of indifference by India. One can argue that the best way to unmask the Pakistani duplicity would have been through accepting its proposal of either signing the NPT or declaring South Asia a NWFZ. At this juncture, Indian authors mention New Delhi's principled stand against the nuclear apartheid in the form of NPT. Hence the Pakistani proposals are termed as ploys to demean the Indian status from a principled great power to a regional adversary of Pakistan—an identity unacceptable to India due to its size and being a civilizational entity.

While some Indian analysts see the Pakistani proposals as a means either of concealing the military aspects of Islamabad's nuclear program or of furthering the West's interests through making such suggestions, there is a third group that finds the Pakistani proposals to be aimed at benefiting China to the cost of India. In this scheme Pakistan is dancing to the Chinese tune to undermine India's stature.[44]

How do the Indian authors sum up the different policy stands of the two countries on the ways to resolve the nuclear issue in the region? Subrahmanyam declares that "the Indian policy is principled and practical" implying that the Pakistani stand lacks principles and is impractical.[45] One inevitably ponders why the Pakistani stand, which is professedly guided by perceiving a security threat from India, is unprincipled or impractical. Guided by the tenets of political realism, Pakistan is trying to safeguard national interests, as defined by the dominant security discourse of the country, by tying its nuclear program to that of India's. In principle, Pakistan appears to be ready to abide by any international or bilateral arrangement that lifts the cloud of nuclear ambiguity in South Asia. Yet these proposals are termed insincere by the Indian writers just because they do not echo the Indian aspirations of being granted the identity of a great power.

Why is it that Pakistan continues to present such ideas? Subrahmanyam decries the "loss of nerve on the part of the Indian leadership that emboldened Pakistan to challenge India in the nuclear field, treat India condescendingly and propose to India calculatedly demeaning proposals."[46] This language of blatant regional hegemonic dreams is at the heart of claims made in the name of a country said to be devoid of any such aspirations.

By now it has become clear, if one accepts the Indian accounts, that Pakistan introduced the nuclear factor in the subcontinent, and the Pokhran in 1974 explosion had hardly anything to do with the present-day situation. The Pakistani nuclear program is variously described as wider in scope ranging from a conspiracy against the Third World to being an instrument in Western and Chinese hands. Pakistani intentions are also suspect when it suggests signing international agreements to curb proliferation. India stands diametrically opposed to these features and is portrayed as a country with noble intentions, concerned with genuine national security matters, sincerely trying for global disarmament, and bereft of any aspirations to become the regional hegemon.

If the early 1980s were marked by the emergence of the Islamic bomb as a patent factor in Indian nukespeak, the decade ended with monumental changes in the international system that neither Indian decision-makers nor security analysts had imagined. Foremost among them was the collapse of the Soviet Union, the key source of arms procurement for India, and the consequent rise of the United States as the global hegemon. In the next section I will look at some of the possible ways suggested by the strategic fraternity in India to deal with the changing situation.

NUKESPEAK IN THE 1990s

The end of the Cold War was either a curse or a blessing for India, depending on how one looked at the new situation. The changing pattern of the international scene was considered a curse when the United States made antiproliferation a key point in its foreign policy agenda. This became most obvious during 1995–1996 when considerable U.S. pressure was mounted on India to be part of the NPT and the Comprehensive Nuclear Test Ban Treaty (CTBT). The post-Afghanistan period was a blessing because Pakistan was no longer needed by the United States as the frontline state to contain communism. Islamabad lost the status of the best ally of the United States in South Asia as well as arms and monetary aid that came with it. It became, and continues to be, a target of U.S. punitive measures because of Islamabad's alleged nuclear program and abetting of international terrorism. As the Arabic proverb "the enemy of my enemy is my friend" suggests, the Indian strategic elite also saw a potential for closer Indo-U.S. ties to combat "Islamic fundamentalism." This was the new catchphrase used in the United States to describe post–Cold War dangers to Washington. On the other hand, opposition to the U.S.-sponsored New World Order (NWO) was seen by India as a common ground to forge closer ties with China, because Beijing also expressed reservations against the NWO. Paradoxes as a result of a combination of this multitude of international developments have characterized the dominant security discourse of India in the post–Cold War period.

Where did India's nuclear option fit in the new scheme of things? The dominant security discourse in India maintains that clinging to the nuclear option would serve multiple functions like standing up to international pressure, warding off the Chinese threat, thwarting prospective Pakistani adventures, raising India's global stature, and providing it with a cost-effective deterrent. Anyone suggesting otherwise is either an external agent or ignorant of the needs of national sovereignty.

K. Subrahmanyam, the authoritative voice on national security matters, consistently favored the exercise of the nuclear option in order to deal with China on an equal footing and deter Pakistan because of the decisive advantages in the Indian favor due to its geography and the location of its large cities far from Pakistan. Above all, after the exercise of the nuclear option, the United States would not ignore India.[47] Abdication of nuclear weapons was considered an invitation to Pakistani or Chinese challenges, and the coercive diplomacy of any nuclear power.[48] Given the Indian inability to verify Pakistan's nuclear status, going nuclear was considered the best way to deal with the situation.[49]

This line of argument does not acknowledge Pakistani proposals to jointly renounce the nuclear option and open the nuclear sites of both countries to International Atomic Energy Agency (IAEA) safeguards. When it remembers these suggestions, they are castigated as insincere or aimed at eroding India's international status. However, Indian analysts do not acknowledge that by not accepting the Pakistani proposals, the burden of the present imbroglio shifts to Indian shoulders. Rather, the argument is made that it is always Pakistan's clandestine nuclear activities that force India to respond in kind. The nuclear wishes of Subrahmanyam are best captured when he passionately expresses them in the following way: "I, for one, would not be apologetic to admit that India has nuclear weapons if I am convinced of it and I shall be only too happy to be so convinced."[50] Probably Dr. Rajgopal Chidambaram, who, according to *India Today*, "was a key member of the core team that secretly designed India's atom bomb," was simply addressing Subrahmanyam's wishes when in response to a question whether India was still making bombs he said, "We have built up an extraordinary range of know-how and expertise on all aspects of nuclear technology . . . there is now nothing India cannot do."[51]

Nuclear weapons are depicted as an effective and cheaper way of deterring enemies and boosting the Indian image. Those who think that defense expenditure eats up much-needed scarce resources for developing India's social sector are politically naive at best or external spies at worst. National security and development are considered "the (two) sides of the coin of nation-state building."[52] The costs of the Indian nuclear program will be quite low because the genius of local scientists can save a lot that the West had to allocate on research and develoment to develop nuclear weapons.[53] Another suggestion to minimize the costs of the nuclear program is to laterally induct retiring servicemen in the civilian sector to make use of their expertise and save on pensions.[54]

India decided not to become part of the CTBT in 1996. The treaty was portrayed as an extension of the discriminatory NPT and harmful to Indian security interests. K. Subrahmanyam argued that Sino-Pakistan cooperation in the nuclear field is a danger to India and despite China being a signatory to the NPT and the CTBT, there is no barrier to prevent it from transferring nuclear technology to Pakistan.[55] The alleged Sino-Pakistan collusion came in handy to justify the Indian refusal to sign the CTBT. Notwithstanding the Pakistani offer to sign the CTBT if India did the same, the argument put forward by the adherents of nukespeak in India was that given China's assistance to Pakistan in the nuclear field, India should conduct nuclear tests and then join the CTBT as a "virtual" nuclear power.[56] *India Today* equated the CTBT signing with the capping of India's nuclear program. The BJP remained the most vocal opponent of the Treaty and Jaswant Singh, now serving as India's minister for external affairs, maintained that "the treaty hurts India's national interests more than it does to others."[57] K. Subrahmanyam echoed this idea by suggesting that "India cannot undertake any step which would be interpreted by others as narrowing or closing down its deterrence options. . . . therefore, any discussion about the pros and cons of the treaty in its existing form is mere waste of time for India."[58]

The anti-CTBT stance of India became an exercise of national sovereignty in the wake of imperialist onslaught by countries that perpetuate nuclear hierarchy. India was portrayed as the only country resisting "a hegemonic nuclear order which will cover the globe." The indefinite extension of the NPT, signing of the CTBT, and the proposal of declaring South Asia as a NWFZ were all ingredients of imperialist designs against India.[59] The accession of 153 non-nuclear-weapons states, most belonging to Third World, to the CTBT was condemned as an act of surrendering national sovereignty.[60] The anti-CTBT stance of India in 1996 was a departure from the earlier official position on the test ban issue; in the past such a treaty was considered a prerequisite for a meaningful global disarmament. While addressing the UN Security Council in 1992, P. V. Narasimha Rao, then prime minister, called upon the international community to "conclude a comprehensive Test Ban Treaty" to pave the way for universal disarmament.[61]

The proliferation issue was seen as an omen of a more hostile atmosphere for India in the midst of an American-dominated international system. Reviving the 1950s dream of a Sino-Indian alliance of two Third World giants was one possible way to consolidate India's global stature. Narasimha Rao tried to do this in 1991 during the visit of Chinese Premier Li Peng to Delhi by emphasizing "the formidability of friendship between China and India." Such a friendship in the wake of the changing international situation was considered a pressing need. Rao lamented that:

> there was an unfortunate period of estrangement between us. Our initial closeness, and the momentum of our mutual endeavor were lost. Difference over the border created serious strains in our relationship. This was regrettable for our two countries, for our two people and for the world.[62]

But he maintained that this period was a thing of the past and believed that "the demand of our times is for reconciliation, consensus and the cognizance that our own interests lie in the reconciliation of the interests of all."[63]

Even the BJP was willing to acknowledge that the Chinese threat did not pose an immediate danger to India, and argued that "it was possible to reach an accommodation with China."[64] Meanwhile, any rapprochement with Pakistan was considered a remote possibility. Convinced of Pakistan's intervention in Indian affairs, the BJP suggested a tough stance against Islamabad in both the conventional and nuclear realms.[65] Strategic analysts echoed similar views by downplaying the chances of a Sino-Indian conflict in the wake of growing cooperation between the two. They were more anxious about Indian security concerns in light of Beijing's cooperation with Islamabad. Staunch anti-China analysts like K. Subrahmanyam and K. Sundarji conceded that China posed "little immediate military threat to India."[66] In sum, the China factor did not appear as "a clear and present danger" in India's strategic discourse in the 1990s. That left Pakistan as the main threat to Indian security.

The theme of a Pakistani threat has been accentuated in the Indian security discourse with the eruption of a violent secessionist movement in Kashmir since 1989. The dominant parlance in India sees the trouble in the region as a Pakistan-sponsored move to dismember India. The insurgency is cast in terms of the rise of militant Islamic fundamentalism in the wake of post-Soviet Afghanistan. Pakistan is seen as the breeding and training ground of disgruntled Islamic fundamentalists from all over the world, and a number of these are fomenting trouble in Kashmir. It is in this context that Indian security analysts have explored possibilities of forging closer ties with the United States to combat the common threat of Islamic fundamentalism. This possibility appears real because both countries shared a belief in liberal democracy and secularism, and wanted to exploit the immense potential for trade between the two countries.

Pakistan continues to occupy a central position in the Indian nuclear discourse either as an independent variable or as part of a broader conspiracy against India by China or the Western powers. A recent study of Indian elite opinion on the issue confirms the perception that the nuclear threat from Pakistan is "the single most important factor . . . to consider the nuclear option."[67] No one seems more convinced of it than BJP's Uma Bharti, who considers Pakistan "a mere plaything in the hands of Muslim fundamentalist states. These countries are using Pakistan against Hindu India." Rather than successfully Balkanizing India, in the end "Pakistan will disintegrate." By facilitating that process India will help in ushering "peace in the subcontinent."[68]

The precipitous rise in the 1990s of the BJP, the party whose leaders term the disintegration of India's neighbors as an omen of peace, and its decision to put nukes on the shelf is the latest stage of a security discourse that has long learned to love the bomb.

POKHRAN II AND BEYOND

The 1998 tests were conducted in the afternoon of May 11 under the same cloak of secrecy that characterized the 1974 explosion. The three chiefs of services and the foreign secretary were informed only a day prior to the impending tests. Little has changed in the general characteristics of the dominant security discourse since the 1998 explosions. A look at the post–Pokhran II public debate shows intensification of the thoughts that have dominated the strategic discourse of the 1990s.

Indian political parties are not particularly keen on delivering on most promises they make during election campaigns. Party manifestos read like magic wands for India's ills, yet they hardly matter in affairs of the state. The BJP's election manifesto for 1997–1998 polls vowed, among other provocative promises, to "re-evaluate the country's nuclear policy and exercise the option to induct nuclear weapons."[69] So it did. The party's decision to go ahead with the overt embracing of nuclear weapons is considered an act of consolidating Indian identity based upon the notion of "one nation, one people, one culture." Enthusiastic adherents of the country's dominant discourse claimed: "India has arrived on the threshold of superpower status, literally with a bang."[70] Noisy congratulations and deafening celebrations following the tests marked the success of the security discourse that recommended the nuclear pill as a vitamin for the fifty-year-old-country. The post–Pokhran II security discourse sustains and continues in the direction set out in the 1980s. The qualitative difference is the near submersion of the position of the nuclear hawks and the government of India led by the BJP. Above all, the new phase further shows how the role of nuclear weapons is intricately linked with the notion of powerful Hindu India in the dominant security discourse in the country.

Atal Bihari Vajpayee synthesized the tenets of political realism and the moral mission of his party to extol nuclear weapons as part of "the national agenda for governance."[71] The explosions were claimed to be a result of a security policy based on "the supreme consideration of national interests," and an expression of a dream of "beginning of the rise of a strong and self-confident India."[72] That is why the tests were termed *Shakti* (strength) because "they have given India strength, they have given India self-confidence." India's neighbors were told not to worry or be alarmed by the tests. It was considered quite natural on behalf of the nation to rise "to salute" nuclear scientists and engineers for doing a splendid job. The dual role of nuclear weapons as means of external and domestic posturing is explained plainly by Brajesh Mishra, principal secretary to the prime minister, by maintaining that "we have to show a credible deterrent capability no only to the outside world, but to our own people."[73]

Exponents of the nuclear discourse fervently echoed the nationalist theme of the BJP. The editor of *India Today* categorized the nuclear tests as a good dose for "a nation fed on a diet of bad news." The media did not "quarrel" with the government's rationale that India was forced by "hostile" neighbors and a discriminatory international order to resort to nuclear testing. Totalizing themes came into full play by blending patriotism, consensus, national self-respect, and disdain for Pakistan with the support for India's nuclear status. Overwhelming support for the explosions was construed as an embodiment of patriotism, and the reluctance of Marxist parties to join the chorus was seen as an expression of a questionable patriotism.[74] Successful conduct of the nuclear explosion was considered a useful ploy to counter Pakistan's efforts to "export terrorists and guns across our borders, wreak havoc even in a city like Bombay and get away with it . . . [and] even dare to lecture us on human rights."[75]

Pokhran II has become an important signpost in the narrative of Indian identity that conceives the country in terms of a "great power" in international hierarchy and worthy of respect by its neighbors. Anyone casting a shadow of a doubt on this characterization could only be a lesser Indian. George Fernandes, minister for defense in the 1998–1999 BJP-led government, saw any internal debate on the issue as an effort that would project "India as a divided nation on an issue concerning its very survival."[76] Fernandes considered it fit to debate "what should be our priorities, on issues relating to social justice etc. But on our very survival, never." Those who still raised questionable voices in connection with nuclear explosions were dubbed forces that would assure India's opponents "that we are not united on our own survival."[77]

The post–Pokhran II discussion is only the latest extension of a dominant discourse on India's identity that has evolved over the years. The May explosions did put an end to the long-held Indian diplomatic position of nuclear ambiguity, raising interesting questions for students of the international nonproliferation regime. On the first anniversary of the nuclear tests, the day was aptly named a "resurgent India day," and L. K. Advani made it absolutely clear that "the primary aim of [the] tests was to make the people of India self-confident."[78]

Barely a year after India and Pakistan became nuclear powers, the unknown Himalayan area of Kargil became a flash point in the media as the Indian air force tried to flash-out what Delhi claimed to be Pakistani-backed "infiltrators" from the Indian side of the Line of Control—the de facto border in Kashmir. The BJP government had lost a vote of confidence in March 1999 after remaining in power for little over a year. Atal Bihari Vajpayee had visited Lahore, Pakistan in February. The trip led to the signing of the much-publicized Lahore Declaration that reiterated that the countries shall try to resolve all outstanding problems through bilateral and peaceful means. The optimism infused by the Lahore trip plummeted when the Indian government decided to use its air force to deal with crisis in Kargil in May. The crisis ended when Nawaz Sharif, then Pakistani Prime Minister, pledged in Washington to request the withdrawal of armed men occupying the hills. The Pakistani retreat was used by the BJP as its key defense policy victory, and it used the incident to beef up the party's fortunes in elections scheduled for September.[79] Features of this textual war remained tied to the logic of binary opposites where Pakistan was portrayed as India's "most obvious, and only serious enemy."[80]

While the campaign was in full swing, the interim government led by Atal Bihari Vajpayee issued a draft of India's nuclear doctrine in August 1999. The draft was prepared by a twenty-seven-member National Security Advisory Board under the chairmanship of K. Subrahmanyam.[81] Nuclear weapons are now considered essential to India's security and the draft stipulates three oft-repeated but contradictory and paradoxical caveats. It pledges India not to be the first to use nuclear weapons in a crisis. For this, it needs a survivable minimum nuclear deterrent composed of land, sea, and air systems. And finally, the command and control of the Indian nuclear weapons is to lie with the Prime Minister. The question of command and control is quite clear, whereas the notion of a survivable minimum nuclear deterrent remains unclear without a well-defined and recognizable nuclear arsenal.

The main paradox of this doctrine remains New Delhi's avowed policy of no first use and its claim that India's nuclear program is not Pakistan-centric. If Indian nuclear weapons are primarily aimed at countering the

Chinese threat, then the policy of no first use makes them devoid of any military value because a much conventionally superior China has adhered to a no-first-use policy since the 1960s. In the scenario of a conventional war between India and China, the nuclear weapons can best work as weapons of the weak. With a no-first-use principle in place between China and India, the Pakistan-specific nature of the Indian nuclear program becomes all the more clear. K. Subrahmanyam unwittingly puts Pakistan at the center of the Indian nuclear program by arguing that the Indian nuclear doctrine "is the appropriate language to communicate to the nuclear warriors who believe in the first use of nuclear weapons."[82] This doctrine would create uncertainty "in the minds of would-be nuclear intimidators, aggressors and interventionists that those actions against this country would not be rational options."[83] Hence, contrary to the portrayal of China as the main impetus to India's nuclear ambitions, the substance of the Indian nuclear discourse is primarily Pakistan-centric.

The BJP-led coalition is governing India after achieving a simple majority of 298 seats of 537 announced results of the Lok Sabha in October 1999. In their earlier thirteen-month rule, the BJP put the nuclear bomb on the shelf and projected it as a step toward self-confidence. In all probability, the echoes of Pokhran II will continue to resonate in an India led by nuclearists like Atal Bihari Vajpayee and K. Subrahmanyam.

CONCLUSION

Since the list of threats to India as outlined by the proponents of the dominant security discourse is based upon binary opposites, the enemies of New Delhi are invariably blamed for problems afflicting the nation. This becomes obvious when we question: what makes India the target of these threats? Two themes emerge as answers to this question. First, regional adversaries are out to harm India because it is a secular, democratic state amid theocratic, obscurantist, and totalitarian regimes. The innocence of India is patent and its secular and democratic credentials beyond doubt, whereas its adversaries are marred by a variety of negative characteristics. Pakistan is relegated to a theocracy and China to a totalitarian state. Historical amnesia comes into full play here by turning a blind eye to counterevidence that might undermine the claims that Indian secularism may be lacking in substance, or that New Delhi is at least partly responsible for infusing fear in its neighbors. Second, the West, especially the United States, pressurizes India because of the latter's leadership of Third World causes. That is why the NPT and CTBT are still portrayed as forms of nuclear apartheid.

It is in the context of how to deal with such threats that the nuclear issue crops up. In present-day India, the dominant security discourse equates keeping the nuclear option with an effective deterrent and a symbol of exercising sovereignty, and is willing to face any international pressures as the price to be paid for pursuing national interests. This chapter demonstrates that the present views on nuclear weapons are in marked contrast with the Nehru-era policy on the nuclear issue. Nehru vowed that under no circumstances would India opt for nuclear weapons. The abstinence gave way to ambiguity in the mid-1960s followed by Indian transformation into a de facto nuclear power in the wake of the Pokhran explosion in 1974. The explosions in May 1998 put India irreversibly on the nuclear path.

The dominant Indian security discourse is based upon the dictum of assigning evil to the Other and considering the Self as a custodian of goodness. The lines between the external and internal become blurred in this narrative when domestic troubles are attributed to external intervention. In the name of secularism and democracy, an effort is made to create an India that suppresses, often violently, claims to other forms of identity. Externally, India is promoted as a genuinely great power. If such an India instills fear among its smaller neighbors, especially Pakistan, the standard line is to dismiss such fears as the figments of imagination of a paranoid neighbor.

In a security discourse conducted in the nationalist idiom and based upon binary opposites, treachery is useful to highlight the dangerousness of the dissenters from within. Under the present regime of strategic truths, the dominant discourse in India has captured the nationalist enterprise in which place and properties of the enemies of the nation are defined predominantly by nuclear hawks in New Delhi.

NOTES

1. Uma Bharti, "Should we help Pakistan swim—or sink?" *Sunday Times of India* (Mumbai), September 29, 1996.

2. David Cortright and Amitabh Mattoo, eds., *India and the Bomb: Public Opinion and Nuclear Options* (Notre Dame, IN: University of Notre Dame Press, A Publication of Joan B. Kroc Institute for International Peace Studies, 1996), p. 6. This volume is an excellent guide to different aspects of the elite opinion on nuclear politics in India.

3. Zafar Iqbal Cheema, "Pakistan's Nuclear Policies: Attitudes and Postures," in P. R. Chari, Pervaiz Iqbal Cheema, and Iftekharuzzaman, eds., *Nuclear Nonproliferation in India and Pakistan: South Asian Perspectives* (New Delhi: Manohar, A Publication of Regional Center for Strategic Studies, Colombo, 1996), p. 103.

4. K. Subrahmanyam, *Indian Security Perspectives* (New Delhi: ABC Publishing House, 1982), p. v.

5. Ibid., p. 68.

6. Ibid., p. 211.

7. Ibid., p. 230.

8. R. R. Subramanian, *India Pakistan China: Defence and Nuclear Tangle in South Asia* (New Delhi: ABC Publishing House, 1989), p. 41.

9. K. Subrahmanyam, "Problems of Indian Security in the Next Decade and Beyond," in K. Subrahmanyam, M. Zuberi, and R. Ramanna, *Problems of Living in Nuclear Age* (Chandigarh: Center for Research in Rural and Industrial Development, 1985), p. 10.

10. D. D. Khanna and Kishore Kumar, *Dialogue of the Deaf: The India-Pakistan Divide* (Delhi: Konark Publisher, 1992), p. 18.

11. Subrahmanyam, *Indian Security Perspectives*, p. 63.

12. Ibid.

13. Generalizations regarding Islam are a common problem in the West as well. For a good view of how Islam is (mis)represented see Edward W. Said, *Covering Islam: How the Media and the Experts Determine How We See the Rest of the World* (New York: Pantheon Books, 1981).

14. Major General D. K. Palit and P. K. S. Namboodri, *Pakistan's Islamic Bomb* (New Delhi: Vikas, 1979), pp. 21–26.

15. General K. Sundarji, *Blind Men of Hindoostan: Indo-Pak Nuclear War* (New Delhi: UBS Publishers, 1993), pp. 3 and 9.

16. Palit and Namboodri, *Pakistan's Islamic Bomb*, p. 115.

17. Air Commodore Jasjit Singh, "Politics of Mistrust and Confidence Building," in Air Commodore Jasjit Singh, ed., *India and Pakistan: Crisis of Relationship* (New Delhi: Lancer Publishers in association with Institute for Defence Studies and Analyses, 1990), p. 104.

18. Ibid., p. 105.

19. K. Subrahmanyam, "Role of National Power," in *India and the Nuclear Challenge* (New Delhi: Lancer International in association with Institute for Defence studies and Analyses, 1986), p. 257.

20. J. A. Naik, *The Pak Bomb and Rajiv's India* (New Delhi: National Publishing House, 1986), p. v.

21. Ibid., p. 23.

22. K. K. Pathak, *Nuclear Policy of India: A Third World Perspective* (New Delhi: Gitajali Prakashan, 1980), p. 201.

23. Subrahmanyam, *Indian Security Perspectives*, pp. 182–183.

24. P. B. Sinha and R. R. Subramanian, *Nuclear Pakistan: Atomic Threat to South Asia* (New Delhi: Vision Books, 1980), p. 115.

25. Ibid., pp. 115–116.

26. *Times of India* (Mumbai), April 2, 1996.

27. P.L. Bhola, *Pakistan's Nuclear Policy* (New Delhi: Sterling Publishers, South Asia Studies Series, 1993), p. 64.

28. Ibid., p. 65.

29. P. K. S. Namboodiri, "Perceptions and Policies in India and Pakistan," in Subrahmanyam, *India and the Nuclear Challenge*, p. 198.

30. Subrahmanyam, *Indian Security Perspectives*, p. 201.

31. Rikhi Jaipal, "The Indo-Pakistan Nuclear Options," in Subrahmanyam, *India and the Nuclear Challenge*, p. 184.

32. This is how Z. A. Bhutto described Ayub's lack of understanding of the nuclear issue as early as 1963. Bhutto attributed these comments to Ayub while reacting to the Indian nuclear explosion in 1974. For a detailed discussion of this see the Chapter "Four" in this book.

33. Sinha and Subramanian, *Nuclear Pakistan*, p. 68.

34. Bhola, *Pakistan's Nuclear Policy*, p. 68.
35. Pathak, *Nuclear Policy of India*, p. 183.
36. This discussion is based upon General K. Sundarji's *Blind Men of Hindoostan* in which he outlines different situations in which a nuclear war between Pakistan and India could break out.
37. Ibid., p. 50.
38. Ibid., p. 55.
39. Ibid., p. 137.
40. Ibid., p. 138.
41. Subrahmanyam, *Indian Security Perspectives*, p. 167.
42. Bhola, *Pakistan's Nuclear Policy*, p. 57.
43. Ibid., p. 73.
44. Pathak, *Nuclear Policy of India* is a good example of this attitude to the Pakistani proposals.
45. Subrahmanyam, *Indian Security Perspectives*, p. 168.
46. Subrahmanyam, *India and the Nuclear Challenge*, p. 258.
47. Subrahmanyam, *Indian Security Perspectives*, p. 207.
48. K. Subrahmanyam, "India's Response," in *India and the Nuclear Challenge*, p. 281.
49. Ibid., p. 284.
50. K. Subrahmanyam, "Nuclear Issue," in Singh, *India and Pakistan*, p. 88.
51. R. Chidambaram, "Say no to regional capping," *India Today*, April 30, 1994, p. 50.
52. K. Subrahmanyam, "Role of National Power," in *India and the Nuclear Challenge*, p. 269.
53. Ibid., p. 274.
54. Ibid., p. 280.
55. K. Subrahmanyam, "India and the CTBT: Deterrence Requires Testing Option," *Times of India* (Ahmedabad), February 21, 1996.
56. V. P. Dutt, "When to Sign CTBT," *Times of India* (Mumbai), March 15, 1996.
57. Raj Chengappa, "India's Nuclear Policy: Testing Times," *India Today*, December 31, 1995, pp. 46–51.
58. K. Subrahmanyam, "India and CTBT: Deterrence Requires Testing Option," *Times of India* (Ahmedabad), February 21, 1996.
59. K. Subrahmanyam, "New Age of Imperialism: Nuclear Hegemony of the Big Five," *Times of India* (Mumbai), September 25, 1996.
60. "Farcical Finale," *Times of India* (Mumbai), September 12, 1996.
61. "Need for a Comprehensive Test Ban Treaty," Statement at the United Nations Security Council Summit, January 31, 1992, in P. V. Narasimha Rao, *Selected Speeches, Vol. I, June 1991–June 1992* (New Delhi: Publications Division, Ministry of Information and Broadcasting, Government of India, 1993), p. 361.
62. P. V. Narasimha Rao's speech at the dinner hosted in honor of Premier Li Peng of China, New Delhi, December 11, 1991, in Rao, *Selected Speeches*, pp. 343–345.
63. Ibid., p. 345.
64. See Yogendra K. Malik and V.B. Singh, *Hindu Nationalists in India: The Rise of the Bharatiya Janata Party* (Boulder, CO: Westview, 1994), p. 123.

65. Ibid., pp. 123–124.

66. M. Granger Morgan, K. Subrahmanyam, K. Sundarji, and Robert M. White, "India and the United States," *Washington Quarterly* 18:2 (spring 1995), p. 157. For more on the changing nature of Sino-Indian relations on positive lines see Shekhar Gupta, *India Redefines Its Role: An Analysis of India's Changing Internal Dynamics and Their Impact on Foreign Relations Adelphi Papers* 293 (London: IISS and Oxford University Press, 1995).

67. Cortright and Mattoo, *India and the Bomb*, p. 17.

68. Uma Bharti, "Should We Help Pakistan Swim—or Sink?"

69. *http://www.bjp.org*. The BJP's website contains detailed information of the party's vision of India.

70. Chandan Mitra, "Explosion of self-esteem," *The Pioneer*, May 12, 1998.

71. AtalBihari Vajpayee, "Interview: India is now a nuclear weapons state," *India Today*, May 25, 1998, p 28.

72. Ibid., p. 29.

73. Manoj Joshi, "Nuclear Shock Waves," Ibid., p. 14.

74. Tavleen Singh, "Nuclear Fallout," Ibid., p. 11.

75. Ibid.

76. *Times of India*, October 12, 1998.

77. Ibid.

78. Ibid., May 12, 1999.

79. The genesis of the Kargil crisis still remains a mystery. For a brief historical overview see Praveen Swami, "The Bungle in Kargil," *Frontline*, June 19–July 2, 1999. As to how the issue was used in the election campaign by the BJP see Sukumar Muralidharan, "A Kargil Election," Ibid., September 11–24, 1999. The Indian Government appointed a committee to look into the matter. The Kargil Commitee's report was published in *Times of India*, February 25, 2000.

80. M. J. Akbar, "Asleep on a Crucial Watch," *Gulf News*, June 1, 1999.

81. For the draft of the nuclear doctrine see *www.indianembassy.org/policy/ctbt/nuclear_doctrine/aug_17_1999.html*

82. K. Subrahmanyam, "A Credible Nuclear Deterrent," *Times of India*, October 4, 1999.

83. Ibid.

Chapter 4

Roots of Rhetoric in Pakistan: 1960s–1977

> It does not matter what types of weapons exist, human beings will fight with each other. Totally disarm them and they will fight with their fists.
>
> —Ayub Khan in 1961[1]

> Pakistan is a small country facing a great monster . . . [who is] determined to annihilate Pakistan.
>
> —Zulfikar Ali Bhutto in 1965[2]

Nuclear weapons are an integral part of the strategic discourse in today's Pakistan. The national consensus on weapons of mass destruction is an article of faith for nuclear hawks in the country. Western analysts hardly question this consensus, and predict dire consequences of a likely nuclear catastrophe in the region. In the wake of the May 1998 nuclear explosions by India and Pakistan, the region is portrayed as the likely site of a nuclear catastrophe in the eventuality of war. This chapter reconstructs the history of the rise of the nuclear factor in Pakistan from the 1960s to 1977 with the help of tools of discourse analysis. A functional model to organize the discussion looks at the dominant discourse's notions of threats and the threatened, reasons behind that situation, security objectives in such a context, means to attain those objectives, and, finally, costs involved in pursuing the suggested means.

A look at the dominant strategic discourse of the 1960s will make it clear that the nuclear factor was conspicuous by its absence in that decade and gradually became an integral part of Pakistan's strategic discourse in the 1970s. These different positions are best personified by the two important political figures at the helm of Pakistan's state affairs, namely, Ayub Khan and Zulfikar Ali Bhutto, during the 1960s and 1970s, respectively. Nuclear option was never considered an effective deterrent or politically useful tool during the days of Ayub Khan, the head of the military clique that ruled Pakistan from 1958 to 1969. It was Bhutto, leader of a truncated Pakistan from 1972 to 1977, who methodically turned this dormant issue into a symbol of national identity.[3] I start with a focus on the thoughts of these two men followed by the discourse on security during the 1971 civil war in Pakistan and interstate war with India in the same year. This is followed by a look at the impact of India's nuclear explosion in 1974 on the security discourse in Pakistan. The chapter ends with the discussion of the way in which Z. A. Bhutto wove the nuclear issue into the web of patriotic rhetoric in the wake of the controversial elections of 1977.

A brief discussion of the period in which the nuclear option was absent from the dominant strategic discourse of Pakistan would show the relevance of the methodological tools suggested in the previous chapters. I intend to emphasize two interrelated points at this juncture. First, the politics of the nuclear option is of recent origin in the body-politic of Pakistan. In spite of invoking external threats to consolidate a fragile Pakistani identity since its inception, the nuclear option as a means to deter such threats entered late in the political discourse. Second, the above point makes it necessary to examine the changing political context in which an issue hitherto considered outside the realm of national security eventually becomes a symbol of an independent national identity.

Looking in this way at an issue that is enmeshed in patriotic rhetoric requires perspectives that go beyond the narrow confines of national security, that is, neorealism and deterrence literature. Insights of discourse analysis are utilized to rewrite the history of the nuclear discourse in a fundamentally different way than what is offered by otherwise available accounts. Rather than being just a set of testable hypotheses, discourse analysis makes it possible to look at familiar narratives in a radically different way.

NATIONAL SECURITY WITHOUT NUKES

Since its *de jure* inception in 1947, efforts to evolve a separate Pakistani identity have been intricately tied to the portrayal of the Indian threat in the dominant political discourse in the country. The political salience of the nuclear issue can be meaningfully understood in this context. As evident in the writings and speeches of Ayub Khan, the nuclear option was conspicuously absent in Pakistan's strategic discourse during the 1960s. The

Indian threat and the construction of a Pakistani identity to counter it still continued to be the central theme of the dominant political discourse.

Ayub Khan's thoughts could be described as a blend of a soldier's reliance on "political realism" and a periodic recourse to the malleable notion of the ideology of Pakistan to legitimize the regime's politics and policies. He was an arch-realist with an unshakable belief in the dictum of self-help as the basic principle of international politics. He maintained that in an anarchic international system, "nobody gives you freedom: you have to fight it for yourself."[4] In such a system, the principal objectives of foreign policy are security and development. Security "embraces preservation of our ideology."[5] The definition of that ideology is situational and closely linked to the identity of the country and the nature of threats to it. The General was fully aware of the fact that in a world of competing ideologies, Pakistan had to fight to preserve its ideology as the ultimate basis of its national existence. He suggested that to ensure independence "we have to establish our identity."[6]

The question arises: what obstacles did he see in the way of establishing an independent Pakistani identity? Foremost among them "is India's inability to reconcile herself to our existence as a sovereign, independent state."[7] But why is it that India cannot reconcile itself to the independence of Pakistan? The explanation offered by Ayub Khan is both instructive and quite relevant even today. He argued that the "Indian attitude can be explained in pathological terms. The Indian leaders have a deep hatred for Muslims . . . [and] from the beginning, India was determined to make things difficult for us."[8] India's "occupation" of Jammu and Kashmir region, the only Indian state with a Muslim majority, is offered as an irrefutable example to substantiate the above claim. Of special interest in the above portrayal is defining the Pakistani identity with exclusive reference to its "difference" from India. Also, the difference between the two entities (i.e., India and Pakistan) is seen as something that goes beyond the dictates of the *realpolitik* and into the realms of religion and Hindu pathology, which cannot come to terms with the idea of an independent Pakistan.

The Pakistani rulers had to be clear regarding the ultimate motives of India in the light of such characterization and the likely ways to counter them. The former was easy to comprehend because India wanted "to absorb Pakistan or turn it into a satellite."[9] The nature of relations between the two countries is seen as a zero-sum game in which the "prospects of normal relations do not appear to be in sight"; therefore, we must "accept the situation of implacable Indian hostility and learn to live with it."[10]

Ayub Khan ruled out utilizing nuclear weapons as a means to deter the Indian threat in spite of the fact that such weapons were in currency as an effective deterrent in the East-West rivalry. The General had no doubts regarding the lasting nature of hostile future relations between the two countries: "Indian nationalism is based on Hinduism and Pakistan's nationalism is based on Islam. The two philosophies are fundamentally different from each other, and cannot combine."[11] This representation of Pakistan and India is a classic example of relying on binary opposites to envisage two diametrically opposite, yet monolithic entities devoid of internal differences. By implication, any shade of nationalism within Pakistan based on any reference point other than Islam would constitute treason, and any deviance from the dominant view of what constituted a Pakistani identity would be attributed to the Indian designs to undo Pakistan. India, on the other hand, was portrayed as no more than a Hindu entity with ill will against Pakistan as its key characteristic.

The contours of the dominant discourse of Pakistani politics during the 1960s, as exemplified by Ayub Khan, exhibited the following characteristics. First, the discourse was characterized by attempts to forge a separate Muslim national identity for the newly formed state. Second, centrality of "Hindu India" as the real threat played a pivotal role in these efforts. Third, the nuclear issue was missing in this strategic matrix. The salience of the nuclear option to counter the Indian threat, and by implication strengthen the Pakistani identity, was one of the hallmarks of Zulfikar Ali Bhutto's politics. A closer look at his thoughts enables us to trace the origins of the nuclear politics in Pakistan.

BHUTTO AND NUCLEAR WEAPONS

Z. A. Bhutto can singularly be credited for introducing and popularizing the politics of the nuclear issue in Pakistan. I have divided his writings (in the form of a collection of speeches, articles, and book-length studies) on the nuclear issue into three periods. First, the Bhutto of the 1960s, when he initially served in Ayub's government in different capacities including as a foreign minister, and then parted ways with Ayub and organized the Pakistan Peoples Party (PPP) into a mass movement. Second, his stint in power in dismembered and defeated Pakistan from 1972 to 1977. Finally, from 1977 to 1979, his days in the death cell where he managed to produce a book discussing in some detail his views and role in Pakistan's nuclear program. This chapter focuses on the first two periods while leaving the third for the next chapter for the sake of keeping chronological order in the story.

The Bhutto of the 1960s was a young man in Ayub's cabinet and later a mass mobilizer against the regime on the basis of its alleged failures in foreign policy issues, especially Ayub's role in reaching an agreement with the Indians at Tashkent after the 1965 Indo-Pakistan war. Citing the Tashkent Treaty as an act of compromise of national interests by the Ayub regime, Bhutto chose to amplify the anti-India theme to discredit the military regime. Bhutto managed to become a credible voice of the dominant discourse in West Pakistan by conveying to masses, especially in Punjab, that he was more anti-India than Ayub Khan.

As early as 1961, he was convinced that the major threat to Pakistan's security emanated from India, but he did not stipulate the nuclear course for Pakistan to deter conventionally superior India. Overlooking the prevalent view in the Western strategic circles that considered nuclear weapons as effective deterrents, Bhutto tied the survival of mankind with disarmament and argued that the arms race was heading toward an accelerating crisis and the world leaders lacked the political and moral courage to lead the world toward disarmament.[12]

The inconclusive 1965 war between India and Pakistan and the consequent debate in Pakistan regarding means to deter India was marked by the absence of exploring the strategic utility of the nuclear option. Addressing the UN general assembly in September 1965, Bhutto described Pakistan's security dilemma in no uncertain terms by asserting that it was a small country "facing a great monster, a great aggressor always given to aggression."[13] The ultimate objective of "the monster," that is how India was referred to, was to "annihilate Pakistan."[14] Bhutto's ideas regarding Pakistan's identity and the relationship between domestic and foreign spheres were spelled out in detail in a marathon speech in March 1966 while commenting on the 1965 war in the national assembly of Pakistan. He had no doubt that "foreign affairs emanate and originate from internal conditions," but he also knew that the foreign policy of a country also affects its internal affairs.[15] To determine the interaction between the two, he posed such important questions as: What is Pakistan itself? What is our state and our status? What are our objectives? What are our motivations? His answers are a good synopsis of Pakistan's dominant security discourse. Pakistan was declared "a great idea," an idea that was "progressive, concrete, and beautiful."[16] Who could turn a blend of the above characteristics into physical attributes of a country? No one but God was Bhutto's answer. Bhutto emphatically claimed that Pakistan "is not a man-made country . . . it is a blessing of Allah . . . a God-made country."[17] An entity that is portrayed as a work of the divine has "nothing ugly" about it.[18]

By introducing the divine element in the process of state management, Bhutto was addressing foreign as well as domestic opponents in the same breath. It implied that only the evil could find faults with the existing structure of the state, and any attempt to challenge the state authorities (presumably sacred as well because they were ruling a God-made country) had to be considered an act defying the divine will. Such a conception of the country convinced Bhutto that "Pakistan is never to be amputated or merged."[19] Coming at the end of the war with "the monster" whose ultimate aim was "to annihilate" Pakistan, and faced with dissidence (which would blow up later) in the then East Pakistan, such a stance was a warning message with two targets in mind, that is, to India and to opponents of the existing political structure within the country. Such assertions were also a reassurance to the remaining countrymen who were not presented with the much-promised victory against India in 1965. Nuclear weapons still do not appear as deterrents in this grand narrative against the Indian threat.

Reference to the Indian threat became integral to the vision of Pakistan based upon religious identity at its center and the challenges mounted by the contending identities (i.e., linguistic, ethnic, or even class in those days) at its periphery. The contentious issue of Kashmir became the symbol of the two contending versions of postcolonial state identities in Pakistan and India. Bhutto's following two comparisons of Kashmir amplify the salience of the issue in Pakistan's quest for a distinct identity and how India assumes a cardinal position in defining that identity. Addressing Pakistani students in London in August 1966, Bhutto claimed that "without Kashmir Pakistan is a body without a head and it is a very beautiful head."[20] It was during this speech that he also metaphorically pledged a thousand years' war with India over Kashmir. Five years later, amid turmoil in the then East Pakistan, Bhutto (who was the undisputed mass leader of Punjab at that time) was still harping on this theme and impressing upon the West that "Kashmir is to Pakistan what Berlin is to the West."[21]

A distinct Pakistani identity presumably guaranteed by God and the centrality of the Indian threat to it emerge as the two main themes in Bhutto's world-view during the 1960s. Both themes are closely connected for him whether he is playing the role of a mass mobilizer or addressing the UN General Assembly. Despite the centrality of India as a major factor in the political discourse in Pakistan, we still do not see the presence of the nuclear factor in the public domain.

Pakistani strategic analysts were equally oblivious to the possibilities of the nuclear option as a viable deterrent against India. *Pakistan Horizon*, the oldest journal on international affairs published in Pakistan, of the 1960s resonates the same themes covered by Bhutto. The journal carried hardly any articles on the nuclear issue. Even after the signing of the NPT in 1968 and its subsequent ratification in 1970, contributions do not suggest any urgency regarding the long-term implications of the Pakistani decision not to become the party to the treaty.

IMPERCEPTIBLE SHIFT

The earliest and somewhat systematic discussion of the utility of the nuclear option to thwart the Indian threat appeared in Z. A. Bhutto's 1969 book *The Myth of Independence*.[22] In a country with less than 25 percent literacy rate and only a fraction of it able to read English, the very medium (English) and the form (a book) suggest the elitist origins of the nuclear issue. It eventually became enmeshed in popular culture and closely tied to the nation's survival as an independent entity. Bhutto does not jump at the nuclear option without setting a stage for it, but he makes contradictory assertions that remain unresolved. It is important to note that these contradictions are also an integral part of the security discourse in Pakistan based on defining the Self through what it is not.

Bhutto starts the story by restating the nature of the threats faced by Pakistan, followed by the reasons behind such threats. It is as the remedy to meet these threats that the nuclear option is introduced. He starts with one of the most commonly ascribed observations on the paradoxical relationship between India and Pakistan, that is, "India and Pakistan have so much in common that the rest of the world sometimes finds it hard to understand why they are in a state of perpetual confrontation."[23] Answering his own rhetorical question, Bhutto outlines the list of reasons behind this animosity. They include "the legacy of history, superstition, and prejudice."[24] On all these fronts, the opponent is held responsible for harboring such vices. The issue of historical legacy is settled by claiming that "it is India not Pakistan that harbors ill will because of 700 years of Muslim rule."[25] This historical legacy comes with its own psychological baggage for the respective communities. Here, "the Indian mentality is troubled with historical complexes and the obsession of defeat" at the hands of Muslims.[26]

Appropriation and allocation of identities is quite instructive in the above instance to understand the common strategies employed in Pakistan's security discourse. Invoking 700 years of different dynasties' rule in North India, who were Muslims by religion, Bhutto considers the post-1947 Pakistan as an extension of that rule. Second, "the Indian mentality" is interchangeably used with the term "Hindu mentality." The overlapping is seen to be so obvious that he does not even find it fit to expand upon the apparent heterogeneity of the contemporary Indian sociopolitical mosaic. This has little to do with Bhutto's lack of knowledge about the Indian society, and more with the logocentric logic whose objective is to create two easily distinguishable monolithic identities at the expense of their complexities in order to consolidate a fragile Pakistani identity.

The depiction of the past is of no intrinsic value. A particular reading of history is a prerequisite to justify and serve the needs of the present. Pakistan's security discourse is no exception when it offers such a reading of the Indian history. Given the centuries of Muslims' rule resulting in deep psychological scars between Hindus and Muslims of the subcontinent, Bhutto asks what would be the ultimate objective of the post-1947 Indian, which is considered exclusively Hindu, leadership? According to the dominant discourse in Pakistan, "India's principal objective is to obliterate Pakistan."[27] The very existence of Pakistan flies in the face of such an Indian objective. Here, we must be told of reasons behind India's failures, which in turn are considered Pakistan's triumphs. "Indian leaders have come to tolerate Pakistan because they do not have the power to destroy it."[28]

Along with the Indians' lack of power to destroy Pakistan, another explanation is the Pakistani resolve to resist the Indian hegemonic moves, manifesting itself in "two wars to establish a separate identity."[29] India, however, remains firm in its mission to "bring Pakistan back to mother India."[30]

What are the likely solutions to this catch-22 situation where India seems unwilling to genuinely acknowledge the existence of Pakistan and the latter jealously guards its separate identity? Bhutto goes back to the Kashmir issue as the key bone of contention and maintains that Jawaharlal Nehru, India's first prime minister, "believed that the resolution of the Kashmir problem will not put an end to Pakistan-India hostility, because it was just a symptom of the bigoted attitudes of theocratic and reactionary Pakistan to secular, progressive India."[31] Here he conveniently forgets his own account in which animosity between Pakistan and India was portrayed as the most recent phase of centuries-old adversarial relations, and argues that "there is no such thing as eternal enmity, and Kashmir is the key problem."[32] At this juncture, Pakistan has to set its priorities.

The dominant security discourse has not been ambivalent in setting these priorities. Bhutto, being one authentic voice in this category, outlines these priorities in the following way. First of all, "Pakistan's security and territorial integrity are more important than economic development."[33] By implication, any group (let us not forget the unease of Bengalis of East Pakistan) seeking to challenge that hierarchy of priorities cannot possibly be true Pakistani. A different version of priorities would be equated with a lack of patriotism and colluding with the external enemy. The principal challenge to Pakistan's security and territorial integrity, according to the dominant discourse, emanates from India; therefore, "we have to find an effective deterrent" against it.[34] Here Bhutto brings up the nuclear option issue by suggesting that "our plans should include the nuclear deterrent."[35] We find in this assertion the first political uses of the nuclear option in the broader security discourse in Pakistan.

Bhutto, being an avid student of international politics and its attendant power relations, was aware of the hurdles lying in exploring the nuclear path. Foremost among them was the Nuclear Non-Proliferation Treaty (NPT), which he described as "an international treaty limiting this deterrent to nuclear powers."[36] Making Pakistan's attitude toward the NPT conditional upon India's nuclear ambitions, Bhutto argued that Pakistan should not "allow herself to be deceived by" that treaty because India will proceed with its nuclear program in spite of the nonproliferation regime. At that stage Bhutto was not cognizant of the future political magnitude of the issue and the subtleties of choosing the right words to describe Pakistan's nuclear ambitions. He bluntly stated that "our problem is how to obtain such a weapon in time before the crisis begins, because India can choose that timing due to technological advantage."[37]

That is how the seeds of a nuclear discourse were sown in Pakistan. Like many other issues, it remained politically dormant for quite some time. Bhutto's book did not invoke an international outcry, nor did it unleash a charged debate over the nuclear option within the country. Yet, it contained elementary arguments that would eventually turn into dogmas of the dominant security discourse.

TRAUMATIC INTERLUDE: 1970–1974

The election in 1970 was a watershed event in the checkered history of Pakistan. It was the first party-based election held in Pakistan's existence that was based on adult franchise. The landslide victory of the Awami League, the Bengali nationalist party, in the then East Pakistan, and the subsequent refusal of the West Pakistani rulers to hand over power to the majority party, led to fratricidal civil strife that ended with the formal breakup of the country in December 1971. Nine months of bloody turmoil in the East Pakistani streets in 1971 and an ideological warfare over the contending versions of Pakistani identity was a blow to the dominant discourse, which viewed Islam as the ultimate unifying force among the disparate social groups of Pakistan.

This section recounts the ways in which the dominant discourse was conducted mainly in *Dawn*, the leading English daily of Pakistan.[38] Such a focus is important for several reasons. First, an event of the magnitude of the Bengali uprising against the Pakistani state forced the society to confront the critical question of defining oneself and one's opponents. The way Bengali dissidents were portrayed in the Pakistani media could be best contextualized as a discourse about the conception of Pakistani identity at that time. Second, the 1971 contest of different versions of the Pakistani identity was a manifestation of a quarter century's failed efforts to evolve a stable Pakistani identity on the one hand, and a model of discourse that would continue in the post-1971 truncated Pakistan vis-à-vis the identity questions of the later years. Third, the centrality of the Indian factor in drawing the battle lines about the Pakistani identity would become obvious. Fourth, those months marked intra- as well as interstate wars; hence the questions regarding creating an effective defense against the "enemy" were paramount. Study of the identity discourse in the critical year of 1971 would set the stage for the strategic discourse of the 1970s in which the salience of the nuclear deterrent significantly increased. The Pakistani state authorities' resort to extreme violence to quell the Bengali identity movement is indicative of the limits of regime of truth based on maintaining a difference between the ruler and the ruled. Along with the formal state authorities, other proponents of a monolithic Islamic identity of Pakistan wholeheartedly endorsed the use of force against Bengalis.

By March 1971, "threat to the integrity" of the country was a common theme in the media. Yet the belief in a united Pakistan's existence was quite strong. By way of further strengthening that belief, *Dawn* reminded the citizens in its Pakistan Day editorial on March 23 that Pakistan was "a unique phenomenon and an unprecedented experiment in modern times."[39] Condemned were those who based their identities on ethnic lines (read Bengalis), with an added warning that such groups were likely to play into the hands of the enemy (read India) who was "fully alive" to exploit such opportunities.

Mujibur Rehman, leader of the Awami League, was charged with treason by Pakistani authorities in late March. Yahya Khan accused Mujib and the Awami League of insulting the national flag and defiling the photograph of the Father of the Nation, Muhammad Ali Jinnah.[40] The Awami League leader was also held responsible for insulting the armed forces, and Yahya concluded that "Mujib and his men (were) enemies of Pakistan."[41] By that time, pro-Mujib rallies had started taking place in New Delhi and West Bengal. In such sensitive times, *Dawn* set its priorities quite unambiguously. In an editorial of March 28, it put "the dictates of the country's integrity and survival" over "all other considerations." Since the "Awami League's movement of civil disobedience was bound to bring the government's wheels to a stop," the paper suggested dealing firmly (which meant violent suppression of the agitation) with them in that "grave time in the nation's life." Arguing on these lines, the paper did not find it fit to mention grounds that had led to total alienation of Bengalis within the existing structure of the Pakistani state. Neither the fact of the Awami League's massive victory in the general election, nor the reluctance on the part of the military junta and other influential segments of the West Pakistani society to transfer power was brought in to put the situation in context.

The Indian Lok Sabha, the lower house of parliament, passed a resolution offering unanimous support to the "freedom fighters" in East Pakistan.[42] Declaring the resolution as a "shameful" act, *Dawn* accused India of playing the "ignoble part" of supporting "treason and secession in Pakistan." While the Bengalis' disenchantment with Pakistan was nearing an irreversible point, the Pakistani dominant discourse adopted a three-pronged strategy to cope with the situation. First, any uprising (not many were reported) in the Eastern wing was considered a handiwork of the Indians. Second, the Awami League and its supporters (which meant an overwhelming majority of Bengalis) were portrayed as stray elements working on Indian instructions. Finally, the Pakistan army's actions were unquestionably supported and any opposition to them was taken as an act of treason.

The movement for the independent state of Bangladesh was viewed as no more than a pipe dream, and India's role in fueling the separatist fire was equated with "brazen-faced hypocrisy" that was guided by the desire to destroy Pakistan. West Pakistan's leading politicians were all passing joint resolutions condemning the Indian intervention.[43] Bhutto considered the Indian intervention in the Eastern wing as a way of distracting the Pakistani leadership from extending moral support to the Kashmiris.[44] Interestingly, the popular leadership of the Eastern wing, exclusively comprising of the Awami League, did not view the situation in the same light. A tiny section of the East Pakistan population led by leaders like the *Jamait-I-Islami*'s (Party of Islam) Ghulam Azam and Muslim League's Khwaja Khairudin remained firm supporters of a unified Pakistan and relied on slogans such as, Pakistan *Zindabad* ("Long live Pakistan"), *Quaid-I-Azam Zindabad*, Yahya Khan *Zindabad*, Tikka Khan *Zindabad* (General Tikka Khan led the Pakistan Army deployed in East Pakistan that carried out the military operation against the Awami League), and "Down with India and its agents." The West Pakistani media depicted such rallies in a positive light without any reference to their lack of popularity among ordinary Bengalis.

By that time supporting Pakistan and the personality of Jinnah was not isolated from supporting Yahya Khan and Tikka Khan. Yahya Khan was an unelected military ruler whose legitimacy was much in doubt among Bengalis. Tikka Khan's position as the head of the Pakistan army's contingent in East Pakistan symbolized the West Pakistani ruling elite's dictatorial view of Pakistan among the Bengalis.

Support for the perpetrators of the military action was not confined to the coterie of politicians in East Pakistan. *Dawn* expressed the same confidence in the policies pursued by Yahya Khan and generalized that feeling for the whole nation in the following way:

> The nation looks up to President Yahya, the soldier-statesman, with the confidence and hope that he will adequately meet this challenge from without just as he firmly faced the threat of disintegration from within when Awami League's obduracy and adamant unreasonableness left no other course open.[45]

Every true patriot was given the duty of praying for the security and solidarity of Pakistan. The solidarity of the country was defined the way the military regime perceived it. Since the Awami League's ideas regarding Pakistan stood in marked contrast with those of the West Pakistani elite, the majority of the country's population, numerically Bengalis, was declared to be agents of a hostile power. And those within West Pakistan who questioned that decision risked being dubbed traitors as well.

Champions of the dominant discourse were in the forefront of outlining the defining criteria of a genuine Pakistani identity and traits that would help in identifying enemies within the country. Justice Hamud Rehman, the Chief Justice of the Supreme Court, who later headed the commission to look into the reasons for Pakistan's debacle, presented the blueprint of a true Pakistani identity in detail; it merits a closer look.[46] The central theme was to map the ways to "infuse national love in citizens." The section of the population lacking that spirit were the Bengalis; therefore, they became the targets to be infused with national love. Crucial importance was given to indoctrination at an early age, and the idea was to start each school day with the singing of the national anthem and "appropriate readings emphasizing the concept of the Pakistani nation." This was to be done with the "important task of defining [the] ideology of Pakistan" in their minds.

The raison d'être of the ideology of Pakistan lies in the "brutalities committed by the Congress governments in the Hindu majority provinces against Muslims." Since the Congress continued to rule India after the independence, it is reasonable to assume, according to the Justice, that the contradiction between Hindus and Muslims has taken the form of rivalry between two sovereign states (i.e., India and Pakistan). Therefore, the flourishing of Pakistani nationalism was made dependent upon depiction of the differences between Hindus (also India) and Muslims (also Pakistan).

In this play of interchangeability of words, Pakistani distinctiveness could not exclusively survive by relying upon anti-Congress historiography of the prepartition days. The next step "should be to develop a sense of nationhood." Since Pakistan's dream was realized by rallying the Muslims of India around the Two Nation theory (dividing the Indian population into two nations on the basis of Hindu and Muslim religions), the idea of asserting a nonreligious basis of identity (especially by Bengalis) eroded the very foundations of Muslim Pakistan. Justice Rehman's reasons to establish grounds for a distinct Muslim nationality in the subcontinent also take a racist turn. He argues that "not all Muslims are descendants of converts. Many are descendants of Arabs, Turks, Afghans, Persians." This echoes the common theme among adherents of Muslim nationalism in India that most Muslims in the subcontinent are ethnically descendants of Muslim rulers who came from far-flung areas, some of which are mentioned by the Justice. The argument goes that, coming from different ethnic stocks, Muslims are physically distinct from their Hindu countrymen. According to the Justice, "there are many in Sylhet (a Bangladesh district) who are of light complexion, tall and well-built with sharp features and aquiline noses." The validity of such claims may be doubtful but the implications are quite clear.

The difference in physical attributes implies a superior/inferior and us/them dichotomy. If Muslims are fair, well built, and tall, and with sharp features, Hindus are considered dark, short, and with dull features. Had there not been any superiority attached to the former features there would be no need to mention these factors. But the story does not stop at physical difference alone. It must also translate in genetically determined behavioral variations between the two communities. Hence Muslims have common dress and cuisine and they "never eat off a banana leaf." But Justice Rehman laments the fact that despite such similarities among Muslims, "false propaganda" unleashed by India regarding the lack of commonalties between Bengali Muslims and the rest of Pakistan seems to be working among the former. There is one difference, that of language, that worries Justice Rehman. Ideally he would like to overcome that difference by making it compulsory for Bengalis to learn Urdu and for the rest of Pakistanis to learn Bengali. In order to make Bengali acceptable for other Pakistanis, he suggests changing the script of Bengali from Devanagari to Arabic. This brief exposition of the views regarding the roots of Pakistani ideology and conditions in which it can flourish enables us to locate the centrality of India in defining Pakistan, and the salience of suppressing difference within the country as the only prerequisites for sustenance of the new identity.

In November 1971 the breakup of Pakistan had become an ominous reality. Fearing it to be a big blow to the role of Islam as a unifying factor for the country, the guardians of the dominant discourse in Pakistan tried to shift the blame for the scenario to India. Zulfikar Ali Bhutto headed a delegation to China in November to seek diplomatic and strategic support against India. It was agreed that "the present situation was a result of India's willful violation of the principles of peaceful coexistence."[47] Accusing India of duplicity in its behavior, the Pakistanis maintained that, although India wanted independence for East Pakistan, it had "destroyed the freedom of the Kashmiri people and which exploits and oppresses Indian Muslims, the Mizos, the Nagas, and the Sikhs."[48] Such references by Pakistanis to the obvious heterogeneity of the Indian society and the inability of India's dominant identity discourse to bring disparate groups under one umbrella are rather paradoxical. On the one hand India is portrayed as a Hindu entity out to destroy Pakistan, but on the other it is also viewed as a problem-ridden, multiethnic society where religion has not been able to quell all differences. As the previous chapters show, India will play the same tune vis-à-vis Pakistan in order to justify its violent suppression of different identity movements.

When Yahya Khan imposed the Emergency in the country in late November, *Dawn* claimed that the action was welcomed by *all* (italics mine) segments of the population.[49] Presumably, Bengalis were effectively left out of the whole that welcomed the move. Now the battle was between the "foreign enemy" (India) and the "resolute nation . . . which wore a rock-like expression of unity." Bengalis in this contest were mere agents of India. Millions of them who had taken refuge in India were a result of "India's conspiracy to instigate, organize, and support the secessionist rebellion in (Eastern) Pakistan."

The 1971 war formally started on December 3, 1971 and lasted for about two weeks. Until the day of the ignominious surrender the demand for Bangladesh was still considered a figment of a few miscreants' imagination. Pursuing that state of denial, *Dawn* told readers in the middle of the war about the "valiant nature of the armed forces due to the Islamic spirit" and claimed that "every citizen of Pakistan is determined to defend his country."[50] The Pakistan army formally surrendered on December 16, 1971. The following day's *Dawn* symbolizes the intransigence of the dominant discourse in West Pakistan in coming to terms with the failure of the twenty-five years of Islamic narrative regarding the identity of Pakistan. The story of the humiliating defeat in Dhaka was euphemistically termed a ceasefire "agreement between the local commanders of India and Pakistan" reached in East Pakistan. The President and the paper praised armed forces for writing "new chapters of glory in defending their country."[51] The future was still seen in terms of a united Pakistan. The political ostrich-like view was evident in the fact that the defeat was not even mentioned in *Dawn*. When Bangladesh became an irrevocable reality, the remainder of Pakistan picked up the strands of the story of Muslim nationalism in the subcontinent.

A detailed account of the dominant Pakistani discourse regarding national identity during the decisive days of the movement for a separate country on the basis of ethnic identity is of crucial importance for a number of reasons. First, the nine months of 1971 tell a lot about the version of Pakistan that was being vehemently opposed and assertively resisted by the Bengalis. Second, the salience of the Indian role in defining the parameters of Pakistani identity becomes obvious during this narrative. And finally, the nuclear factor had not emerged yet as an effective deterrent to fend off the Indian threat. The last point reveals the political significance of the nuclear issue as against the strategic value attached to it by a wide range of analysts of South Asian security. Nuclear weapons had been on the global scene as an effective deterrent for a while. After two wars with conventionally superior India before 1971, the logic of deterrence suggests that Pakistan should have explored the nuclear option prior to the 1971 disaster. This anomaly also minimizes the relevance of the principles of the deterrence theory. With the preceding discussion of Pakistan's security discourse in mind, we now turn to the mid-1970s when India exploded what it termed a "peaceful nuclear device" and assess its effects on the security discourse in Pakistan.

EXPLOSION OF A DEVICE, EXPLOSION OF AN ISSUE

The dismemberment of the country did not put an end to the unresolved identity question in what remained of Pakistan. Societal heterogeneity to date poses a considerable challenge for the unifying discourse based on Muslim nationalism. Changes like the transfer of power to the civilians headed by Zulfikar Ali Bhutto and the promulgation of a new constitution in 1973 were significant breaks from the past, but the lessons from the failure of the centralizing discourse to coopt Bengali Muslims were not learned in truncated Pakistan. Preoccupation with the Indian threat continued to play a key role in setting the contours of the security discourse in Pakistan. The Indian explosion of a nuclear device on May 18, 1974 opened a new chapter in that narrative.

Two weeks before the Indian explosion, Z. A. Bhutto, prime minister of Pakistan, had a wide-ranging interview with the *New York Times*. Little had changed in terms of views on India, which was accused of wanting to see its "shadow all over us [Pakistanis]."[52] Adversarial relations between the two countries were given an aura of eternity.

> We have been the oldest adversaries in the world, much older than anyone else. There have been [a] thousand years of antagonism between the Hindus and the Muslims. From the vantage point of history, therefore, this is too old a situation for it to settle down quickly.

Entangled in interactions perceived by the neighbors in the above manner, India surprised the world by conducting what it euphemistically termed a "peaceful nuclear explosion" (PNE) on May 18, 1974. Not surprisingly the news item hit the headlines in the Pakistani media. The Pakistani foreign office's spokesman was quick to dub it a development that "cannot but be viewed with the degree of concern matching its magnitude by the world and more especially by India's neighbors."[53]

The issue would certainly become one of the important elements in India-Pakistan antagonism and their relations with other nuclear powers, especially the United States. Other neighbors of India, including China, did not accord the same urgency and importance to the Indian explosion that it assumed for Pakistan. The Pakistani foreign office's reaction was more of shock than surprise. It assured the public of the measures, especially those of Z. A. Bhutto, taken by the government to face such a challenge. They included Bhutto's pleas to Ayub in securing Karachi Nuclear Power Project (KANUPP), and his direct supervision of the Pakistan Atomic Energy Commission (PAEC) since assuming power in 1971.[54] Such a statement was like a routine response of the foreign office to any act by the Indian government that did not please Pakistanis. However, there was no pressure on the government by the opposition politicians, foreign policy analysts, or the Pakistani public to outline the Pakistani response on the issue.

Bhutto seized the political initiative in the wake of the Indian explosion and emphasized the magnitude of the issue and critical importance of his efforts to cope with any likely eventuality, that is, a threat to the existence of Pakistan. His thoughts on the issue had three dimensions. First, he claimed that his predecessors were criminally ignorant of the importance of the nuclear option despite his repeated efforts to correct their strategic myopia. Second, he conveyed to the Indians that the nuclear issue was more of a political card than a technical subject. Hence, the nature and direction of the matter would be determined by public enthusiasm regarding the nuclear option. Finally, he tied the issue to the fragile national security theme and became "the sole spokesman" to represent what constituted the national interests of Pakistan. The objective was to sideline his political opponents. In the process, he undeniably laid the foundations of Pakistan's acrimonious nuclear discourse. Two of his public pronouncements on the subject shed light on the embryonic form of nuclear discourse in the country at that time. The Indian evil designs and the near criminal negligence of his predecessors to counter them were the main points of Bhutto's first public reaction to the explosion. Terming the Indian explosion a form of "nuclear blackmail," Bhutto pledged not to succumb to the pressure.[55] The explosion was blended with the outstanding issue of Kashmir and Pakistan's resolve to jealously guard its independent identity in the subcontinent. He pledged to "move in all fields to meet the threat posed by the explosion." Since giving up the Kashmir issue surmounted to accepting Indian hegemony, which negated the whole concept of a Muslim nation-state in the subcontinent, yielding to the "nuclear blackmail" would amount to undermining the existence of an independent Pakistan. Bhutto was aware of the fact that nuclear weapons were unlikely to be used for military purposes and were primarily political weapons. He vowed to continue Pakistan's peaceful nuclear program. Recalling his earlier statements of waging a thousand years' war with India, he added that Pakistanis would "eat grass to ensure nuclear parity with India." And in the process, he expected "brave and patriot" Pakistanis to respond "magnificently to the new development."

A connection was established between patriotism and support for the nuclear option where any disagreement would be equated with cowardice and lack of patriotism. The dichotomy of Us/Them both within the country and externally was established by asserting that "if *we* were to become fearful over India's test it would indicate *we* have already succumbed to the threat. This would be disastrous for *our* national determination."[56] The conscious use of "we" to depict the resolve of the nation implies exclusion of those from the community who question the above version of national identity and its requisites for survival. Second, any reservations against the quest for nuclear parity were interpreted as an act of cowardice as well. In such a scheme of things, a lack of enthusiasm against India's nuclear explosion carried risk at two levels. Politically it meant likely exclusion from the community referred to as patriotic Pakistanis, and socially such behavior signified a coward. The latter term carries a certain weight in a predominantly patriarchal society with feudal norms to judge others. A combination of the two would certainly be "disastrous" for the nation. Bhutto's touchstone statement would intricately enmesh Pakistan's nuclear program in the web of national identity challenged by the Indian enemy.

Bhutto thrashed previous governments, especially Ayub Khan's, for their strategic naïveté in not paying due attention to the nuclear option, and accused them of "the grossest and the most appalling negligence in this respect." Ayub Khan was particularly cited as demonstrating the above traits by recalling a personal experience. In 1963, when young Bhutto had pressed Ayub Khan "to embark on a peaceful nuclear program," the latter had rejected the advice by saying, "If India went nuclear we would buy a weapon off the shelf somewhere." Bhutto retroactively dubbed Ayub Khan's attitude as "fatal to our national survival." Under new circumstances, Bhutto emerges, through personal claims, as a true savior to thwart the challenges to Pakistan's integrity. By accusing a former general, who ruled Pakistan for more than a decade, of committing fatal errors in ensuring national survival, Bhutto was also establishing a link between past and future attitudes on the issue. That would continue to guide proponents of the nuclear option in the nuclear discourse in Pakistan.

The Pakistani parliament debated the implications of the Indian explosion for Pakistan's security in June 1974.[57] Concluding the debate, Bhutto used the nuclear issue to castigate political opponents as less patriotic. The Opposition in the parliament had boycotted the debate for reasons not related to the issue. Bhutto equated the boycott with playing into the hands of India. Since the act of not participating in the debate amounted to telling the world that the Indian explosion did not threaten Pakistan's security, the "irresponsible" act of the Opposition was "in complete conformity with that of the Indian government." The Indian explosion and the consequent boycott of the Opposition not only made them Indian agents, but the explosion laid to rest, according to the government, any charges they had previously leveled against Bhutto of entering into a clandestine deal with the Indian government. This was an allusion to Bhutto's role in reaching the Simla accord with India, which was dubbed by the Opposition as a sellout of Pakistani interests. The Indian explosion came in handy for Bhutto to counter that charge. As the explosion was an "intimidation against Pakistan," it sealed the lips of "sinister-minded individuals . . . who tried to mislead the people by saying he [Bhutto] had made a secret deal with India." The connection between the two, that is, the explosion and the sealing of lips, may appear tenuous, but given Bhutto's cardinal role in Pakistan's nascent nuclear program, the government claimed that the patriotism of Bhutto was unquestionable.

The nuclear issue had entered into Pakistan's security discourse by 1974 and the initiative was firmly in the hands of Bhutto. The Opposition leaders did issue statements condemning the Indian act, but little was done by means of either accusing the government for not doing enough to ensure Pakistan's security, or dispelling the impression created by the government that by not loudly agreeing with the government on the issue they lacked the spirit of patriotism. Opinion-makers were either ignorant or made sparse comments on the matter. Following the explosion *Dawn* published only one editorial on the issue in a span of six weeks. The paper condemned the blast as "fateful" and called it "a minatory sign which Pakistan could ill afford to ignore," but interestingly, it demanded a nuclear umbrella from the nuclear weapon states (NWS) to meet the challenge. The issue was not considered pivotal enough and could be left to foreigners to take care of. However, two signed articles in that period were somewhat different in attitude. Hamid S. Rajput, a political commentator, repeated what Bhutto had already stated, and concluded that now that "India has tested her device, it is bound to have a chain reaction, especially among her neighbors."[58]

Mehrunisa Ali, an early security analyst, critically evaluated different options available to Pakistan.[59] The Indian blast was considered a bid by New Delhi to settle the Kashmir issue on its terms. Pakistan had the options of securing international guarantees, seeking a security pact with China, achieving self-sufficiency in the nuclear field, or accepting the Indian hegemony. Since the last meant negation of the Pakistani identity, and the plausibility of the first two was in doubt, the only real option to ensure the sovereignty of the country was to strengthen the national nuclear program. However, Mehrunisa Ali made it clear that the nuclear program could not be divorced from other domestic issues besetting the country. Lack of internal unity was considered the most important among those issues. We can see that the analysts now combined the nuclear issue with questions of unity and identity as well. However, the intensity surrounding the nuclear debate had hardly attained critical importance as yet. *Pakistan Horizon*, Pakistan's oldest quarterly journal concerned with foreign policy issues, in its 1974 and 1975 volumes did not publish any analysis by a Pakistani scholar regarding implications of the Indian blast. Only Bhutto consistently drew attention to the nuclear issue in the context of Pakistan's security needs up until his removal in 1977.

The nuclear issue in Pakistan was not isolated from the dynamics of general Pakistani politics, which had been at the crossroads again. Pakistan's central authorities were again faced with a crisis of legitimacy due to turmoil in two of the country's four provinces, namely, Baluchistan and the North West Frontier Province (NWFP). The provincial coalition governments led by Baloch and Pashtun nationalists were dismissed on the grounds of alleged conspiracies against Pakistan. The specter of ethnic nationalism was again looming large over the Pakistani horizon. Baluchistan, the largest but the least populated province of the country, had slipped into a civil war with armed forces chasing semitrained tribal guerrillas in the hilly terrain. Echoes of the 1970 chorus concerning a Pakistani identity and threats to it once again began resounding in the country. Bhutto, the armed forces, and an overwhelming majority of the media instantly dubbed the proponents of subnational identities as Indian and Afghan agents. Their actions were considered challenges to Pakistan's sovereignty.[60] Veteran

Pashtun leader Khan Abdul Ghafar Khan, also known as the Frontier Gandhi, was termed the ringleader of Indian agents. Establishing a connection between the Bengali nationalists and the recent generation of the disillusioned Balochs and Pashtuns was one way of legitimizing the dominant discourse concerning a monolithic Pakistani identity. Bhutto claimed that Mujibur Rehman's manifesto of the Awami League was drafted in India, and the insurgents in Balochistan and the NWFP were of the same stock.[61]

The first NPT review conference was held in 1975, a year after the Indian explosion, and Pakistan decided not to take part in it because rules prevented observer states from making a full contribution in strengthening the nonproliferation regime. Discussions regarding the NPT and Pakistan's role in it were determined by the overall political discourse in the country. Guardians of the Pakistani identity portrayed failures of the unifying discourse as a result of a deep-rooted conspiracy of the subnational movements, which were fueled by the external elements. This totalizing discourse left little room for dissent. Any disagreement was quickly construed as yet another example of anti-Pakistan forces at work. Faced with these dilemmas, *Dawn*'s analysis of the proliferation issue and Pakistan's role in it was seen in the context of the "frightful possibilities" presented by the Indian blast and the Israeli admission of carrying on a clandestine nuclear program. Reiterating the Pakistani proposal to declare South Asia a nuclear weapon-free zone (NWFZ), India was blamed for being "hostile to the idea."[62] Concerns about the Israeli nuclear program as a security threat to Pakistan had entered the Pakistani discourse about the issue. They gained prominence during subsequent years. The West's failure to agree upon any meaningful disarmament measures was mentioned but not yet construed as a deep conspiracy against Pakistan.

The nature and direction of relations with India were not divorced from the currents of politics within Pakistan. The nuclear issue was an irritant but still not a major bone of contention to derail any efforts to normalize relations between the two countries. The dominant Pakistani political discourse was undoubtedly based on anti-Indianism but the nuclear issue had not yet become an emotional shield to protect Pakistani identity. India's official stand on the nonproliferation issue was seen by analysts in Pakistan as a part of New Delhi's overall aim to play a hegemonic role in South Asia. A. T. Chaudri, a leading commentator on Pakistan's foreign policy, argued that "Mrs. Gandhi had relapsed in bellicosity" thwarting any efforts to normalize Indo-Pak ties.[63] For Chaudri, India's hegemonic aspirations were evident in "its obdurate stand on the matters of fundamental importance to this region." He argued that the Pakistani offer to declare South Asia a NWFZ was overridden by India because it wanted to have a "veto on denuclearization of South Asia." He called upon all smaller neighbors of India to "take serious note of India's desire to keep the option of setting free its nuclear genie." A small number of politicians had taken up the nuclear cause of Pakistan. Dr. M. Shafi, a Pakistan Peoples Party (PPP) parliamentarian, called for giving priority to achieving nuclear capability.[64] He mentioned Indian nuclear capability as a reason to speed up Pakistan's nuclear program, but the key concern was to use the technology for industrial purposes and not as an effective deterrent.

NUKES IN THE PUBLIC DOMAIN

The politics of the nuclear issue took a decisive shift immediately after the controversial general election in Pakistan held in March 1977. Officially, Bhutto's PPP had won a landslide victory in polls for the National Assembly. The Pakistan National Alliance (PNA), an alliance of assorted political groups led by religious parties, disputed the election results and decided to launch a mass movement against the Bhutto regime. Allegations and counterallegations about opponents' patriotic and religious credentials were rampant.

Bhutto linked the movement against his regime to a U.S. ploy to remove him in the wake of the nuclear reprocessing plant deal his government had struck with France. The floor of the National Assembly reverberated with claims of protecting national sovereignty against external threats. This time however, the alleged threat emanated from the United States, not India, and revolved around the ambitious Pakistani nuclear program rather than "aggressive" Indian nuclear capability. Bhutto argued that the United States had sponsored the agitation against his patriotic government because Washington did not want Pakistan to benefit from the French nuclear plant deal. The acquisition of the plant became synonymous with the prime national interest. The external and internal enemies of Pakistan were allegedly colliding to abort the deal. Bhutto warned the Americans that "the party is not over and will not be over till my mission is complete for this great nation."[65] The reference to the party was made after an alleged remark by the U.S. ambassador in Pakistan that Bhutto's party was over. Surely a party revolving around the nuclear program would only swell in the times to come. The adversaries, the Americans in this instance, were termed "white elephants" and "bloodhounds" that were after Bhutto to destabilize Pakistan.

The nuclear genie as a political force entered the popular domain on April 29, 1977 when Bhutto addressed a huge public rally in Rawalpindi about the nuclear program and the anti-PPP designs of the Americans and its Pakistani allies. Waving the letter of the U.S. secretary of state to Bhutto asking for a quiet dialogue on the nuclear issue, he vowed not to compromise on national interests. He pledged to keep the nation's interest supreme in the wake of all kinds of pressures. Pakistan's nuclear program was portrayed as a symbol of resistance by an independent Islamic state against the U.S. and Indian hegemonic designs. The official media depicted the

PNA's lack of support for Bhutto's nuclear stance as a sign of disregard for national interests. Debate over the site of patriotism would continue to mar the political discourse in Pakistan, but the totalizing tendencies embedded in the politics of the nuclear issue would make it one of the criteria of Pakistan's dominant identity test. It would become a rallying point with which to demonstrate one's affiliation with Pakistan and opposition to it would carry the stigma of being branded as an outsider.

In the wake of Bhutto's confrontation with Washington over Pakistan's nuclear program, the government used the nuclear issue as a means to delegitimize the Opposition's movement. Statements issued by the Pakistani foreign office during that period were addressed as much to the United States and India as to the domestic audience. If the United States was accused of exerting pressure to abandon the nuclear program, India was accused of vicious propaganda against the peaceful character of the Pakistani program. But the Foreign Office drew a line by claiming that "Pakistan is committed to build the plant and no government can go back on it."[66]

While the government was trying to emerge from troubled waters by highlighting the critical importance of the nuclear program for the nation's sovereignty, and condemning the external as well as internal impediments as dangers to Pakistan's sovereignty, the Armed Forces were devising plans to do away with the Bhutto regime. On July 5,1977, General Zia-ul-Haq, then chief of the Pakistan army, declared martial law and promised to hold new general elections in ninety days and hand over power to duly elected legitimate representatives of the people. He, however, remained in power for the next eleven years until the day he died in a mysterious air crash in 1988. The next chapter tells the story of how the nuclear issue became all-pervasive in the dominant security discourse in post-1977 Pakistan.

NOTES

1. Mohammad Ayub Khan, *Speeches and Statements, Volume IV, July 1961–June 1962*, n.p., n.d., p. 56. The Government of Pakistan publishes these volumes but they do not state so.
2. Zulfikar Ali Bhutto, *Reshaping Foreign Policy: A collection of articles, statements and speeches: Politics of the People Series, Volume I, 1948–1966*, Hamid Jalal and Khalid Hasan, eds. (Rawalpindi: Pakistan Publications, n.d.), p. 222.
3. Zulfikar Ali Bhutto (1927–1979) led Pakistan after the 1971 defeat until he was removed in a military coup d'état in 1977. He also served as a foreign minister during the 1960s under Ayub Khan. Bhutto played a key role in bringing the nuclear issue into the political arena of Pakistan through his word, works, and patronage of the Pakistan Atomic Energy Commission.
4. Mohammad Ayub Khan, *Friends Not Masters: A Political Autobiography* (London, Karachi: Oxford University Press, 1967), p. 114.
5. Ibid.
6. Ibid., p. 115.

7. Ibid.
8. Ibid.
9. Ibid.
10. Ibid., p. 117.
11. Ibid., p. 128.
12. Bhutto, *Reshaping Foreign Policy, Volume I*, pp. 140–141.
13. Ibid., p. 221.
14. Ibid., p. 222.
15. Ibid., p. 287.
16. Ibid.
17. Ibid.
18. Ibid., p. 288.
19. Ibid.
20. Zulfikar Ali Bhutto, *Awakening the People: A collection of articles, statements, Politics of the People Series, Volume II, 1966–1969* (Rawalpindi: Pakistan Publications, n.d.), p. 708.
21. Zulfikar Ali Bhutto, *Marching toward Democracy: A collection of articles, statements and speeches, The Politics of People, Volume III, 1970–1971* (Rawalpindi: Pakistan Publications, n.d.), p. 192.
22. Zulfikar Ali Bhutto, *The Myth of Independence* (London, Lahore, Karachi: Oxford University Press, 1969).
23. Ibid., p. 162.
24. Ibid.
25. Ibid., p. 163.
26. Ibid., p. 164.
27. Ibid., p. 173.
28. Ibid., p. 170.
29. Ibid., p. 180.
30. Ibid., p. 113.
31. Ibid., p. 162.
32. Ibid., p. 163.
33. Ibid., p. 152.
34. Ibid.
35. Ibid.
36. Ibid.
37. Ibid.
38. *Dawn* is the leading and the oldest Pakistani daily newspaper published in English from Karachi. Founded by the founder of Pakistan, Muhammad Ali Jinnah, the daily is seen as the credible voice of Pakistan. *Dawn* is a useful site to study the dynamics of the identity discourse as expounded by "true Pakistanis."
39. *Dawn*, March 23, 1971.
40. Jinnah is officially addressed as *Quaid-I-Azam* in Pakistan. The term roughly translated means the Great Leader.
41. *Dawn*, March 27, 1971.
42. *Dawn*, March 30, 1971.
43. *Dawn*, April 2, 1971.
44. *Dawn*, April 3, 1971.
45. *Dawn*, April 4, 1971.

46. Justice Hamud Rehman, "Steps to Strengthen Ideology of Pakistan," *Dawn*, October 14, 1971.

47. *Dawn*, November 9, 1971.

48. Ibid.

49. *Dawn*, November 23, 1971.

50. *Dawn*, December 12, 1971.

51. *Dawn*, December 17, 1971.

52. The transcript of the interview was published in *Dawn*, May 6, 1974.

53. *Dawn*, May 19, 1974.

54. Ibid.

55. *Dawn*, May 20, 1974.

56. Ibid.

57. *Dawn*, June 8, 1974.

58. Hamid S. Rajput, "Indian Nuclear Test: Threat to Peace," *Dawn*, May 30, 1974.

59. Mehrunisa Ali, "Implications of Indian Nuclear Blast," *Dawn*, June 24, 1974.

60. *Dawn*, April 15, 1975.

61. *Dawn*, April 17, 1975.

62. Pakistan initially proposed the establishment of a nuclear-weapons-free zone in South Asia (SANWFZ) after the Indian nuclear explosion in 1974. The matter was originally raised in the UN Ad Hoc Committee on the Indian ocean in 1973. Pakistan has periodically raised the issue in spite of India's categorical rejection of the SANWFZ idea. See Ziba Moshavir, *Nuclear Weapons Proliferation in the Indian Subcontinent* (London: Macmillan, 1991), p. 119.

63. A. T. Chaudri, "The Deadlock at Delhi," *Dawn*, May 25, 1975.

64. *Dawn*, June 15, 1975.

65. *Dawn*, April 29, 1977.

66. *Dawn*, June 26, 1977.

Chapter 5

Nukespeak in Pakistan: 1977–1999

> The Christian, Jewish, and Hindu civilizations have nuclear capability along with communist powers. Only the Islamic civilization was without it, but the situation was about to change. What difference does my life make now when I can imagine eighty million of my countrymen standing under the nuclear cloud of a defenseless sky?
>
> —Z. A. Bhutto in 1979[1]

In May 1998, Nawaz Sharif, then prime minister of Pakistan, clamored about "settling the account with India" while announcing the successful conduct of Pakistani nuclear explosions. Pakistan and Islam had the nuclear bomb too. Ayub Khan, Pakistan's military ruler during the 1960s, thought that Pakistan would buy nuclear bombs off the shelf if needed. Nawaz Sharif, businessman-turned-politician prime minister of Pakistan, put the country's homemade bomb on the shelf, and presumably ensured the safety of 130 million Pakistanis. This chapter tells the story of the security discourse that shows how Pakistan's sovereignty has become intimately tied up with nuclear weapons. Therefore, when India conducted nuclear tests the question was not *whether* Pakistan would follow suit but *when* it would do so.

Pakistan's brief encounter with parliamentary democracy came to an abrupt end in July 1977 when the military, led by General Zia-ul-Haq, began its eleven-year term in power through a coup. The idea of a "nation in danger" was pursued with intensified vigor by the unelected *junta*. The military regime of Zia could not have survived for a decade on the use of naked force alone. It drew its sustenance from monopolizing, manipulating, and creating forms of truth, which became part of the security discourse in the country. The process was never easy or entirely peaceful. It was a mix of demagogy, censorship of some views and promotion of others, and resort to judicial and extrajudicial powers to execute and imprison opponents. The boundaries between the external and internal, which have always been muddy in Pakistan's dominant security discourse, became even more blurred. The dominant security discourse during the Zia period essentially was built on the themes already pervading the political culture. My account traces the politics of the nuclear issue as one factor utilized by the dominant discourse to legitimize the military regime and consolidate a particular form of Pakistani identity. I start with a look at the way in which the new regime kept the essential ingredients of Z. A. Bhutto's nukespeak while physically eliminating him in a controversial death penalty in 1979. This is followed by an analysis of the formation of an epistemic community of strategic experts on the nuclear issue in the 1980s. The narrative continues with an examination of the nuclear discourse in the post-Zia era, ending with a look at contemporary nuclear discourse in Pakistan culminating in the nuclear test in response to the Indian explosions in May 1998.

GET RID OF BHUTTO BUT KEEP HIS NUKESPEAK: 1977–1979

The physical presence of Bhutto, although he was incarcerated, as the most authentic voice on the nuclear issue put the new regime in a dilemma. The populist image of Bhutto was a specter that haunted the military regime from the very beginning. Maligning his image initially and ultimately getting rid of him physically were deemed necessary for the continuity of the military regime. The new regime was quick to make political capital from Bhutto's charged nationalist stance on foreign policy matters, especially on the nuclear issue, in its drive for legitimacy. The incarcerated Bhutto managed to pen his views amid the deafening voices of his opponents through a book written in the death cell. The following is a reconstruction of that period, with a focus on nuclear weapons and the question of the Pakistani identity.

Arthur Hummel Jr., the U.S. ambassador in Pakistan, had a midnight meeting with Bhutto two days prior to the imposition of martial law.[2] On July 6, 1977 newspapers splashed the headline of Bhutto's unceremonial removal and imposition of the military rule after an interregnum of five years of civilian administration. The Jamait-I-Islami, the most organized religious party in Pakistan and one of the leading opponents of Bhutto, was the first political party to assure Zia of all cooperation.

Mainstream media did not waste any time in endorsing the army act by suggesting that "after stumbling from deadlock to deadlock, the nation is now able to look forward to the future without trepidation."[3] Conversely, those who had expressed any hesitation, dismay, or disapproval about the martial law could be considered out of bounds with the imaginary nation, which was demonstrating "a tranquil mood." Rather than taking Zia's pledge to transfer power to civilians in ninety days with a pinch of salt, the leading newspaper of the country argued that "the role the army has assumed now was forced upon it by circumstances." The ban on political activities, which was a euphemism for a crackdown on the Pakistan Peoples Party (PPP), was justified on the grounds of creating "a proper atmosphere for a political debate." Pakistan's dominant discourse commended the coup d'état and credited the military authorities with moving at a "brisk promptitude" to pave the way for general elections—which were to be held on October 3, 1977.[4]

By September 1977 the political intentions of the Zia regime to remain in power became evident when Bhutto was jailed on charges of being an accomplice in the murder of a political opponent. Whereas *Dawn* praised Yahya in 1971 for discharging his professional duties in the East Pakistan crisis, it absolved Zia of any "involvement" in the case against Bhutto. Furthermore, the courts were declared free of any pressures, and skeptics were told that Bhutto "will be tried under the established criminal procedure," and the judicial process should be allowed to take its course without adversely affecting the political process.[5] The military regime was applauded for acting responsibly in the contentious issue.

The nuclear issue became one of the favored national possessions to be saved by the new regime. Statements of the Pakistani delegation in the UN General Assembly became headlines confirming continuity in the foreign policy of the country despite the regime change. The solution of the Kashmir issue and acquisition of nuclear technology for peaceful purposes were declared as the cornerstones of the policy objectives.[6] As the promised election date (October 1977) approached, the champions of the idea of Pakistan as the monolithic Islamic society faced the dilemma of an incarcerated Bhutto capable of undermining the legitimacy of the new setup. Holding an election was presented as a choice between accountability and representative rule. The former was considered a pressing need of the time, whereas the latter only a luxury when the political spectrum was cleared of any potentially dangerous people, and "elections without sorting out the accountability issue" were seen as a recipe for trouble. *Dawn* categorically stated that the armed forces assumed power with a simple mandate of holding free elections. Now that the former prime minister was believed to be involved in a murder, good Pakistanis should shudder at the thought "of allowing people suspected of murder to participate in the elections."[7] The ruling generals wholeheartedly accepted the suggestion of postponing elections. Bhutto became the new demon to haunt the narratives of the dominant discourse after his death. Meanwhile, his writings from the death cell would shed light on the importance of the nuclear program as a potent force in the game of proving one's patriotism and others' lack of it.

The nuclear issue was, at least for Bhutto and his new adversaries, a firm factor in Pakistani nationalism, especially in the wake of U.S. pressure to abandon the program. The theme of a foreign hand and its local allies who harm the national sovereignty was the hallmark of Bhutto's statements on the nuclear issue while he was incarcerated. He accused the Pakistan National Alliance (PNA) and the military *junta* of openly joining hands to "dislocate and destroy Pakistan's nuclear program."[8] Alluding to the United States, he argued that this antinational alliance was taking place in compliance with the interests of a foreign power. Using the political realism's dictum of self-help as the key principle of international politics, he suggested that "foreign governments will follow their own policies," but lamented that "only we, in Pakistan, have regimes which follow the policies of foreign governments."[9] Here, Bhutto's statements after the Indian explosion in 1974 are worth recalling. At that time he accused the then opposition of playing into the enemy's hands by not supporting what he perceived to be the key national interests. Ironically, this time it was the government of the day and its informal allies he was blaming for fiddling with national interests.

Controversy surrounding the deal with France to acquire nuclear weapons was high on Bhutto's mind when he tried to convince Pakistanis that the Zia regime was squandering the agreement his government had signed in March 1976 after three years of intense negotiations. The French government's suggestions to modify the original agreement were portrayed by Bhutto as Paris' preference for a civilian government in Pakistan.[10] Bhutto implied that in light of Zia's record of broken promises to hold elections, the French government was reluctant to take his word regarding the nature of the nuclear program. This line of argument explicitly suggested that the best way to ensure transfer of nuclear technology to Pakistan would be to have Bhutto at the helm of affairs. Bhutto accused Zia of adopting a "flippant and callous approach" on the "issue of the nation's life and death."[11]

In a changed political configuration, Bhutto emphasized that he was still an uncompromising patriot and the people at the helm of affairs in the new regime were a coterie of external agents. What he apparently overlooked is the fact that it was nearly impossible to prevent different actors from assuming the role of custodians of truths hitherto considered to have been discovered by Bhutto. The Zia regime adopted Bhutto's views on the nuclear issue as a cornerstone of the security discourse. Essentially, there was continuity in the nature and direction of the discourse but with different faces. The new regime's ironic dependence on Bhutto's views on the nuclear issue became most obvious when Bhutto's thoughts on the matter chronicled in a book written while he was in prison eventually became a primer for the new regime in its discourse on the nuclear issue. By declaring the nuclear program a matter of life and death for the nation, Bhutto warned that by losing the uranium-reprocessing plant Pakistan would be "at the mercy of those who are professionals in the art of nuclear blackmail."[12] In the new situation, India and the United States had joined hands with the Pakistani *junta* to derail Bhutto's efforts. In the future, Indo-U.S. cooperation to frustrate Pakistan's nuclear program would remain a "truth" but the Zia regime's complicity, as alleged by Bhutto, in the process would become a nonissue.

Faced with the death penalty in a controversial and politically motivated trial, Bhutto turned the nuclear issue into a manifestation of his lifelong dream of strengthening Pakistan's security against India in the geostrategic realm and introducing a qualitative strategic shift in terms of civilizations. Crediting himself for working "assiduously and with granite determination" to "acquire nuclear capability" for Pakistan by sending "hundreds of young men to Europe and North America for nuclear science training," he was not focusing on the narrowly defined interests of Pakistan. In this context Bhutto penned his now widely cited quote that has turned into an article of faith in the dominant security discourse of Pakistan: "The Christian, Jewish, and Hindu civilizations have nuclear capability along with communist powers. Only the Islamic civilization was without it, but the situation was about to change."[13] Pakistan's nuclear hawks see the country's nuclear program not only as an effective deterrent against Hindu India, but a shield to protect the Muslim world against Zionist Israel. The Americans would see such sentiments as definite grounds on which to deny Pakistan's bid to acquire nuclear capability.

The program would also become a sacred sight for the proponents of religious identity in Pakistan. Even while facing the gallows, Bhutto would put the country's key interests well above his physical existence in the following way: "What difference does my life make now when I can imagine 80 million of my countrymen standing under the nuclear cloud of a defenseless sky?"[14] With the decision to send him to the gallows, "the sovereignty and security of the nation have been mounted on the gallows."[15] What he did not realize was the fact that the regime and other sections of the dominant discourse in Pakistani politics would not abandon Bhutto's ideas on the issue. The Zia regime expediently rallied behind the nuclear issue as one way to further an Islamic Pakistan's identity and counter domestic and external enemies. Bhutto was hanged in the middle of the night of April 4,1979 but his legacies on the nuclear issue continued to unfold in hitherto unknown forms.

ZIA'S PAKISTAN, ISLAM'S FORTRESS!

The security discourse during the Zia regime was characterized by familiar themes of external dangers and their domestic allies. The Soviet invasion of Afghanistan in 1979 enabled the dominant security discourse to invoke images of a Pakistan sandwiched between hegemonic Hindu India and expansionist communist Russia. A new kind of player entered the nuclear discourse in Pakistan by 1979: a retired soldier turned strategic expert. Abdul Qayyum was one of the early soldier experts who analyzed the nuclear issue with patriotic zeal.[16] Other high-ranking soldiers would join him in the days to come. A closer look at Qayyum's views in 1979 sheds light on totalizing tendencies that have become a hallmark of the nuclear discourse. To draw lines in the discourse as to what is true and what is false, Qayyum relies heavily on the logocentric logic of creating dichotomies of Them and Us. These dichotomies are based on historical amnesia to lend credence to the new people at the helm of affairs in the country.

Qayyum starts with the statement of two events that prompted him to write. The first was a recent uranium shipment to India by the Americans: a self-explanatory cause of concern for Pakistanis. The second emanated from the U.S. decision to suspend aid to Pakistan. The combination of the two was seen as serious enough to force an inquiry into the dynamics of national politics to determine what should be the best response of the nation in such a crucial situation. The resolve of the military and civil bureaucracy, the direct rulers of the country at that time, to defy any external pressure is never doubted in Qayyum's account. Qayyum then turns to what he calls "the national press" and its strong support for "the nuclear program being pursued by Pakistan." By implication, any segment of the press that lagged behind in strongly supporting the government at that time put its status of being "national press" in jeopardy. The national press was not credited with just supporting the program, it was lauded for urging "the nation to face this cut-off of aid with patriotic courage." If the shock of Bhutto's hanging dampened many Pakistanis' enthusiasm for the nuclear issue, it just showed their lack of patriotism. Even worse, those who contemplated challenging the government for its hanging of an elected leader and opposed martial law at that time must have been handpicked agents of external adversaries. Amid all this, the nuclear program was considered "a matter of consensus in this country and the Government would not make any compromises on this fundamental issue because the entire nation is behind it." The myth of consensus was assumed and imposed on the issue. Any attempts to force Pakistan to give up its program were doomed to fail "for the simple reason that our program is supported by consensus in Pakistan."

A new epistemic community came into being in the Zia years that now constitutes the core of nukespeak in Pakistan. The basic guiding principle of the new pool of experts would be a reference to the national consensus on the nuclear issue. The presumed consensus could only be envisaged with the help of historical amnesia. Qayyum's account, written while Bhutto's death was still fresh in peoples' minds, conveniently forgot to mention the role played by the former prime minister in the history of the nuclear issue in Pakistan. Whenever generals would write about the nuclear program and its history, Bhutto would usually become a victim of selective amnesia. The issue itself would regularly adorn the front pages of newspapers to keep the nation aware of the importance of Pakistan's nuclear program, and would reaffirm the "truth" of consensus on the matter.

Zia usually pledged to hold elections and often deferred the promised date on grounds that national security had priority over electoral politics. In May 1979, Zia again promised to hold elections in November. By now, Islam, stability, and national security became not only the favorite causes of the regime, but they increasingly became mutually dependent on one another in the dominant security discourse. Pakistan's nuclear program became an integral part of the security discourse and a symbol of national unity and sovereignty. These connections were duly made by higher-ups in the Foreign Office. Agha Shahi, then foreign secretary, assured the world of the peaceful nature of Pakistan's nuclear program; and Akram Zaki, ambassador to the Philippines, demanded a nondiscriminatory attitude by the Americans toward Pakistan on the nuclear issue.[17] The American media's negative portrayal of Pakistan's nuclear program became a rallying point for proponents of the dominant security discourse to infuse the issue with patriotism. Commenting on a news report on Pakistan's nuclear ambitions by the American television network Columbia Broadcasting System (CBS), *Dawn* viewed the Western propaganda as a part of "the smear campaign" that had "degenerated into a vilification campaign."[18] The nuclear issue was no longer one concerning the differing views on nonproliferation measures, but one that put "the Pakistan government's credibility at stake."

Zia was by now well aware of the legitimizing potential of the nuclear issue. He ordered the foreign office machinery to "refute propaganda against Pakistan's nuclear program."[19] And those efforts appeared as headlines in the "national press" to forge a closer link between external and domestic dimensions of the program. Any news item in the Western media contemplating a commando action against Pakistan's nuclear installations would easily find its way into Pakistani headlines and a spate of commentaries would follow preparing the nation to safeguard its cherished program. One such report appeared in the *New York Times* in the middle of August 1979, and a Pakistani analyst, Qutubudin Aziz, wrote about an alleged "Zionist conspiracy" against Pakistan that reflected the standard argument used in the dominant discourse.[20] The newly found zeal in the United States against the Pakistani nuclear program was seen as an anti-Pakistan campaign by the Israeli lobby in the West. According to Aziz, "international Zionist hostility" against Pakistan was manifested in "the pro-Jewish *New York Times*" and "the Zionist influenced CBS." Such views were eerily reminiscent of Bhutto's thoughts from the death cell in which he talked of Jewish, Hindu, and Christian bombs.

Gradually, strategic experts, retired generals and ambassadors, and religious ideologues turned the Pakistani nuclear program into a bulwark against Zionism along with a shield against Hindu India and a symbol of defiance against the United States. As the date of the promised polls in November 1979 drew closer, so did the hype surrounding Zia's patriotic rhetoric to safeguard the nuclear program. In a countrywide address on August 30, 1979, Zia stipulated his vision of the country in some detail. This speech offers a good synopsis of the currents of the dominant discourse. The nuclear program ranked top among the items mentioned. Repeating what Bhutto had said in his book, Zia termed the bid for "the acquisition of nuclear energy . . . a matter of life and death for the country."[21] There was a double-edged warning, one aspect of which was addressed to the domestic audience and the other to external enemies. Countrymen were told that "unholy plans are being promoted to destroy our research program." Firmly locating the nuclear program in the context of sacred versus profane values, the politics of the issue was no longer seen as a contest over strategic options but rather a *jihad* (Islamic holy war). Once the nature of the issue was cast in terms of religious beliefs, it became incumbent upon patriotic Pakistani Muslims to lend support to the regime in its "holy" endeavor. The external adversaries were warned that by contemplating such "unholy" plans, they were showing a lack of understanding about "the true mettle of the Pakistani nation and its spirit of self-respect." Zia maintained that "the Pakistani nation is convinced that acquisition of atomic technology . . . is its basic right, which can not be denied by any foreign power nor can any government in Pakistan surrender it."

Now that Zia and the nation had become synonymous, according to him, he knew what the nation would choose in case of an emergency; that is, "this nation will prefer death with honor to domination by others." But the nation, whose course of life and death was so convincingly defined by the words of Zia, had something else in mind too, namely, an election. After a lengthy sermon on the delicate nature of the nuclear issue and delineating lines of holy patriotism, Zia turned to the issue of holding the promised election. It was stated at the outset that the election was a "divisive" issue. Turning to unsubstantiated requests by "*ulema* (religious leaders), intellectuals and worried citizens" not to hold elections in the country, he not only readily agreed, but suggested that "national integrity demands that steps should be taken before elections."

Hinting at a possible postponement of the election, stories of Zia's steps toward fulfilling the demands of national integrity frequently appeared in the media.[22] Zia finally declared electoral democracy as an opposite of Pakistan's security in the following words: "The security and solidarity of the country and the protection of Islamic ideology in any case was much more important than plunging the nation into the electoral exercise."[23] By now, he had assumed the guardianship of safeguarding the country's needs, especially through his efforts to ward off any pressure against the nuclear program. After he had portrayed the electoral process and the country's security as diametrically opposite poles, the announcement of an indefinite postponement of the promised election was made on October 1, 1979.

By late 1979, the new regime prided itself for defending Pakistan's nuclear program in international forums. The Soviet invasion of Afghanistan in December 1979 proved to be the lifeline of the Zia regime. The Islamic identity of Pakistan came to be threatened by Hindu India on the eastern side and the communist threat was knocking at the door from the western side. The Soviet invasion had a lasting impact on the security discourse in Pakistan, especially by providing the pretext of an external threat to suppress dissidence within the country, and also to intensify efforts to Islamize Pakistani polity.

Efforts to unify Pakistan on the basis of Islam received a blow in 1983 when the Movement for the Restoration of Democracy (MRD), a political alliance led by the PPP, called for street agitation against the regime. Rural Sindh, the home province of the Bhuttos and their political stronghold, became the epicenter of the movement. The agitation started with voluntary arrests by political activists, but soon turned into violent encounters between the security forces and Sindhis. Prior to the movement, Zia, whose regime was receiving full U.S. support due to its role in Afghanistan, claimed to have uncovered an Israeli plan to destroy Pakistan's nuclear installations.[24] At the heels of these claims came the MRD movement and violence in Sindh. The regime initially categorized the situation as "regrettable but not disquieting,"[25] considering it the work of a handful of "anarchist elements" with the possibility of foreign support. This conception of reality overlooked the limits of the dominant discourse to effectively bring the whole population of the country under its umbrella. It invoked the role of external powers to explain what was essentially a homegrown phenomenon.

Increasingly, the movement became a nationalist uprising against the dictatorial rule of Islamabad. The guardians of Pakistani nationalism were quick to dub the procession of protestors as "looting mobs."[26] All "right-minded people of Pakistan" were expected to oppose these "mobs." In line with past tradition in the country, A. T. Chaudri, a leading political analyst, drew analogies between the Bangladesh movement and the "violent, rather terrorist" elements in Sindh who were "bent upon enacting the 1971 gory drama."[27] For this group of people the debacle in the then East Pakistan was a result of the Bengalis' intransigence rather than a failure of the basis of Pakistan's ruling elite in forging a national identity. The foreign hand that Zia had suspected earlier was now considered a reality and the Pakistani government officially lodged complaints with the Indian government for meddling in the internal affairs of Pakistan.

Meanwhile, Pakistan's geostrategic location became the much-discussed source of vulnerability among experts on strategy in the 1980s with nuclear issue a rallying point for the new epistemic community's regime of truth. Hasan Askari Rizvi, one of the leading security experts of Pakistan, justified Pakistan's defense spending on the grounds of external threats faced by the country.[28] The 1974 nuclear explosion of India was considered one such threat that called for Pakistan to boost up its nuclear capability.[29] These views were incessantly echoed in conferences and seminars organized by the government-sponsored think tanks.[30]

Pakistan's nuclear program was portrayed in strategic terms with little or no mention of earlier arguments about its uses for the purposes of meeting the country's energy needs. Mushahid Hussain, serving as minister for information in the Nawaz Sharif government, represented a new generation of experts who viewed Pakistan's program as "a response to India's nuclear ambitions."[31] The main objective of Pakistan was "to seek a credible nuclear deterrent against its principal adversary, i.e., India."[32] Gone were the days when experts tried to wrap their argument in the context of energy needs. The teachings of nuclear deterrence prevalent in the West had become staple arguments of Pakistani experts. Conventional weapons were considered incapable of allaying the "deep historical fears" of Pakistanis. The nuclear deterrent was seen as "the best guarantor of Pakistan's security against India" under the changed circumstances.[33] Zia and Hussain had identical views on the nuclear issue. Responding to a question as to why Pakistan wanted a bomb, Zia said, "to ensure security, to create a deterrent."[34]

In sum, it was during the Zia regime that the nuclear issue became the domain of experts who continue to dominate the debate in today's Pakistan. Zia's version of Pakistan was based upon a militarily strong, politically and socially homogenized Pakistan with "Islamic ideology" as the ultimate test of patriotism, and the nuclear option as the best available sword to deter India and convince the nation of the regime's patriotic credentials. A week before his accidental death, Zia asked the people of Pakistan "not to grudge defense allocations . . . as no price is too big for national independence."[35] He expressed pride in the fact that the Armed Forces were his constituency who "were defending the sacred soil of the country at great sacrifice." Bhutto brought the nuclear issue into the security discourse of Pakistan, and Zia continued to make use of it to consolidate an independent Islamic identity for Pakistan by invoking the image of an Indian threat. The 1980s saw the birth of an epistemic community of strategic experts in Pakistan that continued to flourish in the post-Zia period. The nuclear issue would no longer remain tied to the people in power alone. It also became a powerful tool in the hands of the people with knowledge about the issue to determine how patriotic different rulers were. The next section discusses the nature and direction of nuclear politics in Pakistan in the post-Zia period.

THE POST-ZIA PERIOD

Election campaigns provide a good opportunity to assess the salience of various issues in a society. Qualitative shifts in the discourse become transparent in the public assertions of politicians, writings of analysts, and reactions of people to the statements of truth and countertruth. The party-based November 1988 polls centered upon patriotic credentials of the key contenders. The shadows of Z. A. Bhutto and Zia-ul-Haq loomed large over the election campaign of Benazir Bhutto, leader of the PPP, and Nawaz Sharif, a close associate of Zia and the leader of the newly formed Islami Jamhoori Ittehad (IJI), or Islamic Democratic Alliance.

Which issue could have served better than the nuclear issue to measure the contenders' love for national sovereignty! Z. A. Bhutto had accused the United States and its Pakistani allies of pressuring him to give up Pakistan's nuclear program during the post-1977 election agitation. Eleven years later, the IJI was accusing the Bhutto ladies (Benazir and her mother Nusrat) of being the stooges of United States ready to provide Americans access to the nuclear facilities of Pakistan if they came to power. So close were the connections between the enemies of Pakistan and the anti-Pakistan Bhuttos that, according to the IJI, the "Jewish and Hindu lobby was working for PPP's campaign. The objective of Jewish and Hindu lobby was to bring in a government which suits their designs."[36] For Nawaz Sharif, then leader of the IJI, if India was the external enemy, the PPP was the internal enemy bent upon harming the national sovereignty of the country.[37] The Bhuttos offered what they thought was incontrovertible evidence to counter these charges: the fate of the late Bhutto who faced the gallows to protect the nuclear plant of Pakistan. If Z. A. Bhutto could die for the country, doubts about the Bhutto ladies' patriotism were unfounded. All the allegations regarding the sellout of the Bhuttos were made in the cities of the Punjab. The province had traditionally been the bastion of the dominant discourse in Pakistan. During the Zia regime the discourse regarding Pakistan's geostrategic security and Islamic ideological frontiers had taken deep roots in the politics of the Punjab. The IJI knew that the people of Punjab would not accept politicians who would jeopardize Pakistan's nuclear program. The nuclear issue by now had assumed a life of its own and could determine future prospects of politicians in the most populated province of Pakistan.

While Benazir Bhutto played up the theme of democracy versus autocracy in Pakistan as personified by martyrs of two kinds, Bhutto and Zia, respectively, the IJI went on the offensive on the issues of nuclear policy and the threat posed by Benazir to the Islamic identity of Pakistan. Continuation of the nuclear program without yielding to external pressures was one of the cardinal principles outlined in the election manifesto of the IJI.[38] Benazir won the elections with a slim majority and vowed to safeguard the nuclear program of Pakistan despite proclaiming to be a nonproliferationist. The combined pressure of her political opponents and the pundits of Pakistan's security forced her to stick to the policy of nuclear ambiguity. The epistemic community of strategic analysts highlighted the threats to Pakistan's identity in uncertain political times. The centrality of the Indian threat had become an article of faith in such writings, and they argued that the centuries-old rivalry between Hindu India and Muslim Pakistan was unlikely to subside due to the hegemonic designs of India. Pakistan should be prepared to safeguard its "national independence and territorial integrity" at any cost.[39] There was no better way to ensure these two essentials than a "suitable deterrent . . . mix of the nuclear and conventional forces," where nuclear forces would "act as a bulwark against Indian designs."

The 1988 election led to a minority government led by Benazir Bhutto. Coincidentally, the valley of Kashmir slipped into a violent uprising against New Delhi in 1989. Ethnic turmoil in the urban centers of Sindh, especially the port city of Karachi and Hyderabad, was in full swing as well. American aid to Pakistan remained suspended. The dominant security discourse in Pakistan was rife with anti-India assertions and in favor of Pakistan's nuclear program. France decided to renew nuclear cooperation with Pakistan in spite of U.S. displeasure. The new regime portrayed this development as a key triumph to ensure Pakistan's security.[40]

Meanwhile, the Iraqi invasion of Kuwait in 1990 followed by the U.S. victory in the Gulf War had visible effects on the security discourse in Pakistan. At the onset of the Gulf War, the political scene in Pakistan was torn with the dilemma of massive anti-Americanism on the one hand and closer ties with the U.S. ally in the Gulf, that is, Saudi Arabia, on the other. Although Pakistani troops were deployed on Saudi soil to defend the kingdom, General Aslam Beg, then Chief of the Army Staff, was talking in terms of "strategic defiance" to ward off what he believed to be American hegemony in the region. The dominant discourse in Pakistan was calling into question U.S. sincerity in liberating Kuwait, when the former's role in safeguarding the rights of Kashmiris was far from the expectations of Pakistanis. The continuing pressure against Pakistan's nuclear program and threats to put Pakistan on the list of countries supporting terrorism militated public opinion against the United States. The myth of a tripartite Indo-Jewish-American informal alliance against potentially nuclear Islamic Pakistan was gaining credibility. Now Pakistan's nuclear program was not only a shield against "expansionist India," but a symbol of the iron will of the Muslim world to resist the U.S.-Jewish–led march of the new world order.

In the 1990s, Z. A. Bhutto's dream of the Muslim civilization having nuclear capability was vehemently pursued by some of his sworn enemies, namely, the Jamait-I-Islami and retired generals. In today's Pakistan, Islam, security, patriotism, and the bomb are fused together in the dominant security discourse. For the sake of simplicity, there were two sides in the dominant discourse regarding the nuclear issue before the May 1998 explosions. First, 'bomb crusaders,' who thought that Pakistan by virtue of being founded in the name of religion is duty-bound to develop the bomb to further the Islamic cause. Second, adherents of official ambiguity, who acknowledge the stabilizing role of the nuclear factor in India-Pakistan relations and were content with the status quo. These two positions intersected, coexisted, and competed in the same space with each other. Combination of these two groups eventually left no option for the Nawaz Sharif government but to put the bomb on the shelf after the Indian nuclear tests in May 1998. The contours of the contemporary security discourse and the position of the nuclear issue in it can be meaningfully understood by asking questions like: Who is threatening whom? How will nuclear weapons meet those challenges? We will start with bomb crusaders followed by their moderate allies who are more in line with the official government line.

BOMB CRUSADERS

Jamait-I-Islami has been in the forefront of bomb crusaders in Pakistan. Four years before Pakistan formally claimed to have the bomb, Professor Khurshid Ahmad, a leading ideologue of the Jamait, claimed that "even a single person on the streets of Pakistan would not say that we should abdicate our nuclear option."[41] Professor Khurshid Ahmad's thinking is reflective of an identity carved out for Pakistan on the basis of Islamic nationalism. His views manifest tensions that can be expected in a narrative that invokes such diverse strands as pan-Islamism, territoriality, denial of domestic heterogeneity, and principles of modern realist theory of international relations to validate a particular version of discourse about Pakistan's security needs.

In the classic mode of forging an identity through outlining threats, Ahmad's Pakistan is an entity threatened by a host of elements. To lend his views an air of objectivity on the one hand and prescribe Islamic solutions on the other, the portrayal of the threatening entities takes place in a mix of the mundane and the divine. States in the international system are seen as a projection of the individual (who is always male in his narrative) in the state of nature. Like man in the state of nature, the states also have a built-in instinctive defense system.[42] This world-view of international politics leaves little room for the ideological rationale to justify a proposed code of action in the international arena based on ethics. Ahmad fuses his realism with divinity to make room for the conduct of international affairs of an ideological entity. He informs us that "the leading countries of the West . . . in seeking power and its attendant pleasure, have reached a stage where they are doomed to meet disaster."[43] It is clear that the West (which generally means the United States in this account) is a giant heading toward an imminent disaster, but on its way would like to devour Pakistan.

In the "predatory world . . . Pakistani Muslims" correctly understand the nature of threats. The first threat comes from "the Indian mentality and their frenetic arms build-up."[44] A second threat emanates from the "Zionist entity" called Israel, which is no more than a "European colony" grafted in the heart of the Muslim world.[45] Pakistan is the country of its Muslim citizens and only they can correctly understand the nature of these threats. This version of Pakistan practically excludes all religious minorities from the fold of the threatened citizenry. Second, although an overwhelming majority of Pakistanis (about 96 percent) are Muslims, they do not all concur with the idea that religion is the only basis of identity in the country. Proponents of ethnic and other identity-based movements put their patriotic credentials in jeopardy in the above discourse.

In the same vein, General (Retd.) K. M. Arif, a close associate of Zia and now a prolific commentator on Pakistan's security, warned the nation of unified moves by "the Indo-Jewish lobby" to "defame and malign" Pakistan.[46] Guided by dicta of *realpolitik*, General Arif argues that Pakistan cannot rely on any other country's assurances to ensure its national security, especially in the face of the "enduring danger" posed by India.[47] Among the crusaders, the threat to Pakistan's territorial integrity and ideological boundaries is multifaceted. Retaining the nuclear option becomes a pressing necessity to thwart such threats.

The nuclear option can only be understood in the context of threats it is supposed to ward off. As the adversaries were not only militarily powerful but also involved in "evil designs" against Pakistan, (late) Ghani Eirabi, one of Pakistan's leading security analysts, regarded the U.S. pressure on the Pakistani governments to give up the nuclear program as a package deal that also included betraying "the Kashmiris and revise *our* [italics mine] commitment to Islam."[48] Retaining the nuclear option symbolizes Pakistan's twin commitments to Islam and Kashmir. The two are the pillars of the ideological foundations of the state; reneging on the nuclear issue would certainly result in crumbling of the other two. Any hope of the United States playing an impartial role in this context is ruled out because it has helped "India and Israel build substantial nuclear arsenals while penalizing Pakistan."[49] Jafar Wafa, another prominent political commentator, remains convinced of the Israeli "wickedness" in brokering an Indo-U.S. nexus against Pakistan.[50] Such a nexus has ominous implications for Pakistan, especially when "there is hardly any sanity left in the body-politic of India." This insanity blocks any chances of reconciliation between the two countries because the "Hindu psyche" wants to build a "Hindu empire" in the rest of the subcontinent.[51]

In a world marked by such inequities and intrigues, a nonproliferation regime in the shape of the NPT is viewed as no more than a "technological apartheid" aimed at tightening the noose around Pakistan's neck.[52] The Pakistan of Professor Khurshid Ahmad needs a nuclear deterrent not only for its safety and independence but also for the security of the Muslim *Ummah*.[53] Dr. S. M. Koreshi, a former ambassador, argues that compromising such a vital program to meet the requirements of the NPT would constitute an act of treason.[54] Air Chief Marshal (Retd.) Zulfiqar Ali Khan argues that signing of the NPT by Pakistan should not be conditional upon India's denial to abide by the treaty. For him, Pakistan's nuclear program is tied to the Kashmir problem and unless it is resolved to Pakistan's satisfaction, acceding to the NPT would be against the national interests of Pakistan.[55]

Disenchantment with the NPT and the CTBT is an integral part of the crusaders' nukespeak. Seen as no more than an obstacle in ensuring Pakistan's and the Ummah's security, it is termed a dead and outdated treaty. The solution, according to Shireen Mazari, lies in Pakistan declaring itself a nuclear state. This is a course that she thinks will further endear the Pakistani state to the masses of the country.[56] Abida Hussain, a politician from Punjab who briefly served as an ambassador to Washington and a minister in Nawaz Sharif's cabinet, was so frustrated with the U.S. pressure on Pakistan about the NPT that she "seriously thought of going back (to Pakistan) and joining the Jamait-I-Islami."[57]

This brief synopsis of the probomb crusaders' nuclear discourse in contemporary Pakistan demonstrates that the Pakistani "imagined community" for this group is conceived as a Muslim nation devoid of any internal heterogeneity. Any indication in that direction is taken as the work of external enemies and their domestic allies. The external enemies are guided by "evil designs" against the sacred concept of Pakistan. Pakistan in turn is duty-bound to be the vanguard Muslim state with a nuclear shield protecting its territorial boundaries and safeguarding the ideological frontiers of the Muslim world. There is a significant section of adherents of the pronuclear option whose views vary slightly in some respects from the above perspective. A look at the concepts of that view would show that the ambiguity, in their nuclear stand is reflective of ambiguity in their notion of Pakistani identity.

DIPLOMATS' AMBIGUOUS BOMB

Career diplomats were exposed to the intricacies of nuclear diplomacy in the 1960s, and realized the political subtleties of the issue during Z. A.

Bhutto's era. Pakistan's diplomats also played a pivotal role in providing ideological and diplomatic ammunition to General Zia in his bid to use the nuclear issue as a means of gaining regime legitimacy and strengthening a militant Islamic political discourse in the country. Two former diplomats, Agha Shahi and Abdul Sattar, typify the ambiguous position in the nuclear discourse in Pakistan.[58]

Their writings are in marked contrast with those of the crusaders in terms of style and understanding of conceptual aspects of the deterrence literature. A good sample of Shahi s views can be found in articles in the special issue of Islamabad Council for World Affairs (ICWA) journal on "Nuclear Issues in South Asia."[59] Shahi is less concerned with defining what Pakistan is and focuses more on the threat posed by India to the territorial integrity of the country. As the threatened is not perceived in terms of the manifestation of a divine power, the threat is not considered an incarnation of evil. The rivalry between India and Pakistan is understood in terms of the dicta of a Realist world-view in which historical factors have led the two countries to pursue zero-sum bilateral relations. Faced with the superior conventional forces of India, keeping the nuclear option is seen as a viable way to deter India from launching a conventional attack on Pakistan. Considering the importance of the nuclear option in this context, Shahi's thinking is in line with the Waltzian notion regarding the superior deterrent and stabilizing value of nuclear weapons in the contemporary world. Shahi's views on the NPT are low on rhetoric but rooted in the oft-repeated and widely agreed stance among strategic experts in Pakistan that the treaty is discriminatory and incapable of addressing the security needs of developing countries in its present form. Adopting the moral high ground against the NPT, most Pakistani security analysts express identical views with their Indian counterparts. Munir Ahmad Khan, former chairman of Pakistan Atomic Energy Commission (PAEC), held similar views on the NPT and the security dilemma faced by Pakistan.[60]

Abdul Sattar is equally skeptical about the success of the NPT in achieving meaningful disarmament.[61] Pakistan's decision to retain the nuclear option is justified in the light of the Waltzian notion of the deterrent value of nuclear weapons. Sattar argues that the end of the Cold War did not alleviate Pakistan's security concerns that are based upon "India's recurrent use of force to impose 'solutions' of its own preference upon less powerful neighbors."[62] For Pakistan, living next to the bigger and hostile neighbor, the nuclear option works as a means of self-defense in a system without a dependable collective security system. The efficacy of the nuclear factor in stabilizing Indo-Pakistani strategic interaction is considered a self-evident fact.

In sum, the crusaders and the diplomats portray India as a "threat" to Pakistan's security, but the latters' language is couched in diplomatic jargon. Both view the NPT as a discriminatory treaty. The crusaders point to a grand conspiracy aimed at depriving the Muslim world behind the non-proliferation regime, whereas diplomats refer to the limitations of the NPT by virtue of its selective emphasis, preventing vertical proliferation. Before the May 1998 explosions, diplomats saw merits in Pakistan's policy of nuclear ambiguity and the crusaders wanted an open declaration of going nuclear to consolidate the independent identity of Pakistan.

All these subtle differences among proponents of nuclear Pakistan were swept away when the BJP government in New Delhi formally inducted nuclear weapons into India's arsenal in May 1998. The Pokhran tests of May 11 predictably led to Pakistan's nuclear explosions three weeks later. The question of when and where Pakistan would join the nuclear club was answered on May 28, 1998. Chagai, a site in the remote hilly area of Balochistan, became Pakistan's Pokhran. The tests were a technological expression of political value invested in the nuclear option as a guarantor of national sovereignty.

CHAGAI AND BEYOND

Nuclear discourse in the post-Chagai era is a continuation of themes that characterized the nuclear debate during the 1990s. Street indignation that followed the Indian tests and jubilation that accompanied the Pakistani tests further consolidated the nuclear hawks' belief in the nuclear option as a symbol of national self-respect. The centrality of the Indian factor in determining the political as well as technical nature and direction of Pakistan's nuclear program became axiomatic. Indian nuclear tests and rhetoric surrounding them (see Chapter Three) forced Pakistan to join the nuclear club. The Indian factor has been the rallying point of the dominant security discourse in Pakistan. When India opted for nuclear weapons under the leadership of a Hindu nationalist party, proponents of Islamic identity in Pakistan deemed it a national duty to respond in kind.

Issues of national identity, strategic imperatives, and self-respect became dependent upon the immediate conduct of nuclear tests. Euphoria following the nuclear tests signified the success of the dominant discourse in tying the above factors together. General K. M. Arif had no doubt that "faced with a serious threat to its national security Pakistan did what an honorable country was expected to do." The decision to order nuclear tests "earned Prime Minister Nawaz Sharif a place of honor in Pakistan's history."[63]

The United States and other Western countries decided to impose sanctions against Pakistan as a punishment for its nuclear audacity. The dominant discourse considers the nuclear issue a worthy cause to pay the economic price. Nawaz Sharif went a step further and used the nuclear tests as a "golden chance to help Pakistan shift from dependency to self-reliance."[64] Others condemned the United States for wrongly exploiting Pakistan and imposing unfair restrictions on the country when "sanctions should have been imposed only on the country that started the nuclear race in the subcontinent and posed a threat to the region."[65] Under the changed circumstances, the potential role of the nuclear issue also includes helping the country to come out of economic slumber.

As the first anniversary of the nuclear explosions approached, the government of Pakistan announced a nationwide contest to find an appropriate name for the day the nuclear tests were conducted. The person who suggested *Yaum-e-Takbeer* (Day of Pride) was declared winner. Today a huge replica of the Chagai hills welcomes visitors at Islamabad's entrance with glowing lights depicting effects of the nuclear explosions. Similar structures adorn main public parks in all provincial capitals as well. While the government officials were inaugurating these monuments of nuclear power, Pakistani soldiers were exchanging artillery with Indian armed forces and shooting down Indian air force planes in the Himalayan region of Kargil and Dras. World attention turned to the two newest nuclear powers in May 1999 locked in an undeclared war. Pakistan's advances and then ignominious retreat in Washington pledging to respect the sanctity of the Line of Control divided the dominant discourse regarding the potential value of nuclear weapons in strategic interaction with India. The Pakistani establishment's strong belief that the presence of nuclear weapons rules out the possibility of a conventional war between two nuclear powers appears to have played a significant role in initiating actions in Kargil. The heavy retaliations by the Indian forces and New Delhi's assertions that the introduction of nuclear weapons does not rule out the possibility of a conventional war between the two neighbors were apparently underestimated and ignored by Islamabad.[66] Leading voices in the dominant security discourse were divided over the costs and benefits of the Kargil crisis for Pakistan. While K. M. Arif, a retired general, continued to blame India's "self-righteousness" for conflict in Kargil, Abdul Sattar, a former foreign secretary, accused the Nawaz Sharif government of pursuing "shallow and myopic policies" that have inflicted "incalculable damage" on Pakistan's credibility.[67]

Amid unconfirmed but widely reported differences over the handling of the Kargil crisis between Nawaz Sharif and Pervez Musharraf, chief of the army staff, the Sharif government was toppled in a military coup on October 12, 1999. The new military regime has promised no changes in the foreign and defense policy of Pakistan. If the previous military regime's penchant for the nuclear issue is any indication, then nuclear monuments and missiles models will continue to be a common sight in Pakistani society.

CONCLUSION

A functional model to summarize the discussion looks at the dominant discourse's notions of threats and the threatened, reasons behind that situation, security objectives in such a context, means to attain those objectives, and finally costs involved in pursuing the suggested means. In the dominant security discourse, the primary threat to Pakistan emanates from external sources. India, which is portrayed as a Hindu entity, is the nearest and the most potent of them, followed by Israel and the West. The threatened community is that of a Muslim Pakistan whose Islamic identity is endangered by external enemies and their local collaborators. The image of the threatened community is a monolith and any evidence to suggest otherwise is seen as a manifestation of the foreign hand. Explanations of threats are located in so-called objective incompatibility of Islam against the Hindu psyche and other forms of expansionism, that is, Zionism and Western civilization. This objective conflict facilitates a tripartite alliance of Western-Jewish-Hindu forces against the Muslim world (of which Pakistan is a fortress). Faced with this situation, the key objectives of Pakistan's security policy are strengthening of an independent Islamic identity, bringing Kashmir in the fold of Pakistan to complete the unfinished agenda of the 1947 partition, and, finally, building the solid foundations of an Islamic Ummah (community) in world politics.

The nuclear option is firmly fixed in the larger context of the security issue and any suggestion to renounce the nuclear program is portrayed as a compromise of national interests. Nukespeakers also emphasize that since the nuclear program is a symbol of national sovereignty only enemies of Pakistan can recommend or put pressure on the government to abandon this option. Fully aware of these pressures, the dominant discourse expects international pressure on Pakistan to give up the nuclear option. They warn the nation that the resistance to such pressures may cause economic hardship.

The dominant discourse derives its power by referring to Islam and the Two Nation theory as the key foundations of Pakistan's existence as an independent state. Consequently, Islamic nationalism becomes the ultimate arbiter of differentiation between foes and friends in the security discourse conducted in the name of Pakistani national interests. Pakistan, according to dominant discourse, is a country created in the name of Islam because the Muslims of the subcontinent constituted a separate nation within predominantly Hindu India. Considering independent India and Pakistan as a validation of the Two Nation theory, post-1947 India is viewed as a Hindu state and portrayed as a permanent enemy of Muslim Pakistan. The limits as well as ultimate justification of the dominant discourse are set by the concept of Pakistan based upon the Two Nation theory.

Nukespeak in the present form in Pakistan is made possible by a regime of truth that derives sustenance from a particular imagery about the country: a Pakistan that is only conceivable in terms of its incompatibility with India. This scheme is based on binary dichotomies in which Pakistan is a good, superior, and peace-loving country, whereas India is the embodiment of an evil and expansionist power. In the preceding pages I have attempted to explain nukespeak by demystifying the arbitrary bases of knowledge that govern the politics of nuclear weapons in Pakistan. The methodology of discourse analysis enable us to better understand the dynamics and the elements that turn the nuclear issue into an all-powerful matter capable of assuming a political life of its own in the security discourse. The discourse analysis not only helps in demystifying the myths that make the nuclear issue powerful, but this methodology also makes us aware of the limits of the perspectives that seek to alter the nature and direction of Pakistan's nuclear program by pointing out the strategic undesirability and economic unviability of the nuclear option.

NOTES

1. Zulfikar Ali Bhutto, *If I Am Assassinated* (New Delhi: Vikas, 1979), p. 138.
2. *Dawn*, July 4, 1977.
3. Editorial, "A Bridge over an Abyss," *Dawn*, July 7, 1977.
4. *Dawn*, July 16, 1977.
5. *Dawn*, September 5, 1977.
6. *Dawn*, September 29, 1977.
7. *Dawn*, September 29, 1977.
8. Bhutto, *If I Am Assassinated*, p. 107. This book is based on Bhutto's notes while in the death cell.
9. Ibid.
10. Ibid., pp. 135–136.
11. Ibid., p. 136.
12. Ibid.
13. Ibid., p. 138.
14. Ibid.
15. Ibid.
16. Abdul Qayyum, "Nuclear Power and US Dual Standards," *Dawn*, April 26, 1979.
17. *Dawn*, June 9, 1979.
18. *Dawn*, July 6, 1979.
19. *Dawn*, July 7, 1979.
20. Qutubudin Aziz, "International Zionism and Pakistan's Nuclear Program," *Dawn*, August 18, 1979.
21. For the full text of the speech see, *Dawn*, August 31, 1979.
22. In the first week of September 1979, Zia raised the issue of nuclear technology transfer at the Non-Aligned Movement meeting held in Havana. See *Dawn*, September 3, 1979. While he was meeting with S. N. Mishra, the head of the Indian delegation at the NAM meeting, the nuclear issue was on top of the agenda. See Ibid., September 5, 1979. Throughout September 1979, news regarding the nuclear program and Zia's patriotic duty to safeguard it continued to make headlines.
23. *Dawn*, September 27, 1979.
24. *Dawn*, July 4, 1983.

25. *Dawn*, August 24, 1983.
26. *Dawn*, August 24, 1983.
27. *Dawn*, August 27, 1983
28. Hasan Askari Rizvi, "Pakistan's Defense Policy," *Pakistan Horizon* 36:1 (1983), pp. 32–56.
29. Ibid., p. 53.
30. See the special issue of *Strategic Studies*, No. 2 and 3 (winter-spring 1982–1983), which contains papers presented at the First International Conference on the Strategy for Peace and Security in South Asia. In 1987, *Strategic Studies* 10: 4(summer–autumn 1987) was devoted to the issue of Nuclear Non-proliferation in South Asia. This journal is published by the Institute for Strategic Studies, Islamabad.
31. Mushahid Hussain, *Pakistan and the Changing Regional Scenario: Reflections of a Journalist* (Lahore: Progressive Publishers, 1988), p. 223. Hussain now (August 1997) serves as a minister for information in Nawaz Sharif's government. Previously he worked as the editor of Islamabad-based English daily *The Muslim*. Hussain is one of the leading syndicated columnists in Pakistan.
32. Ibid., p. 224.
33. Ibid., p. 226.
34. As quoted in Mushahid Hussain, *Pakistan and the Changing Regional Scenario*, p. 1.
35. *Dawn*, August 11, 1988.
36. *Dawn*, November 2, 1988.
37. *Dawn*, November 13, 1988.
38. For the full text of the IJI's election manifesto see, *Dawn*, November 14, 1988.
39. Air Marshal (Retd.) M. Anwar Shamim, "Pakistan's Security Concerns," *Dawn*, November 2, 1988. Similar views were expressed by yet another member of this community with a civilian background. See Afzal Mahmood, "Priorities in Foreign Policy," *Dawn*, December 14, 1988.
40. *Dawn*, February 22, 1990.
41. Khurshid Ahmad, "Summation: Capping the Nation," in Tarik Jan, ed., *Pakistan's Security and the Nuclear Option* (Islamabad: Institute of Policy Studies, 1995), p. 148. Professor Khurshid Ahmad is a leading ideologue of the Jamait-I-Islami, Pakistan's most organized religious party. He is the director of the party's think tank the Institute of Policy Studies (IPS), Islamabad. He also served as a senator.
42. Khurshid Ahmad, "Introduction," in Ibid., p. 17.
43. Ibid., p. 18.
44. Ibid., p. 19.
45. Ibid., p. 20.
46. General (Retd.) K. M. Arif, "Expanding Indo-Israeli Nexus," *Dawn*, June 17, 1993.
47. General K. M. Arif, "Retaining the Nuclear Option," in Jan, ed., *Pakistan's Security*, p. 122.
48. Ghani Eirabi, "Blackmailing Can Backfire," *Dawn*, April 18, 1993. Professor Khurshid Ahmad also gives two reasons for retaining the nuclear option. First, the country is in danger of losing its territorial integrity at the hands of a wrathful

India. Second, Israel is a major ideological threat. The nuclear shield will safeguard both the territory and the ideology. See Professor Khurshid Ahmad, "Introduction," in Jan, *Pakistan's Security*, pp. 17–26.

49. Ibid.

50. Jafar Wafa, "Our Security Option," *Dawn*, August 3, 1993.

51. Ibid.

52. Professor Khurshid Ahmad, "Summation," in Jan, *Pakistan's Security*, p. 147.

53. Ibid., p. 149.

54. Dr. S. M. Koreshi, "The Method in American Duplicity," in Jan, *Pakistan's Security*, p. 132.

55. Air Chief Marshal Zulfiqar Ali Khan, "Pakistan's Security and Nuclear Option," in *Nuclear Issues in South Asia*, Islamabad Council of World Affairs (ICWA), spring 1995, pp. 14–15. Khan consistently reiterates his views in Pakistani newspapers and academic journals. ICWA is a think tank based in Islamabad and founded by former foreign minister Agha Shahi. It is mainly comprised of former foreign office officials, retired military men, and some serving professors.

56. Shireen Mazari served as the chairperson of the Department of the Strategic Studies, Quaid-I-Azam University, Islamabad. She now edits her own weekly paper, *Link*, which promotes a similar point of view. Shireen M. Mazari, "NPT: An Unfair Treaty that Pakistan Must Not Sign," in Jan, *Pakistan's Security*, pp. 32–35.

57. Syeda Abida Hussain, "Don't Give Up What Is Yours and the World will Come Around!," in , Ibid., p. 110. She has not joined the Jamait but has turned into a nuclear hawk after her stint as an ambassador.

58. Agha Shahi served as Foreign Secretary during the Zia period. He led the Pakistan delegation during the NPT negotiations in the 1960s. Since his retirement in the late 1980s he has been vocal in expressing his views on Pakistan's foreign policy, especially with reference to the country's nuclear program. He is the founder of the Islamabad Council of World Affairs, a think tank comprising senior people from different walks of life. Abdul Sattar is serving as the Foreign Minister after the October 1999 military coup. Earlier, he briefly served as Foreign Minister during 1993. He served in India as High Commissioner for a substantial time. Since his retirement, he frequently contributes in the national media on issues of Pakistan's foreign policy with special reference to relations with India.

59. Agha Shahi, "Extension of the Nuclear Non-proliferation Treaty and the Security Dilemma," pp. 1–11, and, "Preservation of Deterrence for Security," pp. 63–66, ICWA Journal, Islamabad, spring 1995. Also see his "Nuclear Nonproliferation Treaty and the Security Dilemma," in Jan, *Pakistan's Security*, pp. 39–54.

60. Munir Ahmad Khan, "Issues in NPT Extension," in *Nuclear Issues in South Asia*, ICWA Journal, pp. 19–25.

61. For a detailed discussion of Abdul Sattar's views see his "Nuclear Stability in South Asia," in *Nuclear Issues in South Asia*, ICWA Journal, pp. 36–62; and also, "Nuclear Issues in South Asia: A Pakistani Perspective," in Jan, *Pakistan's Security*, pp. 55–90.

62. Sattar, in ICWA Journal, 1995, p. 42.

63. General K. M. Arif, "Signing the CTBT with Care," *Dawn*, November 25, 1998.

64. Nawaz Sharif, "There Is No Warmth Now: An Interview," *India Today*, June 15, 1998.

65. General K. M. Arif, "Signing the CTBT with Care."

66. Haider K. Nizamani, "Nuclear Weapons and Kashmir," *Dawn*, February 22, 1999.

67. K. M. Arif, "India's Intimidatory Tactic," Ibid., June 26, 1999; Abdul Sattar, "Harvest of Folly," *News*, July 15, 1999.

Chapter 6

Dissenting Narratives

> Nuclear weapons pervade our thinking. Control our behavior. Administer our societies. Inform our dreams. They bury themselves like meat hooks deep in the base of our brains. They are purveyors of madness. . . . If protesting against having a nuclear bomb implanted in my brain is anti-Hindu and anti-national, then I secede. I hereby declare myself an independent, mobile republic. I am a citizen of the earth. I own no territory. . . . I'm willing to sign any nuclear nonproliferation treaty or nuclear test ban treaty that's going. Immigrants are welcome.
>
> —Arundhati Roy

There are a number of Indians and Pakistanis who are citizens of Arundhati Roy's rebel land. These dissident voices questioned the tenets of the dominant nuclear discourse in the subcontinent well before Roy spoke about nuclear "meat hooks" in the national brains of India and Pakistan. Before the May 1998 explosions, dissent mainly came from people for whom the nuclear issue was a key concern. But with the BJP more than ever blending the nukes with nationalism, concerned scholars and distinguished individuals now seem to have realized the close connection between the Hindu great power identity expounded by India and the role of nuclear weapons in the situation. With nationalist tempers at an all-time high, the widespread belief of a consensus within India and Pakistan on the nuclear issue has further consolidated. In the process, little attention is paid to the dissenting voices that have deviated from official positions adopted by the two countries. This chapter comparatively analyzes the nature and direction of the dissent by exploring its potentials and limits in affecting the nuclear discourse in the subcontinent. It is an overview of strands of dissenting voices on the nuclear issue in Pakistan and India focusing on writings of a select number of representative dissident voices in both countries followed by a comparative analysis of these voices.

In order to appreciate what the dissenters are up against, it is worth repeating some key features of dominant security discourses in India and Pakistan. These discourses are based upon the portrayal of the Other as an inferior. An example of this in the case of Pakistan's dominant discourse is equating all Indians with Hinduism, a religion considered inferior to Islam. For the proponents of Indian dominant discourse, Pakistan is considered an outcome of a parochial idea based on religion. In both countries, the differences within their territorial limits are repressed in the name of Islam and secularism. Nuclear discourse in Pakistan thrives on conceiving Pakistan in terms of its incompatibility with India. The Indian dominant discourse uses the nuclear issue as a sign of the country's assertion as a regional power capable of resisting the global power structure. Those intelligentsia not subscribing to the mainstream views are portrayed as either actual or potential agents of external powers or newcomers who do not comprehend what is in the national interest. The task of turning the dominant episteme into a normal and unquestioned world-view of the constituent populations is seldom accomplished smoothly. Where there is use of power (which is often coercive) to forge a national identity, resistance to it is immanent in the process. This chapter tells the story of nuclear resistance in the subcontinent.

DISSENTING NARRATIVES IN INDIA

One commonality among the proponents of dissenting ideas in the nuclear discourse is their willingness to explore different options that India can exercise in conducting its nuclear policy. This by no means implies that all such voices recommend unilateral renunciation of the nuclear option by India. Although heterogeneous in composition in terms of ideas, they are minuscule in terms of numbers and pose little meaningful challenge to the existing orthodoxy. Indian environmental and women's rights groups, pressure groups that have traditionally been bastions of antinuclear activities in the West, have not been in the forefront of opposition to the national nuclear policy. What one is left with then is a tiny number of individuals proposing routes other than those adopted by the state and supported by the nuclear hierarchy.

If conceived in terms of a continuum, on the one end are scholars who propose the policy of nuclear abstinence as against the long-held official policy of ambiguity (qualitatively this changed with the May 1998 explosions), and on the other are those who would like India to take the drastic step of saying yes to the Pakistani proposal of declaring South Asia as a Nuclear Weapons Free Zone (NWFZ) or officially sign the nonproliferation treaty (NPT). Nuclear abstinence amounts to changing the present strategy, whereas the call to sign the NPT is a result of dissidents' different vision of Indian security and identity. I have chosen Kanti Bajpai's work as an outline of the abstinence option, followed by a look at Achin Vanaik and Giri Deshingkar's ideas representing a fundamentally different view of Indian security.[1] Views of these individuals are hardly heard in the power corridors of policy-making, academia, or the press in India. The selection is guided more by the varieties of counternarrative found in these writers' works rather than by any institutional position they occupy.

Advocating abstinence comes close to what was until May 1998 official Indian policy. If abstinence refers to a choice "not to do something that is within one's power," then nuclear abstinence "would be a clear-sighted decision not to maintain any kind of nuclear weapon option—not to go nuclear and not to keep the option open—when there is the capacity to do so."[2] If adopted, the policy of the abstinence would require India not to choose the nuclear option. The abstinence proposal is within the dominant framework of Indian security needs and is guided by theoretical tenets of political realism. The policy of nuclear ambiguity was considered a risky course for India to meet the security needs of the changing times. Present-day suggestions of the abstinence proposal are different from the abstinence policy pursued during the 1950s in which the thrust was on moral opposition to the nuclear weapons as a mean of guaranteeing national security. Bajpai argues that abstinence is both viable and advisable although it may be politically infeasible in the near future due to an overwhelming belief in the efficacy of nuclear ambiguity.

Although Bajpai does not rule out the value of the ambiguous nuclear option as a useful deterrent against Pakistan, he suggests that such a policy may not necessarily work in crisis situations. Since the chances of an unforeseen crisis in India-Pakistan relations are high given their geographical proximity and mutual distrust fostered over the years, the bombs in the basements can be mounted quickly on delivery systems. The other reservation of Bajpai, which I consider more important, against the presence of a nuclear deterrent in the subcontinent relates to the inability of India to punish Pakistan through conventional warfare. Since nuclear weapons work as strategic equalizers, India's enormous conventional superiority is rendered obsolete at one level.

The reason behind this suggestion is the same as that of nuclear hawks who blame Islamabad for the hostile nature of relations between India and Pakistan. Bajpai argues that an ambiguous nuclear India "cannot deter perhaps the most important sources of violence in the region, namely, insurgency and terrorism." Because of an ambiguous nuclear parity, "Islamabad is free to export violence." In the event of strategic interaction without the presence of the nuclear factor, Pakistan would consider it "exceedingly dangerous" to continue with its "low-intensity subversion" because India could retaliate by waging an outright conventional war. Therefore, "abstinence would at least return the military initiative to India and in doing so it might staunch the flow of external aid to subversion."[3] This characterization concurs with the dominant security discourse's position that Pakistan is primarily responsible for fomenting trouble in India. Convinced that Pakistan is behind all the major troubles of India, Subrahmanyam and Bajpai differ in recommending means to tackle the problem. Bajpai wants nuclear abstinence in order to enable New Delhi to punish Pakistan conventionally, whereas Subrahmanyam would like India armed with nuclear weapons and take on Pakistan through countersubversive ways. He makes it clear that "Pakistan, beset as it is with the Mohajir problem," cannot take India on now and if it does so, it is warned that "the battle will be fought on Sind territory and Karachi will be involved far more than in 1971."[4] Although he shares antipathy for Pakistan with the Subrahmanyams of India, Bajpai is fully aware of the exclusionary practices of the Indian nukespeak and realizes that espousing nuclear abstinence can be seen by them "as treasonous, cowardly, and luddite."[5] He eloquently summarizes that just by suggesting nuclear abstinence, one risks being accused of playing "the game of India's enemies" and bending "before the Western powers."[6]

Dissenters in the Indian nuclear discourse do not view the scope and intent of nuclear programs of India's adversaries in the same manner as the exponents of nukespeak. Consequently, their answers to the alleged adversaries' proposals to deal with the nuclear issue are also different from those offered by the custodians of the dominant discourse. Different perceptions vis-à-vis the nature of the Pakistani nuclear program are a case in point where dissenters proceed from different conceptual grounds. The Pakistani program is variously dubbed as a part of the broader Islamic or Western designs to undermine India in the discourse of Indian nukespeak, whereas dissidents see it primarily as an India-centered project guided solely by the notion of safeguarding Pakistan's national interests. Therefore, Pakistani nuclear policy is not independent of India. According to Praful Bidwai and Achin Vanaik, Pakistan's program has essentially been "dedicated," that is to say, it has a clear military purpose as its principal *raison d'être*. It is reactive and indicative of obsession with the Indian threat.[7] This is diametrically opposed to Indian nukespeak's perception of the nature and direction of the Pakistani program.

Once Pakistan's program is described primarily as a response to the Indian threat, the dissenters question the peaceful nature of India's program and the suggestion that Pakistan's nuclear ambitions developed independently of Indian nuclear ambitions. Bidwai and Vanaik maintain that those in India who argue that Pakistan's nuclear ambitions are not conditioned by the Indian threat are making an implausible and unconvincing argument. They state that "these arguments are also somewhat self-serving in that they tend to obscure India's responsibility as the key referent or pole in the South Asian nuclear arms race."[8] One may debate whether the nuclear situation in South Asia can technically be termed an arms race or not, but what is more important in the above characterization is holding India responsible for the existing nature and direction of nuclear interaction in the region.

Demonizing Pakistan is at the heart of contemporary nukespeak in India and the counternarratives are cognizant of that. Gautam Navlakha, a relatively less familiar name among nuclear dissidents, observes that "portraying Pakistan as the main threat encourages chauvinistic groups to dictate policy by stopping sports and cultural exchanges because it is an enemy nation and anyone having link with it becomes suspect."[9] Such utterances invite the wrath of the likes of K. Subrahmanyam who sees most of India's domestic troubles as Pakistan's doings. Navlakha responds to that view by arguing that "in India acceptance of the right of self-determination has been taken to mean the end of the Indian state rather than a way to rest it on democratic foundation."[10] The dominant discourse dismisses the demands of various identity-based movements and decentralization as the work of a few insurgents acting upon external instructions by asserting India is a genuinely democratic, secular, and federal society. The dissenters call into question that whole edifice by taking a sympathetic look at the demands of various identity-based movements. New Delhi is allocated the key responsibility for mishandling the contending demands of various groups. The dissenters hesitate to blame the alleged external enemies for instigating troubles in India.[11]

When the opponents' evil is not taken for granted, then one's goodness does not remain a given either. The preceding paragraphs outline grounds on which New Delhi's attitude toward various dissents is questioned. The nuclear detractors disagree with nuclear hawks who consider New Delhi's nuclear program as a peaceful venture. Most dissenters agree that India's nuclear program was entirely peaceful during the Nehru era but the same cannot be said of the post-Nehru period. This is amply proved by fears that Vanaik and Bidwai expressed almost eight years ago; namely, "the threshold country that is perhaps closest to crossing the threshold is India."[12] The reasons that propel India's nuclear ambitions are both internal and external politicostrategic considerations. Vanaik and Bidwai suggest that the PokhranI was aimed at deflecting attention away from the domestic troubles besetting the Indira Gandhi regime in 1974.[13] Giri Deshingkar also questions the peaceful nature of the 1974 test in light of the secrecy surrounding the event and the almost total absence of a governmental account of the reasons to opt for a nuclear explosion. The claim that the test was peaceful does not explain why India did not continue with further such explosions.[14]

With the above doubts regarding India's nuclear ambitions and unwillingness to acknowledge India's adversaries, especially Pakistan, as described by the nukespeakers, the sacrosanctity of the policy prescriptions suggested by the dominant discourse is also questioned by the dissident voices. Postures propounded by the adherents of nukespeak in the best interests of India become contested if we listen to the counternarratives. Being familiar with the outright rejection of proposals like NWFZ or opposition to CTBT by the dominant discourse, we will see how dissident voices support the ideas perceived by the dominant discourse as anti-Indian ploys.

By conceding merit to either the Pakistani proposal of a NWFZ or an international measure like the CTBT, the dissenters are in total contrast with the postulates of the dominant discourse. Achin Vanaik considers the establishment of a NWFZ in South Asia as "the most important and desirable" policy alternative for India.[15] He finds the three common grounds used to oppose the proposal as quite spurious. Opponents argue that a NWFZ will institutionalize nuclear apartheid, would not prevent radioactive fallout from other regions, and finally, South Asian geography is not suitable for implementation of such a scheme. Rather than viewing the proposal as a symbol of nuclear apartheid, Vanaik argues that invoking this theme "is simply a crude appeal to racial chauvinism."[16] Since countries of a variety of racial compositions ranging from Sweden to Egypt have renounced the nuclear option, therefore equating nuclear renunciation with racial superiority or inferiority is no more than a "racial bogey . . . to justify horizontal proliferation in threshold states like India."[17] As far as radioactive fallout and geographical unsuitability are concerned, they miss the point that the NWFZ is primarily a political concept. If India had the political will, the technicalities involved in realizing the goal of a NWFZ could be overcome. In the meantime, it is self-contradictory of Indians to doubt the sincerity of Pakistan because the latter has proposed ideas like a NWFZ.[18]

Deshingkar goes a step further and suggests that, despite the NPT being a discriminatory treaty, "India should still relinquish the nuclear weapon option."[19] Since India has learned to live in an unequal world in various realms, there is no point in opposing the NPT. This opposition, according to Deshingkar, "has served no Indian national interest." Furthermore, he feared that holding out from the CTBT would make India "more of a pariah state."[20] Praful Bidwai also argues that New Delhi's refusal to sign the CTBT would isolate India in the international community. Unlike nukespeakers, he did not see the massive support for the CTBT among developing countries because of "nuclear weapon-states' arms twisting."[21]

While dissenting voices were grappling with the pitfalls of official ambiguity, the BJP decided to introduce nuclear weapons into India's arsenal. It presented the nuclear tests as a triumph of Hindu national India. Nationalist rhetoric initially drowned dissident voices barring those veterans who have been consistent in opposing a nuclear India. Praful Bidwai repeated his long-held position and argued that the decision to go nuclear is "devoid of strategic rational" and is an expression of "the raw power of aggressive nationalism."[22] He believes that the tests were an expression of Hindu nationalism rather than guided by any strategic logic. Since the reasons for the explosions are located at the domestic level, Bidwai dismisses the view that the tests had become necessary because of Sino-Pakistani nuclear cooperation. Most dissenters share Bidwai's perception that the BJP decision was guided more by internal dynamics than external security concerns.

The antinuclear voices following the tests came from people who have not been at the core of dissent. Such voices have been articulated in manners that go beyond the oft-repeated arguments of traditional dissenters. Arundhati Roy used her skills as a novelist to condemn the nuclear tests in August 1998. She disapproves of explosions not because they did not serve India's strategic interests or undermined New Delhi's position in international disarmament forums. Nor does she consider Indian decision-makers less intelligent than their Western counterparts. Hers is a moral outcry against blending of nationalism with weapons of mass destruction for she realized that something "infinitely more precious" died with the nuclear tests. She found the air in post–Pokhran II India "is thick with ugliness and there's the unmistakable stench of fascism on the breeze."[23] And this fascism was expressed by the dominant discourse in terms like "self-esteem" and "national pride." Roy clearly could see the nexus between BJP's nationalism and the bomb when any criticism of the official policy was construed as an antinational and anti-Hindu activity, and there was "talk of cells being set up to monitor anti-national activity."[24] She finds nothing praiseworthy about India's nuclear explosions and finds reasons such as the Sino-Pakistan nuclear collusion and the fight against international nuclear hegemony unconvincing. Dissent in this form seems more capable of reaching the ordinary Indian. Ashis Nandy, well-known political psychologist, also sees the sinister aspect of nuclear weapons in broader terms. Acquisition of nuclear weapons for him is not a mere strategic decision, but an indication of a mentality whereby "acquiring the power to inflict death on millions, and by living with the fantasy of that power, you pathetically try to get some confirmation that you are still alive. However, that confirmation never comes. For in the process of acquiring that power, you may not be dead physically, but you are already dead morally, socially and psychologically."[25] These are indeed serious charges against the custodians of the dominant discourse.

In sum, most examples of dissent regarding the policy alternatives adhere to what has been dubbed by Indian nukespeak as the enemy's voice. Does that make the dissidents anti-India agents? This question is discussed in the comparative analysis section of nuclear dissent in India and Pakistan.

DISSENTING NARRATIVES IN PAKISTAN

Dissent based on different lineages has always been an integral part of the political discourse in Pakistan. Ethnic nationalism has been the most prominent one and continues to shatter the totalizing effects of the dominant discourse. In the 1990s, the security-oriented bomb-centric view evoked a parallel discourse in which unilateralists questioned the utility of the nuclear option to ensure security and development of Pakistan. This position is based upon different conceptions about the identity of Pakistan and new notions of security. This section analyzes these contending views in the nuclear discourse of contemporary Pakistan.

I will enumerate types of the dissenting voices in the nuclear discourse of today's Pakistan where keeping the nuclear option has become a litmus test for judging the patriotic credentials of citizens. This discussion will show how the presumed consensus over the nuclear issue is being challenged by dissenting voices.

The dominant security discourse about the utility of the nuclear option is questioned by a small, but gradually growing, number of people. A number of scientists turned social commentators, a few well-known journalists and academics, and a rare breed of ex-soldiers have made it their mission to voice dissenting opinions in the nuclear discourse of Pakistan even at the risk of earning the title of "traitor." It should be made clear at the outset that I do not consider this position either more pious than that of their counterparts or less patriotic than the pro-option analysts. The argument is that unilateralism or skepticism toward the dominant view is reflective of a different vision of Pakistan's identity and security needs. Since the country is imagined in a different way, security priorities undergo change as well. The objective is to outline the themes of the dissenters based on a different notion of what constitute genuine threats to Pakistanis' security, and how the country can repel these threats. A closer look at works of some leading dissenters will enable us to understand the nature and direction of the dissent in the nuclear debate in Pakistan. For this purpose, I have concentrated on the writings of Khaled Ahmed, a well-known journalist who regularly questions Pakistan's security doctrine; Dr. Zia Mian, a late entrant on the intellectual horizon but the key organizer of an antibomb group; and Pervez Hoodbhoy, MIT-educated physicist and veteran pacifist.[26]

As the idiom of the dominant discourse is wrapped in the language of patriotism, any deviation from it invites allegations of treachery. No one is more aware of this than antibomb intelligentsia in Pakistan. Most writings in this category start with the customary disclaimer that by not adhering to the dominant position they are not indulging in any act of treason. Conduct of the nuclear discourse in the dichotomy of Us versus Them is viewed as a ploy to foreclose any meaningful debate on the issue. Given the popularity of Pakistan's nuclear program, dissenters argue that "any appeal to common sense or common reason is immediately dubbed as unpatriotic."[27] Dr. Inayatullah, former chairman of Department of International Relations at Islamabad's Quaid-I-Azam University, argues that the present consensus "was imposed from the top" during the Zia regime, and over the time it has become "an article of nationalist faith." Critics, of whom Inayatullah is one, who questioned the dominant logic had to face the "unfounded allegations and insinuations" of being Indian or American agents.[28]

Since the dominant rationale is considered a manifestation of manufactured consent, the dissenters had to look elsewhere for foundations upon which to rationalize their position. Liberal rationality bestowed by enlightenment has become the dissidents' weapon to demystify the dominant myth, and create "rational" and "scientific" grounds to conduct the debate. While the pro–nuclear option people are dubbed as guardians of emotionalism, the dissidents claim to be custodians of "objective thinking." Arguments of harbingers of reason are grounded in a moral milieu, which envisages security in a fundamentally different way. Combination of the two, as argued by this group, makes their position more in line with the fast-changing reality of world politics and better able to further the true national interests of Pakistan.

Dissenters argue that going nuclear is counterproductive and provides a false sense of security. At worst the acquisition of weapons of mass destruction by Pakistanis can be dangerous for the international order as well. Opponents to the existing concept of nuclear politics draw their intellectual inspiration from different sources. Khaled Ahmed's thinking is more in line with the dominant American view that nuclear weapons in the hands of leaders of developing countries is dangerous due to the latters' tendency to decide matters on whim rather than reason. Scientists such as Pervez Hoodbhoy and Zia Mian agree with their counterparts in the West who are against the possession of nuclear weapons in general because of the possibility of accidents and accidental usage.[29] Finally, sporadic dissent comes from former soldiers who argue that reliance on the nuclear option to ward off external threats undermines and erodes a conventional defense system that is more reliable.

Khaled Ahmed's suspicion of the Pakistani leadership's capability to handle nuclear weapons emanates from his belief in the embedded "irrationality" of the non-Western world.[30] The West is credited with developing reason as "an intellectual tool for survival" over the past ten centuries. The non-Western world, meanwhile, is considered a realm of "primitives," "irrational," "suicide-bombers," in which nationalists and dictators act "at some animal level." Third World leaders tend to think "if you have the bomb, you are a 'big power' perched permanently in the UN security council, vetoing what you do not like." This vituperative rendering of the part of the world to which Ahmed himself belongs is not without its own myths about the relative superiority of the West and the absolute inferiority of the rest.

Based on this vision of the world, Ahmed argued that the effects of nuclear weapons vary in two fundamentally different worlds. In the West, the bomb had a "sobering" impact; and the will of the non-West to acquire similar technology is "irrational" because it is not backed up by scientific and economic advances. Third World countries' reiteration of basic principles of modern deterrence thinking does not convince Khaled Ahmed to consider them fit to handle nuclear weapons because the leadership here suffers from "personality disorders." Fears of state-level irrationality are not the only concerns that guide Ahmed; alarmism leads him to argue that nuclear devices can land in the hands of splinter groups who would not hesitate to annihilate their enemies.[31] This mode of thinking is applied to analyze the dynamics of nuclear politics in South Asia, and we need not say that Pakistan and India are seen as inherently incapable of tackling the tricky weapons meant only for descendants of the Age of Reason.

Khaled Ahmed's analysis of Pakistan's conduct of foreign relations, especially its Kashmir policy and relations with the United States over the nuclear issue, helps to explain the alternative vision of Pakistan's identity and its security needs. Pakistan in its existing shape is seen "as a corrupt and politically divided state," which has the "potential to become the cockpit of international terrorism."[32] Under these circumstances, Pakistan's bid to acquire nuclear capability is an "adventurism" that appeals to its disenchanted public.[33]

A select group of Pakistani scientists claiming enlightened social consciousness also opposes the existing parameters of nuclear politics, but for somewhat different reasons than those expounded by Khaled Ahmed. Zia Mian relies heavily on graphic details of destruction caused by radioactivity in the areas where superpowers conducted their nuclear tests as a warning for Pakistan to desist from the nuclear path.[34] He considers the nuclear option a risky way to ensure security and a path fraught with dangers to meet energy needs. He gives examples of accidents that led to terminal illnesses of workers and residents affiliated with nuclear sites in the relatively safety-conscious West. If mishaps cannot be prevented in the advanced Western countries, Mian considers it a moral duty to enlighten the Pakistani public of the dangers of the nuclear option.

Hoodbhoy has been drawing attention to the likely dangers of an unsafe nuclear program and the tenuous grounds on which security analysts justify the program.[35] Hoodbhoy's concerns are based upon what is commonly termed C3 (command, communication, and credibility)-related problems inherent in any situation where nuclear deterrence is at work. He argues that prestige may be a paramount factor in shaping India's nuclear ambitions. However, he dismisses it as the thinking of a bygone era when nuclear science was equated with scientific excellence. Today's bomb can be assembled with good engineering, competence, and dedication, none of which requires scientific genius.

This synopsis of the three representative figures shows that the nuclear myths in Pakistan are challenged by parallel myths about developing countries' inferiority and the horrors of nuclear accidents. Implicit in their accounts is a countervision of Pakistan's identity. Let us see what they mean by "their" Pakistan, and how best its security needs may be addressed.

Zia Mian is skeptical of the notion that a nuclear program is an effective and cheap deterrent. Given the steadily high defense spending in Pakistan, he thinks the argument for cheap security is less valid. What he is concerned about are "the hidden social and human costs of the lost opportunities for building schools, hospitals, water and sewage system."[36] This implies a zero-sum relationship between the nuclear program and other issues highlighted by Mian. Dispelling the overriding concerns of an Indian threat as a tool for the tiny ruling clique to bolster their narrow interests in the name of national security, Mian thinks that "true" security can come only with good education and proper health care. This vision of Pakistan's security pits it squarely against the dominant discourse in which protection of "territorial integrity" and "ideological boundaries" takes precedence over material gains that can be accrued by giving up the present strategic policy. Similar views are expressed by I. Hassan, a prominent political commentator, who thinks Pakistani peoples' pressing needs are shelter and education. Sticking to the present nuclear policy "impoverishes" the masses of Pakistan.[37] Rather than denouncing the NPT as a means of undermining the sovereignty of Pakistan, Hassan argues for renouncing nuclear ambitions by signing the NPT and relying on the United States to pressure India to do likewise.[38] The same unilateralism is obvious in Inayatullah's account, which calls for signing of the NPT.

Ahmed is not overtly concerned with the well-being of downtrodden classes, but acutely aware of the poor state of the Pakistani economy. He sees a close connection between Pakistan's refusal to sign the NPT and the devastated state of its economy. Rather than proposing a unilateral course on the proliferation issue, Ahmed believes that Pakistani rulers will have no choice but to succumb to the international (read American) pressure on the NPT if the country wants to become economically self-reliant. Once the connection between economic self-reliance and the nuclear policy is established, it becomes a matter of choice to give up one for the other. Ahmed unambiguously favors signing of the NPT as "a way out of economic collapse."[39] Since the dominant view in Pakistan makes any move in the direction of nonproliferation conditional upon similar initiatives by India, Ahmed implicitly advises the Americans to offer positive incentives to persuade Pakistan to "sign on the dotted line (of nonproliferation) while India keeps its nuclear arsenal."[40] The economic determinism of Khaled Ahmed is in total contrast with the strategic determinism of the dominant discourse. For Ahmed "economic reality is the only reality on the basis of which to calculate one's chances of survival."[41] That is why he does not see any "American conspiracy" in financing informal dialogue between opinion-makers of India and Pakistan to further the cause of economic liberalization as the most viable form of ensuring security in both countries.

Odds against nuclear dissent were raised with Pakistan's nuclear test in May 1998. The nuclear nationalism that gripped the country after the Indian tests made it doubly difficult for dissident voices to air their doubts about the utility of the nuclear option.[42] Gradually the nuclear euphoria is giving way to concerns about Pakistan's shattered economy that is further affected by international sanctions. Dissenters are resigned to the idea of nuclear Pakistan as a fait accompli, and their immediate focus seems to be emphasizing the need for the country to sign the CTBT.[43] Second, given Pakistan's dependence on international donor and financing agencies, some leading economists are indirectly questioning the rationale of Pakistan's nuclear policy.[44] Yet is unlikely that Pakistan's dominant discourse would yield to these arguments in the near future.

COMPARATIVE ANALYSIS

In order to contexualize the nature and direction of dissenting voices, I return to the framework used to discuss the main features of the dominant discourse. As against the prevalent views on the nuclear issue, let us examine the counternarratives' notion of threats and the threatened, reasons behind that situation, and how to meet these challenges. The counternarratives in the security discourse find threats at the internal level, in the shape of economic disparities, social problems, and bad governance. Among the threatened are the masses of Pakistan and India. Pakistani dissenters would also list liberal intelligentsia as being among the threatened.

According to the dissenting voices in Pakistan, the reasons behind this situation go back to rule by a military clique in conjunction with a feudal bourgeoisie and clergy. They argue that the dominant notions of national security are created by the ruling classes to sustain higher military spending. The objective of the dissident voices is to make Pakistan a liberal state with either a semisocialist economy or a market economy based on good governance. Such a Pakistan will have friendly relations with India and close ties with international markets. The best way to achieve these objectives is through drastic cuts in defense spending, including renouncing the nuclear program, and moderation in Islam-based rhetoric. The costs of creating

Pakistan on these lines would possibly include close ties with international capital and a drastic reduction in Pakistan's military strength. This in turn would tamper the militaristic rhetoric and possible deals with India on issues like Kashmir.

The counternarratives in India, as well, question the dominant discourse by not considering the Others of the dominant discourse as a manifestation of evil. They do not see Pakistan as the main culprit behind troubles that plague contemporary India. Rather, they consider most of India's internal troubles as an outcome of the unresolved aspect of the question of Indian identity and bad governance on the part of New Delhi. By espousing such views these intellectuals risk being termed traitors. Under the present regime of strategic truths, the dominant discourse in India has captured the nationalist enterprise in which place and properties of the enemies of the Indian nation are defined with reference to external enemies, especially Pakistan, and the internal detractors are seen as agents of the enemy. When a dissenter says that the existing policy is not in the national interests of India, the nuclear hawk strikes back with the question: Which nation are you talking about? India of the dominant discourse is an entity with no hegemonic attitude toward its neighbors, whereas most internal movements challenging the dominant identity are portrayed as works of intrusive hostile powers. If the dissenter wants India to share responsibility for regional tensions, does not see the dominant discourse's Others as an incarnation of evil, would like India to sign the NPT, or allay smaller neighbors' security concerns by eschewing the big brother role, then she is envisioning India in terms entirely different from and opposed to the parameters of the dominant security discourse.

Limits of dissent under present circumstances become apparent when seen against the traits of the dominant discourse. The Pakistani dominant discourse derives its power by referring to Islam and the Two Nation theory as the key foundations of Pakistan's existence as an independent state. Consequently, Islamic nationalism becomes the ultimate arbiter of differentiation between foes and friends in the security discourse conducted in the name of Pakistani national interests. Pakistan in the dominant discourse is a country created in the name of Islam because the Muslims of the subcontinent constitute a separate nation. Since post-1947 India is viewed as a Hindu state, it is considered a permanent enemy of Muslim Pakistan. For New Delhi's dominant discourse, India is a genuine secular democracy, which has the special responsibility of ensuring peace and stability in South Asia. By virtue of its size, population, and history, India ought to be respected by its neighbors and treated as a major power by the international community. Pakistan, which is seen as a historical anomaly, is perceived as an archenemy.

The dissenters in both countries attempt to undo these national perceptions by offering alternative views on security. For dissidents of Pakistan, the ultimate reference is the Renaissance model of rationality with the individual's material progress as the ultimate criterion to distinguish good from bad. What the dissenters are suggesting would fundamentally alter the basis of Pakistan as we know it today. Expecting or demanding to change the fundamentals of that discourse in the name of "reason" seems unreasonable. The territorial security-centric and Islamist view of Pakistan does not reject the socioeconomic costs caused by high military spending or costs accrued due to aid cutoff because of the nuclear policy. But yielding to those pressures or temptations of material well-being alone is a betrayal of the very ideals Pakistan was created to serve. Invariably, transgression of limits imposed by this identity version of Pakistan risk the transgressor being put in any category but a true Pakistani. Since the dominant security discourse is couched in either the modern dictum of nationalism or wrapped in religion, transgressors are either "traitors," "external agents," or "heretics." Conversely, someone who is a "traitor" for Zia-ul-Haq may be a good example of enlightened reason for his/her liberal cohorts. The individual who is the focal point of the alternative discourse sees nothing but bigotry in the dominant discourse. His efforts to fundamentally change the parameters of truth in the existing discourse are met with resistance at different levels. Dissenters tend to decry the repressive nature of the rules of the game set out by proponents of the dominant discourses. Dissenters appear to overlook the historical limits of their imaginations in which power to set the criteria of truth will be invested in the reasoning liberal social democrat. This is a different concept of truth in which today's custodians of the national security risk are termed lunatics.

Similarly, the dissenters in India would like to change the present parameters of the national security discourse. Rather than viewing India as custodian of regional order, the dissidents would like New Delhi to abandon policies that are construed by smaller neighbors as hegemonic. Furthermore, exponents of dissent would like India to be signatory to the NPT and other international nonproliferation measures.

In sum, dissenting narratives are limited by the respective concepts of national identities they espouse for India and Pakistan. And these identities involve fundamental restructuring of the bases on which postcolonial India and Pakistan exist. Since such overhauling is not in the offing, in all probability, it appears that in the near future dissenters will remain marginalized like many other peripheral voices within India and Pakistan. What does this entail for the future of dissenting voices in the nuclear debate in the subcontinent? These voices are likely to have marginal influence due to the clamor of nuclear lore that has intensified since the explosions in both countries. At the same time, overt nuclearization opens up new avenues for dissent as well. With the dominant discourse putting its ultimate card on the table, dissenters can show the intricate connection between the identity issue and the politics of nuclear weapons. Dissident voices can attempt to show the futility of nuclear weapons by demonstrating that these weapons alone hardly entitle a country to a great-power status. For this, the dissent has to abandon its traditional arguments and show innovation in its approach.

NOTES

1. Kanti Bajpai teaches at Jawaharlal Nehru University, New Delhi. Achin Vanaik is a regular commentator on security issues whose ideas are in marked contrast with the concepts of the dominant discourse. Giri Deshingkar is a veteran dissident in the community of security experts. He was associated with Center for Study of Developing Societies (CSDS), the well-known independent-minded think tank founded by India's leading political scientist Rajni Kothari.

2. The discussion of abstinence relies almost exclusively on Kanti Bajpai's chapter "Abstaining," in David Cortright and Amitabh Mattoo, eds., *India and the Bomb: Public Opinion and Nuclear Options* (Notre Dame, IN: University of Notre Dame Press, 1996), p. 23.

3. Ibid., p. 45.

4. K. Subrahmanyam, "Missile Proliferation: US Must Heed India's Concerns," *Times of India* (Ahmedabad), July 13, 1995.

5. Bajpai, "Abstaining," p. 24.

6. Ibid.

7. Praful Bidwai and Achin Vanaik, "Indian and Pakistan," in Regina Cowen Carp, ed., *Security with Nuclear Weapons? Different Perspectives on National Security* (New York: SIPRI and Oxford University Press,1991), p. 260.

8. Ibid., p. 265.

9. Gautam Navlakha, "Pakistan-India: The Chill Factor," *Economic and Political Weekly*, February 17, 1996, p. 379.

10. Ibid., p. 383.

11. Taking into account the use of supposed external and internal enemies by the Indian elite, especially since the days of Mrs. Gandhi, for political expediency and to legitimize the increasing use of force in the body politic of India, Rajni Kothari has termed it the "rise of a Terrorist State." See Rajni Kothari, *Politics and the People: In Search of a Humane India*, Volume II (New Delhi and London: Aspect Publications with arrangements with Ajanta Publications, 1990); also see Rajni Kothari, *State against Democracy: In Search of Humane Governance* (New Delhi: Ajanta Publications, 1988)

12. Bidwai and Vanaik, "India and Pakistan," p. 271.

13. Ibid., p. 267.

14. Giri Deshingkar, "India," in Eric Arnett, ed., *Nuclear Weapons after the Comprehensive Test Ban: Implications for Modernization and Proliferation* (New York: SIPRI and Oxford University Press, 1996), p. 42.

15. Achin Vanaik, "Political Case for a NWFZ in South Asia," *Economic and Political Weekly*, November 30, 1985, p. 2115.

16. Ibid., p. 2116.

17. Ibid.

18. Ibid., p. 2117.

19. Deshingkar, "India," p. 50.

20. Ibid., p. 48.

21. Praful Bidwai, "India's Veto of the CTBT Is Futile," *Times of India*, September 12, 1996.

22. Praful Bidwai, "Dangerous Descent: Flawed Logic of Nuclear Tests," *Times of India*, May 15, 1998.

23. Arundhati Roy's essay appeared in *Frontline*. I have used the website version of it. Arundhati Roy, "End of Imagination," *Frontline* 15:16, August 1–14, 1998. p 7. http://www.the-hindu.com/fline.

24. Ibid. p. 8.

25. Ashis Nandy, "The Epidemic of Nuclearism: A Clinical Profile of the Genocidal Mentality," www.mnet.fr/aiindex. This website has number of antinuclear articles by Pakistani and Indian authors.

26. Khaled Ahmed is a prolific commentator in this group. In the past he has served as the editor of two English language dailies, namely, *The Nation* (Lahore) and *The Frontier Post* (Lahore). At present he writes in the Lahore-based weekly *The Friday Times* and is the editor of the Urdu version of this paper. Dr. Zia Mian is a physicist by training and worked as a Research Fellow at an Islamabad-based research organization, the Sustainable Development Policy Institute. He is also a founding member of an antinuclear group called the Campaign for Nuclear Sanity. Pervez Hoodbhoy teaches physics at the Quaid-I-Azam University, Islamabad and writes and comments frequently on social and political issues.

27. Lieutenant General (Retd.) Mujib-ur-Rehman, "A False Sense of Security," in Zia Mian, ed., *Pakistan's Atomic Bomb and the Search for Security* (Lahore: Gautam Publishers, a publication for the Campaign for Nuclear Sanity and the Sustainable Development Policy Institute, Islamabad), p. 32. This volume is probably the only book-length collection of articles written by dissidents on the nuclear issue. Contributors to the book regularly voice their views in the national media.

28. Dr. Inayatullah, "The Nuclear Arms Race and Fall of the Soviet Union: Some Lessons for Pakistan," in Mian, *Pakistan's Atomic Bomb*, p. 83.

29. The *Bulletin of the Atomic Scientists* is in the forefront of analyzing scientific, social, and economic repercussions of nuclear weapons. The *Bulletin*'s influence is evident in writings of these Pakistani writers.

30. Khaled Ahmed, "After Hiroshima, Why Do We Still Love the Bomb?," *The Friday Times*, Lahore, August 17–23, 1995. A detailed analysis of this article is of paramount importance to understand the alternative narrative.

31. In this regard he names Altaf Hussain, leader of Pakistan's Urdu speaking ethnic group and its party the Muhajir Quomi Movement(MQM), as the kind of nonstate actor who might acquire such weapons and use them against his rivals.

32. Khaled Ahmed, "Pakistan's America Problem: Crisis of Defiance," *The Friday Times*, Lahore, March 24–30, 1994.

33. Khaled Ahmed, "NPT: More Troubles Ahead for Pakistan," Ibid., December 1–7, 1994.

34. Dr. Zia Mian, "Cost of Nuclear Security," in *Pakistan's Atomic Bomb*, pp. 39–82.

35. For a good overview of Hoodbhoy's views on the issue see Pervez Hoodbhoy, *Nuclear Issues between India and Pakistan: Myths and Realities* (Washing-

ton, DC: Henry L. Stimson Centre, Occasional Paper No. 18, July 1994); also "Nuclear Myths and Realities," in Mian, *Pakistan's Atomic Bomb*, pp. 1–30.

36. Dr. Zia Mian, "Costs of Nuclear Security," in *Pakistan's Atomic Bomb*, p. 61.

37. I. Hassan, "Seizing the Nuclear Moment," in Ibid., p. 126.

38. Ibid., p. 127.

39. Khaled Ahmed, "The NPT and Pakistan," in Mian, *Pakistan's Atomic Bomb*, p. 115.

40. Khaled Ahmed, "NPT: More Troubles Ahead for Pakistan," *The Friday Times*, December 1–7, 1994.

41. Khaled Ahmed, "Is 'Neemrana Dialogue' a Conspiracy?," Ibid., December 29–January 4, 1995.

42. Samina Ahmed, and David Cortright, eds., *Pakistan and the Bomb: Public Opinion and Nuclear Options* (Notre Dame, IN: University of Notre Dame Press, 1998). This is one of the very few book-length studies where dissident voices in the nuclear discourse in Pakistan expound their views. Although written before the May explosions, contributors rightly thought that in the event of Indian tests Pakistan would certainly follow suit.

43. Akhtar Ali, "CTBT: The Options before Pakistan," *Dawn*, September 18, 1998.

44. For a sample of these views see Shahid Kardar, "Waiting for the Bailout," *Dawn*, August 22, 1998.

Chapter 7

Summary and Assessments

> History, it would seem, has decreed that we in the postcolonial world shall only be perpetual consumers of modernity. Europe and the Americas, the only true subjects of history, have thought out on our behalf not only the script of colonial enlightenment and exploitation, but also that of our anticolonial resistance and postcolonial misery. Even our imaginations must remain forever colonized.
>
> —Partha Chatterjee[1]

The voices of nukespeakers in the subcontinent to date remain conceptually colonized and wedded to modernity.[2] Products of modernity, in this case, include neorealist theories of international relations and strategic studies. These, in turn, are only conceivable within the theoretical framework of nation-states. Few states in the new millennium could boast that they celebrated the acquisition of weapons of mass destruction with the fanfare that was witnessed in India and Pakistan. New Delhi called the anniversary of the May 11, 1998 explosions "resurgence of India day," and Islamabad termed its feat a Day of Pride. Since the May 1998 explosions, the world's two newest nuclear powers have passionately embraced nuclear weapons as essential to ensure national security. The relationship between the policy, discourse, and dynamics of nuclear politics in the subcontinent has become even more obvious in the postexplosion period. This chapter explore this nexus by summing up and comparing the main themes of politics of nuclear weapons in Pakistan and India by outlining similarities and differences between the two. While doing this I will also look at the relevance, or lack of it, of various theoretical perspectives discussed in the first chapter. It is pertinent in this regard to heed the warning of Bradley Klein that "there is a danger in any critical enterprise of its bearers announcing their particular truth as the latest and greatest newly dominant paradigm."[3] I have exercised utmost caution and do not claim to have uttered the final word or discovered the ultimate explanation of the nuclear issue in the subcontinent. Nevertheless, I maintain that the methodology of discourse analysis demystifies and shows the historical specificity of the canons of the dominant security discourses in Pakistan and India. It also demonstrates the limited analytical ability of existing problem-solving perspectives to explain the dynamics of the nuclear discourse in Pakistan and India. The first section of this chapter assesses various similarities of the nuclear discourse in India and Pakistan and their impact on the nature and direction of the dominant security discourses. This is followed by an analytical summary of the differences between nuclear discourses of the two countries. The final section outlines the manner in which the methodology of discourse analysis helps to explain the multifaceted nature of the politics of nuclear weapons.

SIBLINGS OF THE SAME THEORY

The most striking similarity between the nuclear hawks of Pakistan and India is their shared reliance on political realism as the guiding intellectual inspiration despite its adherents' frequent use of higher moral grounds to justify their position. This reliance on political realism is a result of these intellectuals' preoccupation with the problem-solving goals of theorizing. This trait, in turn, makes existing accounts of nuclear politics prone to presenting their subjective analyses as objectively true depictions of strategic reality. By presenting one's subjective account as a rendition of the objective situation, problem-solving theories tend to discard alternative views just because they do not follow the dictums of the dominant discourse. Nukespeakers in both Pakistan and India have equal contempt for dissident voices on the nuclear issue in their respective societies.

Another striking similarity between nukespeaks in Pakistan and India concerns the role of political parties with religious agendas. The Jamait-I-Islami in Pakistan and the Bharatiya Janata Party (BJP) in India are outspoken supporters of the nuclear option and play a significant role in influencing the nature and direction of the nuclear discourse. Finally, dissenting voices on the nuclear issue in both countries remain on the political margin and are unlikely to pose any meaningful challenge to the existing orthodoxies in the near future.

These similarities are not merely accidental, rather these are logical results of a security discourse conducted in the name of national interests relying on and promoting a particular view of the truth. Each of the above-mentioned similarities requires a closer look and can be best understood through the methodology of discourse analysis employed in this study.

Political realism's postulate of conceiving national states as entities with objective interests and ensuring survival in an anarchic international system, being the key concern of all states, has been considered sacrosanct in traditional strategic studies. Under this scheme, threats to national security are described as objective conditions in order to cloak the subjectivity of survival plans proposed as national defense policies and prescriptions. The overwhelming influence of this characterization of the international system and the role of national states is amply reflected in the nuclear discourses of today's Pakistan and India. The ultimate justification for retaining the nuclear option derives sustenance from listing external threats to the national security. If the Sino-Pakistan threat and the uncertainties of the international system are rallying points for India's nukespeakers, then the fear of being devoured by a conventionally superior India has made retaining the nuclear option an article of faith and patriotism for Pakistani policy-makers and opinion-makers.

Security of the state in a discourse guided by assumptions of political realism is considered foremost in terms of preserving territorial boundaries of a given entity. For example, Z. A. Bhutto placed safeguarding geographical borders of Pakistan over any other issue proposed as a security need of the country.[4] Once security is primarily conceived in terms of territoriality, threats to it are usually located in the external realm. In the case of Pakistan's dominant security discourse, India is portrayed as the key external danger. It is in this context that Bhutto called for plans to include the nuclear option as a deterrent against India. Leading Indian nukespeakers also view the world through this lens. As Chapters Two and Three show, India is portrayed as a country genuinely interested in universal disarmament, and often analysts assert in self-congratulatory style that "India's track record on arms control is excellent."[5] The origin of New Delhi's nuclear ambitions is found in the external realm by arguing that "the Chinese bomb is the reason underlying India's nuclear weapons program."[6] Fixation of India's dominant discourse on territorial nationalism was most obvious during the May–July 1999 Kargil crisis. The government, the opposition, and mainstream security analysts agreed that there was a consensus in the country when it came to ensuring the geographical sanctity of India. K. Natwar Singh, former minister of state for external affairs, made it clear that "where the security, territorial integrity and sovereignty of India are concerned, the country is united."[7]

Because of the dependence of the Indo-Pakistan nuclear discourses on political realism, I presented caveats of that framework at the start of the first chapter to make it easier for the reader to be conscious of theoretical bearings of the dominant discourses in the respective countries. In all fairness to nukespeakers of the subcontinent, their discourses do go beyond the supposed amoral attitude attributed to diehard neorealists. Subcontinental nukespeak is laced with the jargon of patriotism and invokes moral grounds to justify nuclear programs. The dominant discourse in India claims a high moral ground while opposing the "discriminatory" nuclear nonproliferation treaty. Inequities of the international system are seen as an affront to a country like India, which is portrayed by proponents of the nuclear discourse as a genuine contender for great-power status. For example, K. Subrahmanyam views India's near isolation in international forums on the issue of CTBT as his country's resolve to resist a "hegemonic nuclear order."[8] Pakistani nukespeakers see moral value in their nuclear program as it provides a symbol of Islamic power and a viable means to counter Hindu India's hegemonic designs against Islamic Pakistan. Ghani Eirabi, one exponent of this position, considers Pakistan's nuclear program as an example of the Islamic world's advancement in the atomic field as well as a means to support the anti-India struggle of Kashmiri Muslims.[9]

Purporting to be exponents of objective reality on the one hand and justifying respective nuclear programs as expressions of high morality leads to paradoxes in the dominant security discourse of Pakistan and India. On one hand, theoretical models aiming at an objective view of reality have little room for ethical considerations in the conduct of security policies. On the other, policies guided by morality alone run the risk of being subjective. Nuclearists, both in India and Pakistan, have yet to resolve this paradox in their positions.

Along with this mix of normative reasoning and reliance on political realism as the guiding light, the other conceptual similarity between the two nuclear discourses is their shared contempt for domestic opponents of the dominant positions. As per the argument of the dominant discourse, since dangers to national security emanate primarily from outside the territorial boundaries of their countries, any voices within these states deviating from the prevailing regime inevitably come from people whose patriotic credentials are in doubt. Dissenting voices, though they exist only on the margins in both countries, are mainly muffled by creating binary dichotomies like patriots/agents, intelligent/naive, objective/subjective, realists/utopian, and so forth. These voices are always branded as foreign agents or naive analysts who do not understand the imperatives of national interest. I have shown in Chapter Six the limits of the dissent and the power of the dominant discourse by discussing how the latter defines the rules of the game to participate in the debate on national interests. In this regard, the analytical value of the discourse analysis becomes apparent by exposing the logocentric logic used by the dominant discourse in creating binary opposition, where superior values are always associated with the adherents of nukespeak, to conduct the debate.

This similarity is indicative of a larger problem in which postcolonial

Indian and Pakistani states and the dominant discourse have failed to coopt a variety of dissident voices in the so-called "national" mainstream. The following remarks of Partha Chatterjee mention only India but are equally true for Pakistan.

> The continuance of a distinct cultural "problem" of minorities is an index of failure of the Indian nation to effectively include within its body the whole of [the] demographic mass that it claims to represent. The failure becomes evident when we note the formation of a hegemonic "national culture" was *necessarily* built upon the privileging of an "essential tradition," which in turn was defined by a system of exclusions.[10]

Previous chapters show that both nuclear discourses in particular and national security discourses in general are certainly based on an "essentialist" tradition, which cannot operate without its set of exclusions. Therefore, the problem of the intellectual minority of nuclear dissidents is, in all probability, here to stay as long as the nuclear discourses are based on a concept of national interest. In this chain, nuclear discourses cannot be envisaged without the paradigm of national interest and the latter's dynamics dictate that it needs antinational elements both from within and without to keep going. External adversaries and internal dissent serve as nukespeak's Others in the subcontinent. Through discourse analysis I am able to show how certain statements are considered reflections of patriotism and the others as traitors.

Besides these conceptual similarities, there is a common situational denominator between the two discourses, namely, a near monopoly by a select number of individuals in India and Pakistan over the nature and direction of these discourses. As has been frequently observed by scholars and examined at length in this study, the core of nukespeakers in Pakistan and India comprises a small number of strategic scholars, military and civil officials, and a handful of politicians. The total effects of these discourses have more to do with the strategies used by nukespeakers than their numbers. The power of the strategic epistemic community is evident in the manner in which political parties with huge support bases have to abide by the rules of participation in the discourse that are defined by a select group of nukespeakers. For example, I. K. Gujral, when he was Prime Minister at that time, had to withdraw the nomination of Bhabani Sen Gupta, a renowned security analyst, as an advisor to the Prime Minister on foreign policy issues because Professor Gupta had expressed reservations against India's official policy on the NPT in a letter to the *New York Times* almost thirty years earlier. Nukespeakers saw the appointment as a bad omen for India's national interests, and Gujral had to yield to these pressures. Similarly, Benazir Bhutto, who claims to be an avowed believer in nonproliferation, has to echo Pakistani nukespeakers whenever she is in power.

The above similarities make strange bedfellows and nuclear stances of political parties in Pakistan and India best illustrate this point. Parties on the right of the political spectrum relying on religion as their ideology are vociferous advocates of the nuclear option. In India, it is the BJP, which pledged and then put the bomb on the shelf, and in Pakistan it is Jamait-I-Islami, which relentlessly pursued the cause of nuclear weapons. This similarity is suggestive of a closer relationship that has been established between the respective nuclear programs and national identities based upon the dominant religions of the above parties. Due to such combinations, nuclear programs are not only portrayed in patriotic terms but presented as sacred symbols of religious nationalism.

Before proceeding to enumerate differences between Pakistani and Indian nukespeak, two points have to be made here. First, the dynamics of the nuclear discourse in the subcontinent have striking similarity with the nature of the dominant security discourse in the United States. The idea of external danger plays a pivotal role in defining the American self, and David Campbell and Simon Dalby have very well analyzed this in their studies of the U.S. security discourse. This shared trait among an exemplary "strong state," namely, the United States, and "weak" states like India and Pakistan warns that the artificial division of the world into "strong" and "weak" states may lead to imposing arbitrary differences that cloud the actual process of security policy-making across the globe.

The second point is more specifically concerned with the subcontinent and must be kept in mind while discussing nukespeak in Pakistan and India. A dominant discourse does not necessarily imply a successful discourse. The dominant discourse sets out the rule of participation in the name of national interests, but it does not mean that all sections of the society will subscribe to such views. In this regard, the postcolonial experience of identity formation in the subcontinent shows that at times a large number of populations have remained outside the purview of the dominant security discourses and occasionally the limits of the dominant regime of truth have undermined the very foundations of the state in whose name the regime operates. The ultimate example of such limits was the failure of the dominant discourse in Pakistan to remain intact in the wake of total alienation of the Bengalis. Since the basis on which the dominant discourse of the then Pakistan operated, it excluded the vast majority of Bengalis from becoming a part of the so-called national identity. This incompatibility of the dominant discourse and dissent over the issue of identity led to dismemberment of Pakistan in 1971. Similarly, present-day dominant discourse in India portrays the trouble in Kashmir as a work of Pakistan; this attitude by implication makes the majority of Kashmiri Muslims potential or actual agents of Pakistan in the eyes of New Delhi. Traditional literature on the nuclear issue in the subcontinent has never analyzed these aspects of national security politics, which I believe are crucially important to understand the dynamics of the nuclear issue. This study has been a step in the direction to fill that lacuna. The account of similarities does not imply that the nuclear discourses are identical in the two countries because they differ significantly in some respects. Let us turn to the differences.

DIFFERENT HISTORIES, DIFFERENT SCOPES

> Circular sexualist India my *foot.* No. Bleddy tongue twister came out wrong. Secular-socialist. That's it. Bleddy *bunk.* Panditji sold you that stuff like a cheap watch salesman and you all bought one and now you wonder why it doesn't work. Bleddy Congress party full of bleddy fake Rolex salesmen. You think India'll just roll over, all those bloodthirsty bloodsoaked gods'll just roll over and *die.*
>
> —Salman Rushdie[11]

Panditji (as Nehru was affectionately addressed) sold other watches too and they do not work either in today's India. His policy that India should exercise nuclear abstinence is one of them. The present Indian nuclear discourse has undergone a fundamental shift by totally abandoning the Nehruvian ideal of an India rich in atomic energy but firmly opposed to manufacturing atomic weapons. In Pakistan, the dominant discourse had no well-charted nuclear policy until Z. A. Bhutto envisioned the value of the atom for both economic and defense purposes in the late 1960s. Since then, Pakistan's dominant discourse has never severed intellectual ties with ideas expressed by Bhutto. In comparative terms, contemporary India's nuclear stance is not only different but contradicts the thrust of Nehruvian views on the issue. Pakistani discourse, on the other hand, has shown a remarkable continuity in spite of traumatic changes in the political landscape of the country, including the hanging of Z. A. Bhutto.

Postindependence leaders in India, especially Nehru in the political realm and Homi Bhabha in the scientific sphere, were well aware of the economic as well as military potentials of atomic energy. Nehru, who personified the dominant discourse of India from the 1950s to the early 1960s, emphasized that India needed atomic energy for modernizing its economy, but he was unequivocal in his opposition to India using the atom for military purposes. India's status in the international system or its defense needs were not made dependent upon keeping the nuclear option open, whereas present-day dominant discourse sees the nuclear option as a means to deter adversaries and ensure higher status for the country in the international hierarchy. Inder Kumar Gujral was well aware of a close relationship between India's nuclear program and the country's defense needs when he suggested that India requires self-reliance in the nuclear field because it will make her feel more "secure and proud."[12] Such self-reliance is considered by the Indian dominant discourse as a means to be treated by the world "as equal partners."[13] The BJP became the ultimate torchbearer of the nuclear program of India that was put on the path of weaponization by Rajiv Gandhi. *Times of India* argues that India should be grateful to Rajiv Gandhi for ordering weaponization that helped India to fight the international nuclear hierarchy that reduced India "to an inferior status."[14] This shift signifies continuity in the overall aspirations of the Indian dominant discourse but a change in the means to realize them. An international power of some reckoning is still considered the only proper place for India in the international system, but today the nuclear option has become one of the important means to lay claims to an independent great-power status.

Pakistani nuclear discourse has remained quite consistent in its basic tenets since Z. A. Bhutto introduced the nuclear issue in the security discourse. During the 1950s, as well as the 1960s, the nuclear issue hardly appeared in Pakistan's dominant discourse. Bhutto called for utilization of the nuclear option to deter India in 1969, and later expanded the scope of Pakistan's nuclear program by portraying it as a harbinger of the Islamic bomb.[15] Twenty-five years later, Shireen Mazari echoed these views and suggested that the Pakistani state will gain popular support as well as strategic clout against India by overtly going nuclear.[16] In light of the Chagai tests, the proponents of the nuclear discourse seem to wholeheartedly accept Mazari's assertion.

This change in one country's case and continuity in the other's can be partly explained with reference to difference in discourses regarding the respective identities proposed by the adherents of the dominant views in India and Pakistan. In Pakistan's nuclear politics, India is the only external figure, whereas the Indian nukespeakers' list of adversaries is more diverse. Pakistan's dominant discourse defines the country as a Muslim nation opposed by hostile India where the nuclear option serves as a credible deterrent against the nuclear-capable and conventionally superior India. The dominant Indian discourse portrays the country as a worthy great power that is not given its due place in the international hierarchy. The nuclear option works as one of the means to fulfill that aspiration.

REVISIONING NUCLEAR DISCOURSE

It is easy to criticize the existing approaches for what they do not offer, but it is another matter to come up with an alternative method to analyze common issues that constitute the agenda of security studies. This has been the most common, and to an extent valid, criticism against analysts sympathetic to critical theories in strategic studies. I have made a modest attempt to look at a security issue, namely the politics of nuclear weapons in the subcontinent, with the help of methodological tools found in the works of modern social and cultural theorists. It is time to look back and see how the methodology of discourse analysis has helped in reimagining the nuclear issue in the subcontinent. Answering the following questions will help in this regard. What has been the defining difference in my approach from those commonly used to analyze this issue? Has my approach resulted in a better understanding of the nuclear issue in the subcontinent?

All narratives are inevitably partial and mine is no different. Lenses employed in this study are products of the modern-day West. Whether we are talking about neorealism or the "weak states" model, these are Euro-centric frameworks in spite of their claims to universality and particularity, respectively. Therefore, these theories should be read "as aspects of contemporary world politics that need to be explained [rather] than as explanations of contemporary world politics."[17] Such a reading becomes possible if theories are considered discourses, which validate some opinions as true and consider other views false. Interestingly, it is political realism, in one form or the other, that serves as the underlying theoretical framework for security analysts in South Asia. This is interesting because South Asian nukespeakers insist upon the uniqueness of their situation and justify their nuclear stance on the grounds that such an option is necessary due to the objective conditions prevailing in the region. This reference to objectivity is a hallmark of political realism.

In broader theoretical terms, I have drawn attention to the embedded determinism of traditional strategic studies as well as the "weak states" model. Determinism in the former is based upon its claim of being a universalist theory about international politics, whereas the latter's emphasis is on the uniqueness of the Third World state and its distinct security problem. Proponents of the "weak states" model convincingly show the hollowness of the universalist assertions of neorealism, but the "weak states" perspective relapses into an orientalist trap that views the Third World as the West's external other. The postcolonial world is conceived in terms of "weak states" for the simple reason that these entities are different from their Western counterparts, that is, "strong states." Pitted against the "developed" and "strong" West, the rest of the world is pronounced "weak." The only way the Third World state can become "strong" is to become like the West. In the meantime, all explanations of security predilections of the postcolonial world are ultimately reduced to a single explanation, namely, the problem of "weak states." This, as Chapter One shows, leads to circular logic and predetermined explanations that cloud complexities rather than clear our understanding of the Third World.

This study, above all, draws attention of students of security issues of the postcolonial world to the dual pitfalls of the methodological extremes of either security orientalism on the one hand and "oriental exceptionalism" on the other. If security orientalism privileges the West over the rest and puts the postcolonial world in a race to become like the West, then one hallmark of "oriental exceptionalism" is its emphasis on the uniqueness of, say, India or Africa while overlooking the "depth to which the processes of the modern state have taken root in the contemporary history" of postcolonial societies.[18] Since the postcolonial world can neither undo the legacy of colonialism nor live in the faint hope of becoming like the West one day, one possible way to come to grips with the distinct nature of postcolonial situations is by listening to and arguing with those theorists who view postmodernism as "European culture's awareness that it is no longer the unquestioned and dominant center of the world."[19]

Challenging the objectivity of the role of nuclear weapons as a means of ensuring national interests, I showed how such a body of knowledge endorses and sanctifies certain language and modes of reasoning while vilifying other forms of knowledge. This study demonstrates that neither threats to national security nor identities that are portrayed to be under threat are without problems. The dominant discourses attempt to objectify these processes but usually face dissent in a variety of forms. My methodology is fundamentally different from the neorealist and the "weak states" models. If the former assumes the existence of threats to the so-called national interest, the discourse analysis problematizes construction of these threats and attempts to show temporal limits and historical specificities of such construction. If the "weak states" model assumes a fundamental difference between the weak and strong states, the discourse analysis tries to draw attention to similarities between the First and Third World countries when it comes to creating threats and devising appropriate responses to them. This similarity does not mean that there are universal rules guiding all actions of all states in the international system. Hence, the United States' dominant security discourse as search for and creation of "enemies" after the collapse of the Soviet Union and finding some in the shape of Islamic fundamentalism or international terrorism is not much different from India and Pakistan portraying each other as threats to their national securities.

Certain arguments emerge as the key points of the book. First, strategic truths are human constructs and not objective conditions waiting to be named. Employing Foucault's notion of "general politics of truth" as it operates in postcolonial Pakistan and India with a focus on examining the way nuclear discourses operate in these societies, the nuclear factor is located in the web of threats construed as inimical to the national identity. In this process both the nature of threats and the role of nuclear weapons to meet them have undergone several changes in both Pakistan and India. This study shows the historical specificity and changing nature of the nuclear issue in which there are no eternal truths. For example, in India if the nuclear weapons were portrayed as an evil during the dominant discourse in the Nehru years, today the custodians of the dominant discourse present them as a viable option. Similarly, in today's Pakistan the nuclear option has become synonymous with national identity while in the 1960s it was a nonissue in the dominant discourse.

The story of nuclear discourse in the subcontinent is that of a love-hate relationship between nuclear hawks of the two countries. The key channels of communication between strategic analysts of India and Pakistan on the nuclear issue are between strategic epistemic communities of nukespeakers. Essentially this communication is indicative of two monologues rather than a dialogue. There are two reasons for this situation. First, nuclear proponents on either side of the border see the world through a "realist" perspective and that makes one's monologue communicable to the other. A second, and more important, reason that makes communication possible between adherents of nukespeak lies in their respective positions whereby they have assumed the role of the true representatives of the national interests of their countries. Patriotism of an Indian or Pakistani nuclear hawk is patent and his beliefs are considered beyond doubt. No matter how much they talk to each other, since these are two monologues, the assumption is that no side will yield to the other. Therefore, it is only K. Subrahmanyams and Mushahid Hussains of the subcontinent who get regular opportunities to talk to each other. This scenario closes off any avenues for a meaningful dialogue. Ironically, these people who are at the helm of affairs can affect an orderly change for the better in the bilateral relations between India and Pakistan.[20] Where Pakistani or Indian security discourses are monopolized by a small group of individuals, the probability of links between the voices of dissent in both countries is low. Dissenting voices that are already ostracized by nukespeakers will only consolidate the impression of being less patriotic by establishing a dialogue across the border. There lies the real power of a regime of truth operating in the name of national security policies.

Second, this study shows how a select number of individuals have appropriated the nuclear issue by tying it to the web of issues like national identity, external dangers, and internal dissent. Third, intertwining the nuclear issue as a symbol of national identity and the nuclear discourse works as a double-edged sword where it thwarts external danger and suppresses internal dissent. This strategy makes it incumbent upon the nukespeakers of Pakistan and India to cast the opponents of the dominant discourse as enemies of their respective nations. Fourth, the discussion of the dissenters in the nuclear discourses tells us that these accounts are based upon different notions of national identity. This imposes its own limitations on the effectiveness of such narratives. The potential of these views to be realized in the realm of nuclear policies is dependent upon changed bases of national identities. Since that is unlikely to happen in the near future, fundamental changes in the nature or direction of the nuclear discourses in Pakistan and

India would be no less than a miracle. The fifth conclusion of this study would be that under present circumstances, efforts to institute confidence building measures (CBMs) based on the Soviet-American model are unlikely to yield desired results as envisaged by their main sponsors, namely, the Americans.[21] However, this does not mean there is an imminent danger of a nuclear war between Pakistan and India in crisis situations. Although there is no guarantee that such a war will not break out, this study suggests that the nuclear programs in the subcontinent are extensions of the political projects of the dominant discourses on national identities rather than pure military means to settle scores on the battlefield.

Nuclear weapons have been used in the subcontinent. The May 1998 explosions by India and Pakistan are the most recent examples. These weapons have been put to multiple uses ranging from uplifting the national ego to ensuring self-respect. Exclusive focus on the strategic aspects of nuclear weapons at the expense of their political uses misses even the most important point made by traditional deterrence theory; that is, nuclear weapons are primarily political weapons. The interaction of the subcontinent with nukes amply testifies that these are political weapons.

NOTES

1. Partha Chatterjee, *Nation and Its Fragments: Colonial and Postcolonial Histories* (Princeton, NJ: Princeton University Press, 1993), p. 5.
2. "Modernity" is more appropriately what Aaron Sheldrick, a student of Tom Young, terms "westernity." See, Tom Young, " 'A Project to Be Realized': Global Liberalism and Contemporary Africa," *Millennium: Journal of International Studies* 24:3 (winter 1995), p. 527. "Modernity," as is widely understood, has a close relationship with Enlightenment. On issues related to the problematic nature of "modernity" see Michel Foucault, "What Is Enlightenment?," in Paul Rabinow, ed., *The Foucault Reader* (London: Penguin, 1984), pp. 32–50.
3. Bradley S. Klein, "Conclusion: Every Month Is "Security Awareness Month," in Keith Krause and Michael C. Williams, eds., *Critical Security Studies: Concepts and Cases* (Minnesota: University of Minnesota Press, 1997), p. 363.
4. Zulfikar Ali Bhutto, *The Myth of Independence* (London, Lahore, Karachi: Oxford University Press, 1969), p. 103.
5. T. T. Poulose, "India's Nuclear Option and National Security," in P. R. Chari, Pervaiz Iqbal Cheema, and Iftekharuzzaman, eds., *Nuclear Non-proliferation in India and Pakistan: South Asian Perspectives* (New Delhi: Manohar, A Publication of Regional Center for Strategic Studies, Colombo, 1996), p. 57.
6. Ibid., p. 44.
7. K. Natwar Singh, "The Kargil Conflict and Beyond," *Hindu*, June 25, 1999.
8. K. Subrahmanyam, "India and the CTBT: Deterrence Requires Testing Option," *Times of India*, February 21, 1996.
9. Ghani Eirabi, "Blackmailing Can Backfire," *Dawn*, April 18, 1993.
10. Partha Chatterjee, *Nation and Its Fragments*, p. 134.

11. Salman Rushdie, *The Moor's Last Sigh* (Toronto: Alfred A. Knopf, 1995) p. 166.

12. *Dawn*, September 29, 1997.

13. Ibid., September 30, 1997.

14. "The Nuclear Legacy," *Times of India*, May 26, 1998.

15. See Z. A. Bhutto, *Myth of Independence*, and *If I Am Assassinated* (New Delhi: Vikas, 1979).

16. Shireen M. Mazari, "NPT: An Unfair Treaty that Pakistan Must Not Sign," in Tarik Jan, ed., *Pakistan's Security and the Nuclear Option* (Islamabad: Institute for Policy Studies, 1995), p. 32.

17. R. B. J. Walker, *Inside/Outside: International Relations as Political Theory* (Cambridge: Cambridge University Press, 1993), p. 6.

18. Partha Chatterjee, *The Nation and Its Fragments*, p. 257.

19. Robert Young, *White Mythologies: Writing History and the West* (London: Routledge, 1990), p. 19.

20. A somewhat closer analogy would be the last years of the Soviet Union where Mikhail Gorbachev played an important role in changing the nature and direction of the superpower rivalry. For example, see Richard Ned Lebnow and Thomas Risse-Kappen, eds., *International Relations Theory and the End of the Cold War* (New York: Columbia University Press, 1995).

21. For a list of various CBM efforts and their organizational forms, see Navnita Chadha Behera, Paul M. Evans, and Gowher Rizvi, *Beyond Boundaries: A Report on the State of Non-official Dialogues on Peace, Security and Cooperation in South Asia* (Toronto: University of Toronto–York University Joint Center for Asia Pacific Studies, 1997).

Selected Bibliography

Abraham, Itty. *Making of the Indian Bomb: Secrecy and the Postcolonial State.* London: Zed Books, 1998.

Adler, Emanuel, and Peter M. Haas. "Conclusion: Epistemic Communities, World Order, and the Creation of a Reflective Research Program," *International Organization* 46:1 (winter 1992): 367–390.

Ahmad, Emajuddin. "Regional Cooperation in South Asia and India's Role," *Institute of Defense and Strategic Analysis (IDSA) Journal* 15: 3 (January–March 1983): 405–422.

Ahmar, Moonis. "Security Perceptions in the Indo-Pak Relationship," *Pakistan Horizon* 37:1 (1984): 100–119.

———. "War Avoidance between India and Pakistan: A Model of Conflict Resolution and Confidence Building in the Post-Cold War Era," *Strategic Studies* 16:1–2 (autumn-winter 1993): 5–26.

Ahmed, Khaled. "Pakistan's America Problem: Crisis of Defiance," *Friday Times* (Lahore) March 24–30, 1994.

———. "Where Have We Got on Kashmir?," *Friday Times* (Lahore), September 29–October 5, 1994.

———. "NPT: More Trouble Ahead for Pakistan," *Friday Times* (Lahore), December 1–7, 1994.

———. "The Status of Indo-Pak Trade," *Friday Times* (Lahore), December 15–21, 1994.

———. "Is 'Neemrana Dialogue' a Conspiracy?," *Friday Times* (Lahore), December 29–January 4, 1995.

Ahmed, Samina. "Indian Ocean Peace Zone Proposal," *Pakistan Horizon* 32:1–2 (1979): 98–141.

———. "Pakistan's Proposal for Nuclear-Weapon Free Zone in South Asia," *Pakistan Horizon* 32:4 (1979): 92–130.

Ahmed, Samina, and David Cortright, eds. *Pakistan and the Bomb: Public Opinion and Nuclear Options*. Notre Dame, IN: Notre Dame University Press, 1998.

Akram, A. I. "South Asia and the Bomb," *Regional Studies* 4:1 (winter 1985): 3–19.

Ali, Akhtar. *Pakistan's Nuclear Dilemma: Energy and Security Concerns*. Karachi: Economic Research Unit, 1984.

Ali, Sheikh R. "Pakistan's Islamic Bomb Reconsidered," *Middle East Review* 17:3 (spring 1985): 52–58.

Anderson, Benedict. *Imagined Communities: Reflections on the Origin and Spread of Nationalism*. Revised Edition, London, New York: Verso, 1991.

———. "Exodus," *Critical Inquiry* 20 (winter 1994): 314–327.

Appadorai, A., ed. *Selected Documents on India's Foreign Policy and Relations: 1947–1972*, Vol. 1. Delhi: Oxford University Press, 1982.

Art, Robert J., and Kenneth N. Waltz, eds. *The Use of Force: International Politics and Foreign Policy*. Second Edition, Lanham: University Press of America, 1983.

Arya, D. K., and R. C. Sharma. *Management Issues and Operational Planning for India's Borders*. New Delhi: Scholars Publishing Forum, 1991.

Ashley, Richard K. "The Poverty of Neorealism," in *Neorealism and Its Critics*, ed. Robert O. Keohane, New York: Columbia University Press, 1986.

Ayoob, Mohammed. *The Third World Security Predicament: State Making, Regional Conflict, and International System*. Boulder, CO: Lynne Rienner, 1995.

Azam, Kousar, ed. *India's Defense Policy for the 1990's*. New Delhi: Sterling, 1992.

Baldwin, David A. "Security Studies and the End of the Cold War," Review Article, *World Politics* 48 (October 1995): 117–141.

———. "The Concept of Security," *Review of International Studies* 23 (1997): 5–26.

Banerjee, D. B. "India-China Relations and Chinese Military Capabilities," in *India's Borders: Ecology and Security Perspectives*, eds. Ramakrishana Rao, and R.C. Sharma, 80–102. New Delhi: Scholars Publishing Forum, 1991.

Baral, Lok Raj. "SARC, but No 'SHARK.' South Asian Regional Cooperation in Perspective," *Pacific Affairs* 58:3 (fall 1985): 411–426.

Baweja, Harinder. "Indo-US Relations: Clearing the Air," *India Today*, April 15, 1994, 32–36.

Bhargava, G. S. *South Asian Security after Afghanistan*. Lexington: Lexington Books, 1983.

Bhatia, Shyam. *India's Nuclear Bomb*. New Delhi: Vikas, 1979.

Bhimaya, Kotera M. "Nuclear Deterrence in South Asia: Civil-Military Relations and Decision-Making," *Asian Survey* 34:7 (July 1994): 647–661.

Bhola, P. L. *Pakistan's Nuclear Policy*. New Delhi: Sterling Publishers, South Asia Series, 1993.

Bhutto, Zulfikar Ali. *Reshaping Foreign Policy: A Collection of articles, statements and speeches: Politics of the Peoples Series*, Vol. 1: 1948–1966, eds. Hamid Jalal and Khalid Hasan. Rawaplindi: Pakistan Publications, n.d.

———. *Awakening the People: A Collection of Articles, Statements: Politics of the*

Peoples Series, Vol. 2: 1966–1969, eds. Hamid Jalal and Khalid Hasan. Rawaplindi: Pakistan Publications, n.d.

———. *The Myth of Independence*. London, Lahore, and Karachi: Oxford University Press, 1969.

———. *Marching Toward Democracy: A Collection of Articles, Statements and Speeches: Politics of the People Series*, Vol. 3: 1970–1971, eds. Hamid Jalal and Khalid Hasan. Rawaplindi: Pakistan Publications, n.d.

———. *If I Am Assassinated*. New Delhi: Vikas, 1979.

Bidwai, Praful. "India's Veto of the CTBT Is Futile," *Times of India* (Mumbai), September 12, 1996.

Bidwai, Praful, and Achin Vanaik. "India and Pakistan," in *Security with Nuclear Weapons? Different Perspectives on National Security*, ed. Regina Cowen Carp. New York: SIPRI and Oxford University Press, 1991.

Booth, Ken. "Security and Self: Reflections of a Fallen Realist," in *Critical Security Studies: Concepts and Cases*, eds. Keith Krause and Michael C. Williams. Minneapolis: University of Minnesota Press, 1997.

Bose, T. C. "The United States and South Asia: The Nuclear Proliferation Dimension," *Strategic Analysis* 16:12 (March 1994): 1597–1616.

Bratersky, M. V., and S. I. Lunyov. "India at the End of the Century: Transformation into an Asian Regional Power," *Asian Survey* 30:10 (October 1990): 927–942.

Bruce, Robert H. *Nuclear Proliferation in South Asia and the Middle East*. Perth: Indian Ocean Centre for Peace and Studies, 1992.

Budhraj, Vijay Sen. "The Politics of Transfer of Nuclear Technology: A Case Study of the Tarapur Agreement," *Australian Outlook* 38:1 (April 1984): 21–25.

Burchell, Graham, Gordon Colin, and Miller Peter, eds. *The Foucault Effect: Studies in Governmentality, with Two Lectures and an Interview with Michel Foucault*. Chicago: University of Chicago Press, 1991.

Burrows, William E., and Robert Windrem. *Critical Mass: The Dangerous Race for Superweapons in a Fragmenting World*. New York: Simon & Schuster, 1994.

Buzan, Barry. "New Patterns of Global Security in the Twenty-First Century," *International Affairs* 67:3 (1991): 431–451

Buzan, Barry, Charles Jones, and Richard Little. *The Logic of Anarchy: Neorealism to Structural Realism*. New York: Columbia University Press, 1993.

Buzan, Barry, Ole Waever, and Jaap de Wilde. *Security: A New Framework for Analysis*. Boulder, CO: Lynne Rienner, 1998.

Buzan, Barry, and Gowher Rizvi, eds. *South Asian Insecurity and the Great Powers*. London: Macmillan, 1986.

———. *People, States, and Fear: An Agenda for Security Studies in the Post-Cold War Era*. Second Edition. New York: Harvester Wheatsheaf, 1991.

Buzan, Barry, and Gerald Segal. "Rethinking East Asian Security," *Survival* 36:2 (summer 1994): 3–21.

Cambone, Stephen A., and Patrick J. Garrity. "The Future of US Nuclear Policy," *Survival* 36:4 (winter 1994–1995,): 73–95.

Campbell, David. *Writing Security: United States Foreign Policy and the Politics of Identity*. Manchester: Manchester University Press, 1992.

Carp, Regina Cowen, ed. *Security without Nuclear Weapons? Different Perspec-*

tives on National Security. New York: SIPRI and Oxford University Press, 1991.

Chari, P. R. *Indo-Pak Nuclear Standoff: The Role of the United States*. New Delhi: Manohar Publishers, Under the Auspices of the Center for Policy Research New Delhi, 1995.

Chari, P. R., Pervaiz Iqbal Cheema, and Iftekharuzzaman, eds. *Nuclear Non-Proliferation in India and Pakistan: South Asian Perspectives*. New Delhi: Manohar, A Publication of Regional Center for Strategic Studies, Colombo, 1996.

Chatterjee, Partha. *Nation and Its Fragments: Colonial and Postcolonial Histories*. Princeton: Princeton University Press, 1993.

———, ed. *Texts of Power: Emerging Disciplines in Colonial Bengal*. Minneapolis: University of Minnesota Press, 1995.

Chellaney, Brahma. "The Challenge of Nuclear Arms Control in South Asia," *Survival* 35:3 (autumn 1993): 121–136.

Chengappa, Raj. "Nuclear Business(?)," *India Today*, April 30, 1994, 46–54.

———. "India's Nuclear Policy: Testing Times," *India Today*, December 31, 1995, 46–51.

Chilton, Paul, ed. *Language and the Nuclear Arms Debate: Nukespeak Today*. London and Dover: Francis Pinter, 1985.

Chomsky, Noam. *Deterring Democracy*. Seventh Print, New York: Hill & Wang, 1995.

Clad, James. "India in 1996: Steady as She Goes," *Washington Quarterly* 19:4 (1996): 103–111.

Cohen, Stephen P., ed. *The Security of South Asia; American and Asian Perspectives*. Urbana-Champage, IL: University of Illinois Press, 1987.

———, ed. *Nuclear Proliferation in South Asia: The Prospects for Arms Control*. Boulder, CO: Westview, 1991.

Cortright, David, and Amitabh Mattoo, eds. *India and the Bomb: Public Opinion and Nuclear Options*. Notre Dame, IN: University of Notre Dame Press, 1996.

Dalby, Simon. *Creating the Second Cold War: The Discourse of Politics*. New York and London: Guilford & Pinter, 1990.

Deshingkar, Giri. "India," in *Nuclear Weapons after the Comprehensive Test Ban: Implications for Modernization and Proliferation*, ed. Eric Arnett, 41–54. New York: SIPRI and Oxford University Press, 1996.

Dubey, Muchkund. "India's Foreign Policy in the Evolving Global Order," *International Studies* 30:2 (April–June 1993): 117–129.

Foucault, Michel. *Discipline and Punish: The Birth of the Prison*, trans. Alan Sheridon. New York: Vintage Books, 1979.

———. *The Foucault Reader*, ed. Paul Rabinow. London: Penguin, 1984.

———. *The Uses of Pleasure: Volume 2, History of Sexuality*, trans. Robert Hurley, New York: Pantheon Books, 1985.

———. *The History of Sexuality, Volume I: An Introduction*, trans. Robert Hurley, New York: Vintage Books, 1990.

———. "Two Lectures," in *Critique and Power: Recasting the Foucault Habermas Debate*, ed. Michael Kelly. Cambridge, MA: MIT Press, 1994.

Freedman, Lawrence. "Great Powers, Vital Interests and Nuclear Weapons," *Survival* 36:4 (winter 1994–1995): 35–52.

Gopal, B. "India, Pakistan and the Nuclear Non-proliferation Treaty," *Punjab Journal of Politics* 17:1 (June 1993): 15–26.

Gosh, Partha S. "Nuclear Rivalry in South Asia: Strategic Imperatives and National Pride," *Conflict Studies* 274 (September 1994): 1–22.

Grieco, Joseph M. "Anarchy and the Limits of Cooperation: A Realist Critique of the Newest Liberal Institutionalism," *International Organization* 42:3 (summer 1988): 485–507.

Gupta, Rakesh. *India's Security Problems in the 1990's*. New Delhi: Patriot, 1989.

Gupta, Shekhar. "On a Short Fuse," *India Today*, March 15, 1994, 26–31.

———. "India's Nuclear Stand: Worried, but Ready," *India Today*, September 15, 1994, 32–35.

Gupta, Shekhar, and Sudeep Chakravarti. "Sino-Indian Relations: Vital Breakthrough," *India Today*, September 30, 1994, 22–27.

———. *India Redefines Its Role: An Analysis of India's Changing Internal Dynamics and Their Impact on Foreign Relations. Adelphi Papers* 293. London: Oxford University Press for IISS, 1995.

Haas, Peter M. "Introduction: Epistemic Communities and International Cooperation," *International Organization* 46:1 (winter 1992): 1–36.

Hagerty, Devin T. *The Consequences of Nuclear Proliferation: Lessons from South Asia*. Cambridge: MIT Press, 1998.

Harrison, Selig S., and Geoffrey Kemp. *India and America after the Cold War* Washington, DC: Carnegie Endowment for International Peace, 1993.

Harrison, Selig, and K. Subrahmanyam, eds. *Superpower Rivalry in the Indian Ocean: Indian and American Perspective*. New York: Oxford University Press, 1989.

Holsti, K. J. "War, Peace, and the State of the State," *International Political Science Review* 16:4 (1995): 319–339.

———. *International Politics: A Framework for Analysis*. Seventh Edition. Englewood Cliffs, NJ: Prentice-Hall, 1995.

———. *The State, War, and the State of War*. Cambridge: Cambridge University Press, 1996.

Hoodbhoy, Pervez. *Nuclear Issues between India and Pakistan: Myths and Realities*. Washington, DC: Henry L. Stimson Centre, Occasional Paper 18, July 1994.

———. "Nuclear Myths and Realities," in *Pakistan's Atomic Bomb and the Search for Security*, ed. Zia Mian, Lahore: Gautam Publishers, 1995.

Hussain, Mushahid. *Pakistan and the Changing Regional Scenario: Reflections of a Journalist*. Lahore: Progressive Publishers, 1988.

Jain, J. P. *Nuclear India*, Vol I and II. New Delhi: Radiant Publishers, 1974.

Jalal, Ayesha. *Democracy and Authoritarianism in South Asia: A Comparative and Historical Perspective*. Cambridge: Cambridge University Press, 1995.

Jan, Tarik, ed. *Pakistan's Security and the Nuclear Option*. Islamabad: Institute of Policy Studies, 1995.

Jervis, Robert. *The Meaning of Nuclear Revolution: Statecraft and the Prospects of Armageddon*. Ithaca, NY: Cornell University Press, 1989.

———. "The Future of World Politics: Will It Resemble Past?" *International Security* 16:3 (winter 1991–1992): 3–37.

Jones, Rodney W. *Nuclear Proliferation: Islam, the Bomb, and South Asia*. London: Sage, 1981.

Joshi, Manohar. "Challenges to Regional Stability: Inter-state Regional Conflicts," in *Indo-US Relations in a Challenging World*, ed. Jasjit Singh, 255–286. New Delhi: Lancer and Institute of Defense Studies and Analysis, 1992.

Kalam, Abdul A. P. J., with Arun Tiwari. *Wings of Fire: An Autobiography*. Hyderabad: Universities Press, 1999.

Kapur, Ashok. *India's Nuclear Option: Atomic Diplomacy and Decision Making*. New York: Praeger, 1976.

———. *Pakistan's Nuclear Development*. London: Croom Helm, 1986.

Keeley, James F. "Toward a Foucauldian Analysis of International Regimes," *International Organization* 44:1 (winter 1990): 83–105.

Keohane, Robert O., ed. *Neorealism and Its Critics*. New York: Columbia University Press, 1986.

Khan, Air Chief Marshal Zulfiqar Ali. "Pakistan's Security and Nuclear Option," in *Nuclear Issues in South Asia*. Islamabad: Islamabad Council of World Affairs, 1995.

Khan, Feroz H. "Power Curves and Wars in South Asia," *Strategic Studies* 16:1–2 (autumn-winter 1993): 44–63.

Khan, Mohammad Ayub. *Speeches and Statements, Volume 4: July 1961–June 1962*. n.p., n.d.

———. *Friends Not Masters: A Political Autobiography*. London and Karachi: Oxford University Press, 1967.

Khan, Munir Ahmad. "Problems with NPT Renewal," *Dawn*, March 3, 1995.

———. "No-First Use Doctrine," *Dawn*, April 11, 1995.

———. "Price of Nuclear Rhetoric," *News*, September 14, 1995.

Khan, Rashid Ahmad. "Pakistan, India and Regional Cooperation in South Asia," *Pakistan Horizon* 37:3 (1984): 37–48.

Khanna, D. D. *Strategic Environment in South Asia during the 1990's*. Calcutta: Naya Prokash, 1986.

Khanna, D. D., and Kishor Kumar. *Dialogue of the Deaf: The India-Pakistan Divide*. Delhi: Konark Publishers 1992.

Koreshi, S. M. "NPT Revision and Extension Conflict," *Nation* (Lahore), January 24, 1995.

Kothari, Rajni. *State against Democracy: In Search of Humane Governance*. New Dehli: Ajanta, 1988.

———. *Politics and the People: In Search of a Humane India*, Volume I and II. New Dehli: Ajanta, 1990.

Krause, Keith. "Critical Theory and Security Studies." YCISS Occasional Paper 33, 1996.

Krause, Keith, and Michael C. Williams, eds. *Critical Security Studies: Concepts and Cases*. Minneapolis: University of Minnesota Press, 1997.

Kress, Gunter. "Discourses, Texts, Readers and the Pro-nuclear Arguments," in *Language and the Nuclear Arms Debate*, Paul Chilton, ed., London and Dover: Francis Pinter, 1985.

Krippendorff, Ekkehart. "The Dominance of American Approaches in International

Relations," in *The Study of International Relations: The State of the Art*, eds. Hugh C. Dyer and Leon Mangasarian. Basingstoke, U.K.: Macmillan, in Association with *Millennium: Journal of International Studies*, 1989.

Kumar, Satish, ed. *Documents on India's Foreign Policy: 1974*. Delhi: Macmillan and Jawaharlal Nehru University, 1977.

Lamb, Alastair. *The China-India Border: The Origins of the Disputed Boundaries*. London: Oxford University Press, 1964.

Lapid, Yosef, and Friedrich Kratochwil, eds. *The Return of Culture and Identity in IR Theory*. London and Boulder, CO: Lynne-Rienner, 1996.

Lennon, Alexander T. "The 1995 NPT Extension Conference," *Washington Quarterly* 17:4 (1993): 205–227.

Levy, Jack S. "The Causes of War: A Review Essay," in *Behavior, Society, and Nuclear War*, eds. Philip E. Tetlock et al. New York: Oxford University Press, 1989.

Madan, T. N. "Anthropology as Critical Self-Awareness," in *The Multiverse of Democracy: Essays in Honour of Rajni Kothari*, eds. D. L. Sheth and Ashis Nandy. New Delhi, Thousand Oaks, and London: Sage, 1996.

Majeed, Akhtar. "Indian Security Perspectives in the 1990's," *Asian Survey* 30:11 (November 1990): 1084–1098.

Malik, Mohan J. "India Copes with Kremlin's Fall," *Orbis* 37:1 (winter 1993): 69–87.

Malik, Yogendra K., and V. B. Singh. *Hindu Nationalists in India: The Rise of the Bharatiya Janata Party*. Boulder, CO: Westview, 1994.

Mattoo, Amitabh. "India's Nuclear Status Quo," *Survival* 38:3 (autumn 1996): 41–57.

Maxwell, Neville. *India's China War*. London: Penguin, 1972.

Mian, Zia, ed. *Pakistan's Atomic Bomb and the Search for Security*. Lahore: Gautam Publishers, A Publication of the Campaign for Nuclear Sanity and the Sustainable Development Policy Institute, Islamabad, 1995.

Mirchandani, G. G. *India's Nuclear Dilemma*. New Delhi: Popular Book Services, 1968.

Morgan, M. Granger, K. Subrahmanyam, K. Sundarji, and Robert M. White. "India and the United State," *Washington Quarterly* 18:2 (spring 1995): 155–179.

Moshaver, Ziba. *Nuclear Weapons Proliferation in the Indian Subcontinent*. London: Macmillan, 1991.

Mueller, John. *Retreat from Doomsday: The Obsolescence of Major War*. New York: Basic Books, 1989.

Muni, S. D. "India and the Post–Cold War World: Opportunities and Challenges," *Asian Survey* 31:9 (September 1991): 862–874.

———. "India and Its Neighbors: Persisting Dilemmas and New Opportunities," *International Studies* 30:2 (April–June 1993): 189–206.

Munro, Ross H. "The Loser: India in the Nineties," *Strategic Studies* 16:1–2 (autumn-winter 1993): 80–89.

Naik, J. A. *The Pak Bomb and Rajiv's India*. New Delhi: National Publishing House, 1986.

Nandy, Ashis. "The Bomb, NPT and Indian Elite," *Economic and Political Weekly*, Special Issue, 7:31–33 (August 1972): 1533–1540.

———. "Between Two Gandhis: Psychological Aspects of the Nuclearization of India," *Asian Survey* 14:11 (November 1974): 966–970.

———. *The Savage Freud and Other Essays on Possible and Retrievable Selves.* Princeton: Princeton University Press, 1995.

Naqvi, M. B. "South Asian Cooperation," *Pakistan Horizon* 36:3 (1983): 21–36.

Navlakha, Gautam. "Pakistan-India: The Chill Factor," *Economic and Political Weekly* 17 February (1996).

Nehru, Jawaharlal. *India's Foreign Policy: Selected Speeches, September 1946–April 1961*. Publication Division, Government of India, n.d.

Nizamani, Haider K. "Change and Continuity in Indo-Russian Relations," *Strategic Perspectives* (Institute of Strategic Studies, Islamabad) 1:4 (summer 1993): 58–73.

———. "Indo-US Security Relations in the Post–Cold War Period," *Strategic Perspectives* 2:3 (summer 1994): 20–38.

Nuruzzaman, M. "The Arms Race in South Asia: Some Approaches to Stability," *Strategic Studies* 16:1–2 (autumn and winter 1993): 27–43.

Orwell, George. *Nineteen Eighty-Four*. London: Penguin Books Edition, 1984.

Pakistan Horizon, Special Issue: Focus on South Asia, 36:4 (1983): 3–140.

Pakistan Horizon, Special Issue on South Asia, 43:2 (April 1990): 13–159

Palit, Maj. Gen. D. K., and P. K. S. Namboodri. *Pakistan's Islamic Bomb*. New Delhi: Vikas, 1979.

Paranjpe, Shrikant. *U.S. Nonproliferation Policy in Action: South Asia*. New Dehli: Sterling, 1987.

Pathak, K. K. *Nuclear Policy of India: A Third World Perspective*. New Delhi: Gitanjali Prakashan, 1980.

Paul, T. V. *Reaching for the Bomb: The Indo-Pak Scenario*. New Delhi: Dialogue Publications, 1984.

Perkovich, George. *India's Nuclear Bomb: The Impact on Global Proliferation*. Berkeley: University of California Press, 1998.

Poulose, T.T. "Nuclear Polycentrism and Denuclearization of South Asia," *Asia Pacific Community* 31 (winter 1986): 106–115.

Price, Richard. "A Genealogy of the Chemical Weapons Taboo," *International Organization* 49:1 (winter 1995): 73–103.

Rais, R. B. "The U.S. Nonproliferation Policy in South Asia," *Pakistan Journal of American Studies* 1:1–2 (1983): 17–27.

———. "Pakistan's Nuclear Program: Prospects for Proliferation," *Asian Survey* 25:4 (April 1985): 458–472.

Ramanna, Raja. *Years of Pilgrimage: An Autobiography*. New Delhi: Viking, Penguin, 1991.

Rao, P. V. Narasimha. *Selected Speeches, Vol.1, June 1991–June 1992*. New Delhi: Publication Division, Ministry of Information and Broadcasting, Government of India, 1993.

Rao, Ramakrishana, and R. C. Sharma. *India's Borders: Ecology and Security Perspectives*. New Delhi: Scholars Publishing Forum, 1991.

Ritcheson, Philip L. "Nuclearisation in South Asia," *Friday Times*, March 22–28, 1994.

Roy, Arundhati. *The Cost of Living*. Toronto: Vintage, 1999.

Rushdie, Salman. *Midnight's Children*. London: J. Cape, 1981.

———. *The Moor's Last Sigh*. Toronto: Knopf, 1995.

Sagan, Scott D., and Kenneth N. Waltz. *The Spread of Nuclear Weapons: A Debate*. New York: W. W. Norton, 1995.

Said, Edward W. *Orientalism*. London: Penguin Edition, 1978.

———. *Covering Islam: How the Media and the Experts Determine How We See the Rest of the World*. New York: Pantheon Books, 1981.

Sattar, Abdul. "Nuclear Stability in South Asia," in *Nuclear Issues in South Asia*. Islamabad: Islamabad Council of World Affairs, 1995.

———. "Nuclear Issues in South Asia: A Pakistani Perspective," in *Pakistan's Security and the Nuclear Option*, ed. Tarik Jan. Islamabad: Institute of Policy Studies, 1995.

Segal, Gerald. *The Consequences of Arms Proliferation in Asia-I, Adelphi Papers* 276. London: Oxford University Press for IISS, 1993. 50–61.

Sen, Gautam. *India's Security Consideration in the Nuclear Age*. New Dehli: National, 1986.

Sethi, Najam. "There Was No Threat of Indo-Pak Nuclear War in 1990," *Friday Times*, June 2–8, 1994.

Shah, Prakash. "Nuclear Non-proliferation Implications and the NPT Review: An Indian Perspective," *Strategic Analysis* 16:2 (May 1993): 139–146.

Shahi, Agha. "Preservation of Deterrence," *Dawn*, January 10, 1995.

———. "Extension of the Nuclear Non-Proliferation Treaty and the Security Dilemma," in *Nuclear Issues in South Asia*. Islamabad: Islamabad Council of World Affairs, 1995.

———. "Preservation of Deterrence for Security," in *Nuclear Issues in South Asia*. Islamabad: Islamabad Council of World Affairs, 1995.

Simpson, John, and Darryl Howlett. "The NPT Renewal Conference: Stumbling toward 1995," *International Security* 19:1 (summer 1994): 41–71.

Singh, Jasjit, ed. *India and Pakistan: Crisis of Relationship*. New Delhi: Lancer International in association with the Institute for Defense Studies and Analyses, 1990.

———, ed. *Indo-US Relations in a Challenging World*. New Delhi: Lancer and Institute for Defence Studies and Analyses, 1992.

Singh, Jaswant. *Defending India*. London: Macmillan, 1999.

Singh, Sampooran. *India and the Nuclear Bomb*. New Dehli: C Chand and Co., 1971.

Singh, Swaran. "National Security Structures: A Comparative Study of India, Pakistan and China," *Strategic Analysis* 16:2 (March 1994): 1535–1553.

Sinha, P. B., and R. R. Subramanian. *Nuclear Pakistan: Atomic Threat to South Asia*. New Dehli: Vision Books, 1980.

Subrahmanian, R. R. "India vs Pakistan: The Nuclear Option," *Foreign Affairs Reports* 34:5 (May 1985): 59–68.

———. *India, Pakistan, China: Defence and Nuclear Tangle in South Asia*. New Dehli: ABC Books, 1989.

Subrahmanyam, K. *Our National Security*. New Delhi: Economic and Research Foundation, 1972.

———. *Defence and Development*. Calcutta: Minerva Associates, 1973.

———. *Indian Security Perspectives*. New Delhi: ABC Publishing House, 1982.

——, ed. *India and the Nuclear Challenge*. New Delhi: Lancer International in association with the Institute for Defence Studies and Analyses, 1986.

Subrahmanyam, K., M. Zuberi, and R. Ramanna. *Problems of Living in Nuclear Age*. Chandigarh: Centre for Research in Rural and Industrial Development, 1985.

Sundarji, General K. *Blind Men of Hindoostan: Indo-Pak Nuclear War*. New Delhi: UBS Publishers, 1993.

Tamir, Yael. "The Enigma of Nationalism: Review Article," *World Politics* 47:3 (April 1995): 418–440.

Thakur, Ramesh. "American Policy in South Asia: Regional Fallout of Global Strategy," *Political Science* 36:2 (December 1984): 145–161.

Thomas, Raju G. C. "India's Nuclear and Space Programs: Defense or Development?" *World Politics* 38:2 (January 1986): 315–342.

——. *Democracy, Security and Development in India*. New York: St. Martin's, 1996.

Todorov, Tzvetan. *The Conquest of America: The Question of the Other*, trans. Richard Howard. New York: HarperPerennial, 1992.

The United Nations and Nuclear Non-Proliferation. United Nations Blue Book Series, Vol. III, New York, 1995.

Vanaik, Achin. "Political Case for a NWFZ in South Asia," *Economic and Political Weekly* 30 November (1985): 2115–2120.

Walt, Stephen M. *The Origins of Alliances*. Ithaca: Cornell University Press, 1987.

——. "The Renaissance of Security Studies," *International Studies Quarterly* 35: 2 (1991): 28–39.

Waltz, Kenneth N. *Theory of International Relations*. Reading: Addison-Wesley, 1979.

——. *The Spread of Nuclear Weapons: More May Be Better, Adelphi Papers* 171. London: Oxford University Press for IISS, 1981.

——. "The Emerging Structure of International Politics," *International Security* 18:2 (fall 1993): 44–79.

Weismann, Steve, and Herbert Krosney. *The Islamic Bomb*. New York: Times Books, 1981.

Young, Robert. *White Mythologies: Writing History and the West*. London: Routledge, 1990.

Young, Tom. " 'A Project to be Realized': Global Liberalism and Contemporary Africa," *Millennium: Journal of International Studies* 24:3 (winter 1995): 527–546.

NOTE

Most newspaper and magazine articles cited in the study are not included in the bibliography. At present, daily editions of most leading English dailies of India and Pakistan are available on the Internet. Following are URL (Uniform Resource Locator) addresses of four, namely, *Dawn, Hindu, Times of India*, and *News*, leading English daily newspapers of India and Pakistan. These addresses, however, keep changing.

Dawn: http://dawn.com
Hindu: http://www.hinduonline.com
Times of India: http://www.timesofindia.com
News: http://www.jang-group.com/news

Index